29-1-99

TARGET ENGLAND

FLYING WITH THE LUFTWAFFE IN WORLD WAR II

TARGET ENGLAND

Edmund Blandford

Airlife

England

Copyright © 1997 Edmund L. Blandford

First published in the UK in 1997
by Airlife Publishing Ltd

British Library Cataloguing-in-Publication Data
  A catalogue record for this book
  is available from the British Library

ISBN 1 85310 901 0

Typeset by Hewer Text Composition Services, Edinburgh
Printed in England by St Edmundsbury Press Ltd,
Bury St Edmunds, Suffolk

Airlife Publishing Ltd
101 Longden Road, Shrewsbury, SY3 9EB, England.

CONTENTS

	Foreword	7
1	Air Sports	9
2	A 'Luftwaffe'	18
3	Quality First	40
4	In a Grey Dawn	47
5	'Nazi Air Pirates'	54
6	Spearhead in the Air	70
7	'Bombs on England'	79
8	'Too Many Faces Had Gone Missing'	111
9	'Coventrated'	134
10	'Drop the Bombs and Get Away'	154
11	The 'Baby Blitz'	175
12	Hitler's Luftwaffe Failed	189
13	Escapees Were Soon Rounded Up	201
Appendix 1	Luftwaffe Ranks and Uniform Markings	212
2	Luftwaffe Aircraft	214
3	German Aircraft Production and Losses	215
4	Battle of Britain	217
5	Luftwaffe Slang Terms	218
6	Luftwaffe Badges	220
	Index	222

FOREWORD

The German Air Force of the Nazi period was unique in the sense that it was the first of its kind designed exclusively as a tactical air arm. As such it paved the way for Hitler's armies. But once its political masters decreed its move into strategic air warfare the Luftwaffe began its road of decline, and long before the end of the Second World War its striking power had shrunk to practically nil.

I would like to express my thanks to all those ex-members of the German Luftwaffe without whose assistance this book would not have been possible.

Edmund L. Blandford

CHAPTER ONE

AIR SPORTS

One month after the First World War began in August 1914 the Chief of the Imperial German Naval Staff wrote a minute which included the following:

'I hold the view that we should leave no means untried to crush England, and that successful air raids on London, in view of the already existing nervousness of the people, would prove a valuable means to that end.'

On 9 January 1915 the Kaiser gave permission for raids to start, but insisted that only military targets should be attacked – London was not to be bombed. In view of this injunction a German Zeppelin first raided King's Lynn in Norfolk, and on returning to base the airship commander reported that he had been 'heavily attacked by guns and engaged by searchlights'. In fact, no such defences then existed. But by 1918 things were very different: the menace of German air attack had resulted in Britain's capital being protected by 284 anti-aircraft guns, 377 searchlights and 11 fighter squadrons in an organisation called the Air Defence of Great Britain, a title that was to be temporarily resurrected in the next war.

The German General Hans von Seeckt has been marked down as the true originator of the later Luftwaffe, for in a secret paper prepared for the Reich's War Ministry in 1923 he laid down that a future air force must be part of the war machine and an instrument of the army. His country had built up a formidable air arm in the late war, only to lose it all under the terms of the Treaty of Versailles in 1919, with many thousands of planes and engines being confiscated by the victorious Allies.

Forbidden a new air arm by the same Treaty, certain German generals, in secret agreement with the new Bolshevik government in Russia, set about building a clandestine training organisation at Lipetsk. This facility was commanded by an airman, Hugo Sperrle, who would later go on to lead the German Condor Legion in the Spanish Civil War, then become chief of Air Fleet III in the Western Campaign of 1940 and the subsequent air operations following the Battle of Britain.

The Allies had soon lifted the ban on civil aircraft building in Germany, and this, coupled with encouragement and funds from the Reichswehr and clandestine Air Ministry, enabled a small aviation industry to be kept alive throughout the 1920s. It also enabled the German designers to keep pace with technical developments.

Similarly, the maintenance of a pool of pilots was vigorously promoted by the *Deutschen Luftsport Verbandes* (German Air Sport Movement), the Nazis' own National Socialist Air Corps (NSFK), the firm of Rhon-Rossitten-Gesellschaft and Aero Clubs of Germany. These organisations became a front camouflage for the planned new air force. President of the DLV Air Sports was an ex-wartime flying captain, Bruno Loerzer, who was to become *Reichskommissar* for German Airlines, and one of Göring's highest Luftwaffe adjutants. The DLV was organised into three groups: powered aircraft, gliding, and ballooning. It did much to create the ground organisation of the coming Luftwaffe, so that even before the unveiling of the new air force in March 1935 its officers were clad in uniforms virtually identical to those worn later. Many of the DLV's 50,000 members became a cadre for the Luftwaffe, and also provided a pool of men as reserves.

The Nazi Air Corps (NSFK) had been developed from the 'storms' of air-minded SA (*Sturm Abteilung*) brownshirt detachments, plus some from the SS units. They were very active in promoting their aims among German youth, enrolling any who were interested in taking up an aeronautical career. To do this the NSFK set up training schools on small airfields across Germany, instruction in flying and all technical aspects being provided by ex-WW1 veterans. Before 1935, those who were willing were transferred into the still secret Luftwaffe, receiving new ranks and uniforms in March 1935 when everything came into the open.

During the 1930s, Germany became the most air-minded nation in the world, largely encouraged by the Nazis and a new Wehrmacht, for under Hitler a strong air arm was desired to pursue the fight for 'rights' and '*lebensraum*' (living space), but in reality it assisted the Führer's aggressive aims in Eastern Europe. The organisations mentioned ensured a steady flow of young recruits already well trained in aviation matters before they even entered the air force proper, and provided a great and well indoctrinated core of aircrew. Some 4,000 glider fields sprang up across Germany and Austria, 16 of these run by the NSFK, while large numbers of Hitler Youth boys were co-opted into aviation through model plane building and gliding.

As indicated, a nation such as the Germans refused to accept the dictat of Versailles which forbade them a military air arm. While men like General von Seeckt enlisted like-minded comrades and Russian assistance to create a new air force, others in Germany, namely old hands who had joined the Nazi Party, started up their own 'Air Corps' as an adjunct to the air sports clubs which began to spring up across the land. The aim of the National Socialist Flying Corps was to attract both veterans with experience and any air-minded youth who, while not interested in politics, would still seize the chance to work on or fly in aeroplanes. Such a lad was Reinhard Fuschler who was bored stiff in his first job in an accountants' office:

'I was only really interested in planes, or at least how they were made and maintained. I had heard that the new and vociferous Nazis were looking for suitable young men to join their technical units, including aviation. A friend told me that if I called at the local Nazi Party office I could find out more. So I did this and learned that I could enrol as a technical assistant in the Party's new air arm, such as it was, and learn all about the maintenance of aircraft. I was very excited by this prospect, though failing to understand how a political party which had failed in Bavaria could boast an "air arm".'

Fuschler is of course referring to the so-called '*putsch*' in Munich which Hitler and his cronies attempted in 1923. By this time, however, Hitler had long been released from the jail term awarded him and managed to resurrect his movement into which the fledgling aviation corps was born.

'The only aviation I knew of in Germany was carried on by the few mail and passenger planes operating, plus of course some glider clubs. When I enquired further I was told the NSFK ran a kind of club, a non-military organisation, and that if I was interested in joining I should go home, pack a few belongings and return as it would mean leaving home. I was not at first happy about this, but soon adjusted to the idea. When I discussed it with my parents they asked me about wages, and I confessed I had forgotten to ask!'

Having been told off for his silliness, Reinhard returned to the Nazi Party office to find out what remuneration he would receive:

'The official laughed at me and assured me I would be well taken care of. So within a few days I left home in Essen and was taken by car with a few more aspiring air mechanics to an airfield outside the city where we found hut accommodation and a few planes bearing civil registration. We were then introduced to instructors who were members of the NSFK, an organisation we had never heard of. They told us we were "in on the ground floor", and that their aim was to build a National Socialist Air Force. We soon learned that the NSFK was a widespread organisation run on military lines, including its own rank system and with many old comrades of the former Fliegerabteilungen of the war.'

Fuschler was indeed 'in on the ground floor', so new was everything that no uniforms were available, only NSFK stickpin badges. Nevertheless they entered the course, and received expert instruction on aircraft and aircraft maintenance. There were some twenty students in all who ate in a mess hall and were required to parade for a certain amount of military training. After a few weeks they were given tests and assessments, then:

'We received a big surprise, a visit from Göring himself.'

Göring was not in charge of the NSFK, but as an ex-fighter ace he impressed the class:

'Not by his appearance, he was like a big, fat, overgrown schoolboy, but full of enthusiasm and with strong words of encouragement; you could not help liking the man.'

Göring inspected the school and helped fire their enthusiasm by recounting some of his wartime experiences, assuring the lads he had enjoyed it all.

The course was very thorough, the tutors knew it all and were very determined to re-create a powerful new air arm.

'It seemed I had a natural aptitude so I passed all the tests with flying colours. The Nazis were in the ascendant and at last Hitler gained power, by which time I had long completed my schooling and wore a smart new uniform complete with swastika armband for formal wear.'

After a while a transformation took place: the personnel were called together and told that a regular air force was being organised, which although still secret would soon be unveiled to the world, and that if any of the men wished to transfer into it they could volunteer at once, and be made NCOs and officers without delay.

'My passion for planes induced me to step forward like most of the other lads who thereby agreed to leave the NSFK and join the clandestine air force. In the summer of 1934 the commanding officer told us we were now part of the new air arm and the official transfer took place the same day. We discarded our blue-grey NSFK uniforms and were given new outfits in Luftwaffe blue. When I went home next weekend my family were amazed. Back at our base our CO informed us we were the cadre of a new fighter unit, we were then transported to another base, an airfield largely devoid of buildings and no aircraft in sight.'

The NSFK, having been a semi-secret organisation, was not driven out of existence by the emergence of the official Luftwaffe, which was disclosed to the world by Göring in March 1935, but it was not until April 1937 that the old 'training' air corps was officially formulated, with its *Korpsführer*, Friedrich Christiansen, who would go on to command the German forces occupying Holland in 1940. It was because of a certain amount of grounding via the Nazi NSFK that aviation experts in Allied countries came to view the new Luftwaffe as the most 'Nazified' of the three German services, though it is a fact that by 1939 the great majority of recruits into the Luftwaffe were simply conscripts, for compulsory

military service had been instituted in November 1935. Although earlier
entry through the NSFK had certainly ensured NCO and officer status
for many.

However, other Germans who were air-minded and anxious to see
Germany restored militarily (apart from seeking adventure) went into
the Luftwaffe by a different route, in the case of Wolfgang Schauer via
politics:

*'I was born in Magdeburg into a middle-class family, my father was
a jeweller and I had two sisters, both a little younger than myself. When
I left high school there was no job to go to as things were very hard
in Germany after the war, and unfortunately I had no chance to enter
my father's profession. For a start I was not interested, and I had no
aptitude for such things; in any case his business was in dire straits.*

*'Before long I grew sick of accepting welfare food and benefit pay
which was very small, so I decided to try and join a political organisation
as a paid trainee. In those days there were many such organisations, the
State was in political turmoil, with all kinds of different parties vying for
power, including of course the Nazis and the Reds. It so happened that
the brownshirt Nazis were always looking for youngsters with brains to
assist their organisation, especially among the so-called 'better' classes,
for they were trying to win wider support. So I was enrolled by the local
Nazis as a trainee political officer for a small wage. It wasn't much, but
it gave me something positive to do and I was assured I would have
a bright future. Being young of course I could not see how it would
all end up. I was fired by their political, nationalistic and patriotic
propaganda, and really believed that my small efforts would help to
get Germany back on its feet again. This seemed to be a worthwhile
aim, and my parents did not object, even though they were not totally
in favour of the Nazi brownshirts who included many roughnecks and
adventurers in their ranks.*

*'I managed to do quite well, but by the time the worst of our country's
economic crisis was over our Party membership had swollen greatly and
I had been promoted. We now had our own air and marine units and
all kinds of subsidiary sections, and it was to the air side that I became
greatly attracted. I formed a young man's enthusiasm for flying, and
as an officer had no trouble in taking free flying lessons from the very
people I had helped to organise. These were of course ex-World War
flyers in charge of the training and their enthusiasm was very potent. So
I became more and more interested in flying and less so in politics.'*

Schauer recounts how the Nazi leaders brazenly announced the
existence of a new air force, something forbidden by the Treaty of
Versailles:

*'Incorporated into this were some of the very units I had helped to
organise from the SA brownshirts who then simply transferred into the*

new Luftwaffe and took on fresh uniforms. It was all very exciting and quite glamorous and I applied to join at once. My request was granted as my usefulness as a political officer had ceased. I now felt I had the chance to become a flyer in the real sense of the word and take up an air force career. With my political background there was no problem and I was entered into the lists as a regular officer of proven worth. It was then up to me to prove myself however, for although I had learned to fly I was still very much a novice and not sure which branch of the service to pursue.'

It can be seen from this testimony that Wolfgang Schauer, like others, went into political and then military service through economic necessity. It is doubtful if any National Socialist dogma had much effect when he entered combat, though his case was grist for the mill of those outside Germany who saw the new Luftwaffe as a Nazi creation with personnel imbued with National Socialist ideals.

The case of Christian Rossler offers in some ways a similar route, though with a slightly bizarre twist in the beginnings:

'I was born in Breslau into a strictly Catholic family, two boys and two girls brought up to believe in God and all the associated religion which it contained. I'm afraid I saw much of this as false dogma. However, I was bound to attend a Catholic school and when ready to face life as a working man, I decided to follow my father's advice and enter the priesthood. I was not in fact too sure of this course as I could not see how a decent living could be made from such a vocation, and in the prevailing climate earning one's daily bread was of paramount importance. However, I was accepted as a novice, took my vows and decided to try and make a go of it.

'I soon found that compared to most of the young men in the seminary I was a little headstrong, I did not react very well to the instructors and the strict discipline. I could not see the commonsense in many of the rituals and chants; in short, I did not really fit in with the life at all. I made my disquiet known to my parents and they were most disappointed, but in the end they agreed that perhaps it was for the best. After all, we were quite a big family and at my age I should be a breadwinner. Times were hard and every pfennig counted, so I gave up the priesthood within a few weeks of starting. I don't think they were sorry to see me leave.'

The young Rossler then found work in a flour mill, but found it hard and dusty, rebelling against it and making his father angry.

'I didn't know what to do. I was not stupid, I had a mind of my own, but work was hard to find. Yet I knew I had to do something to support myself, though I did not want to work as any kind of labourer, I preferred to use my head. I had ideas and felt I could be useful as an organiser, if only I could meet someone to give me a helping hand.'

Fate assisted, guiding Christian into an opportunity that would provide the stepping stone into the air force.

'One evening I was drinking beer in our local when I saw an old school friend who greeted me and we fell into conversation. I soon discovered he was doing very well for himself and wondered how I could benefit. It seemed he had joined some kind of political organisation who actually paid him for talking to the ordinary workers. He saw himself as the representative of a rising political party of which we had too many. His job was to win over the workers to the views of him and his party.'

When his friend showed him some leaflets Christian realised he was a Nazi, a member of the brownshirts he had often seen marching around the city streets waving their banners and shouting slogans. His friend offered to take him along to one of their meetings where an important speaker would address the audience. The speaker proved to be Adolf Hitler himself, and Christian had a first-hand chance to see how the political demagogue worked, though not until after he had seen his chum acting as warmer-up on the platform.

Not until later did Christian realise how craftily and effectively the erstwhile 'Führer' worked in such meetings, deliberately arriving late, keeping the audience waiting in a state of expectation, the excuse being that the leader had been visiting wounded comrades in hospital. When he did finally arrive and began to speak it was to arouse those before him with taunting shouts such as: 'When are you going to wake up? Are you going to let the bloody Reds and Jews take over?' They had never before heard anyone like this man Hitler who in no time had them in the palm of his hand, so that though few, if any, among the audience were already Nazi supporters, they were soon converted. Hitler played on all their fears, obsessions and expectations, their prejudices and doubts:

'He had the common touch, he knew these people, even though he was not German by birth, he knew their way of thinking, their nerves and sympathies, as if he were one of them, like a doctor who acted as if he alone could solve their problems.'

Hitler was a master actor in such situations, at times turning silent, looking downcast, so that Christian and all before him were nonplussed, amazed by his performance, especially when he actually produced tears; at last raising his abject face to speak in hushed tones of his 'dead *kameraden*' of the war years, the *frontsoldaten* who had been stabbed in the back by the crooked politicians, black marketeers, and of course the Jews and Bolshevik revolutionaries at home. He then screamed vengeance on these scum, raising the listeners to high approval, so that Christian and everyone were sold and shouted and roared their approval.

'The audience stamped their feet and pandemonium ensued. That was the very great effect such a demagogue had on young men like myself. The brownshirts including my friend came into it by shouting 'Heil! Heil! Heil! and breaking into their Horst Wessel song.'

Christian Rossler was hooked, and when his pal suggested he visit the Nazi Party HQ he quickly did so and was at once offered a lowly paid job as a researcher. In this he survived, but by 1933 he became bored, not only with his work but with some of the people involved: 'There were many who were opportunists, adventurers or pure roughnecks with little intelligence, but plenty of animal cunning.' He now used his position to effect a complete change, needing only to lift the telephone receiver and connect with the right *parteigenossen* (Party comrades), in other words, he pulled one or two strings and in no time at all had exchanged his brown Nazi Party uniform for one of Luftwaffe blue; it was as simple as that and could only have happened in the new Nazi Germany.

In a very short time Rossler became an officer of the Luftwaffe and had himself posted to a bomber Wing HQ, where he at once 'became enthralled with the big birds'. We shall return to his career later.

Arthur Tieker was born into a good family in Berlin and always wanted to fly, but owing to the prevailing economic situation was obliged to enter his father's business which was concerned with the manufacture of foodstuffs:

'It was terribly boring and I didn't feel like sticking it out. But my parents were very strict and I had no choice.'

Everything changed of course with the advent of a Nazi government and before 1935 was out Arthur Tieker was conscripted into the army and to his disgust found himself tramping around a barrack square in jackboots and equipment, including of course a rifle.

'I did not enjoy this, though I must admit I had some fun. Many of the lads were very rough types and not my "cup of tea" in terms of company. However, I grew to like some of them. But one day I saw some aircraft on a field and my old love was rekindled. Without telling my parents I volunteered for the new Luftwaffe and to my great delight was accepted as a trainee pilot.'

If there was one strain of recruit the Nazis most desired to enlist it was the men of proven military merit and good background. No matter how much Hitler himself may have despised the military aristocracy, and especially the Prussian élite. Although in the main the elders of such families regarded Hitler and his followers as rabble, the younger set were often fired up by the Nazis energy and obvious patriotism.

Peter Harmel was born into one such military family, his father had been a cavalry Colonel in the recent great war. It seemed natural Peter should enter the Potsdam military academy to 'learn the ropes of soldiering', as he put it. But once Hitler came to power and set in motino a new 'Wehrmacht', Peter decided he must become a pilot. He volunteered for and was accepted into the fledgling air arm, exchanging his grey-green jacket for an outfit of grey-blue. Following recruit training his application for flying duties was approved and he went off to flying school.

For many German youths those days were an exciting adventure.

CHAPTER TWO

A 'LUFTWAFFE'

T he young Germans who began flooding into the new Luftwaffe late in 1935 were joining a force still in its infancy, one that their officers and NCO veterans of the Great War were striving to build on the honour and glory gained by men such as Richthofen, Boelcke, Immelmann and Udet. The Royal Air Force had gained a substantial lead in this respect since the days of the illustrious Royal Flying Corps, instilling traditions into their young service and developing an *esprit de corps* which was second-to-none. Lacking the customs of their coming rivals, the Luftwaffe chiefs attempted to inspire their force with the names mentioned, and it was these titles bestowed on new fighter squadrons which caught the public imagination. True, they were all fighter aces who gained fame in the early days of aerial combat, and those names given to the less glamorous bomber units would never quite mean as much.

Every recruit into the Luftwaffe came already trained and disciplined into the military way of life, thanks to prior service in the Hitler Youth and Labour Corps. The latter had physically toughened them so that, even though tedious, the recruit training on the barrack square did not test them overmuch. Furthermore, the youngsters were thoroughly indoctrinated by the state controlled media into the justness of their country's cause, only a few perhaps rebelled at being hoisted out of career prospects in civilian life.

Horst Juventus was born in Berlin in 1915 and had a brother and sister younger than himself. Having done his time in the Hitler Youth and Labour Corps, he was conscripted in 1936 and chose the Luftwaffe and volunteered to become a pilot:

> '*After my recruit training; which was quite tedious, I was assessed fit for aircrew duties and was sent with a few dozen other lads to Berlin-Gatow where we were shown into barrack rooms. We then began our interviews as to suitability for various categories of flying. I told them I wanted to be a pilot and nothing else, and I well remember the Sergeant-Major telling me it would all depend on my capabilities and that if I did not learn to discipline myself a little I would end up in the army infantry. This was because I believe I was a little outspoken.*
> '*In the event I was accepted as a trainee pilot and, with some others,*

shown over a few biplane trainers and began to receive lectures on the theory of flight etc. We were then taken up in old Arado and Stosser biplanes and I enjoyed my first flight which was marvellous. However, not all the lads took to it, some were airsick and dropped out, and I must admit that when the weather was cloudy and conditions were bumpy I did not enjoy it quite as much. At this stage we were merely being assessed as pilots with no idea what we would fly, but I had already expressed a preference for bombers.

'In a week several of the lads had been dismissed from the course as unsuitable for pilot training and left the base. I believe they were sent elsewhere to be re-assessed for other duties in aircrew or even ground trades. But I managed to carry on until I had mastered the controls, with an instructor in the other cockpit, and all went well. I managed to carry out simple manoeuvres, and then one day the instructor told me I was ready for my first solo flight. I was very excited and nervous as he watched me taxi away and then take off into the wind. I did my best to remember all I had been taught and managed to get the crate into the air and do a gentle circuit over the airfield. There were other pupils in the air so I had to keep a sharp lookout in all directions, and I soon came in for my first landing which went quite well despite a strong cross-wind. My instructor was very pleased and sent me up again at once. I did so, and by the end of the day had completed four take-offs and landings with no mishaps.

'I was very surprised by my ability as I thought my nervousness would upset everything. However, several of the lads failed to grasp the business of co-ordination and had to be taken off the course. Two of them crashed and I witnessed one of these events. I did not know the fellow well, but had seen him in the barracks; I believe he was called Karl and seemed perfectly confident on the ground. But he came in to land too fast and misjudged his approach completely and struck a tree well off the runway, burned and had no chance to escape. It made a bad impression on all of us but would not be the last crack-up we would see. The instructors got us into the air again as quickly as possible and there were no more fatalities that day.

'I did about two months of very thorough training and passed out as a qualified pilot and was given the choice of fighters or bombers, so chose the latter.'

Karl Haulmeier was an only child from Hamburg and as a boy evinced a great interest in aircraft, making models when a member of the Hitler Youth and attending classes on aeronautics while in the Labour Corps. He volunteered for the Luftwaffe after his call-up in 1935, his great desire was to fly in a plane in some capacity. After the usual recruit training he was sent to a selection centre and even though having no great confidence or even desire to control an aircraft he applied to become a pilot:

'You see, I was in love with the planes themselves, so long as I could climb inside them I was happy. At my interview the officer seemed *doubtful, but forwarded me with many others to flying school: "They will soon sort you out," he told me.*

'Which was exactly what happened. I had no aptitude for controlling a plane at all, and although the instructor could see my great interest in these machines I was unable to co-ordinate my actions to control an aircraft. So within a couple of weeks I was removed from the pilot course and told to report to the observer school, and there I made rapid progress. I learned all about navigation, which was very interesting, and all about bomb sights and bombing, for I had decided I had no interest in fighter planes, although I used to watch them. In short, I was very suited to fit into aircrew. So after some weeks I was assessed as most competent and sent off with others to more advanced training.'

Hans Gilbert was born in Dessau and lived with his parents and two older sisters in a 'reasonable life' despite the difficulties caused by the aftermath of the Great War. As a youth he worked in a coal merchant's office, but after Hitler gained power he joined the Nazi Flying Corps or NSFK to learn all about aircraft in which he was very interested:

'As it happened the Junkers firm were in my town, and although I received instruction at the NSFK school alongside the local airfield we were also taken into the aircraft factory to see the planes being made which I found extremely interesting, especially when we were allowed to get into one of the finished products, such as the Ju 52 and 86. Fascinated though I was by their construction, I had an even greater desire to sit in the pilot's seat and fly one of them.

'After about three years I had qualified as an air mechanic, but after transferring into the new Luftwaffe I volunteered for aircrew and was sent away for suitability assessment. I passed this hurdle and with others was sent away to Berlin-Gatow to learn the rudiments of flying, both in the lecture rooms and on planes which were Stossers and Fieselers. Things went well and I went up for the first time with an instructor which was very exciting, and within a few days I was controlling a machine myself. Then I took my first solo flight which was quite nerve wracking, but I passed this hurdle and had soon made a number of hours flying solo. After a few weeks I had been assessed qualified and was given my pilot's badge. We were then re-assessed, some being sent to fighter school, but I wanted to fly one of the bigger machines such as those I had seen being made at Dessau, so with other lads I was sent to a bomber school where my first flights were in a Focke-Wulf Weihe before we passed on to the larger and more problematical Junkers 86.

'The next few weeks proved far more difficult than I had anticipated, with several accidents occurring at the school which shook the pupils. I had seen one small incident at the first flying school in which the pupil pilot escaped. But at the bomber school it was more serious. We were watching a pupil about to go solo in a Ju 86 when it slewed off the runway and hit another aircraft and caught fire. All were burned

and this was horrible. The Ju 86 was seen by us as an unforgiving type of plane, if you made a serious error your chances of survival in certain cases were small. We had parachutes, but the problem was in even reaching the escape hatch.

'But we gradually mastered the crates and thankfully said goodbye to them and went on to the newer and far more agreeable Dornier. These were quite easy to fly and I enjoyed my first solo flights although we had instructors with us and at least one other pupil in the cabin. Eventually, those of us who proved competent were assessed bomber pilots and sent home on leave. Although my parents looked on me as some kind of hero I still felt a novice.'

By contrast, Georg Kessler became an air gunner on Heinkels. Also born in Hamburg he too loved planes and attended aviation classes in the Hitler Youth. After conscription he entered the Luftwaffe and eventually volunteered for aircrew, being sent to an assessment centre where he opted to become an air gunner:

'We went to a school near Hannover which was very open, with few huts and ranges on which various weapons were set up. We began our training, learning the different calibres and how to take them apart and then defensive work on bombers. There were mocked-up gun turrets in lecture rooms and on the ranges where special trollies with weapons carried the trainees who learned to fire in movement at targets moving along wires. It was all very interesting and I enjoyed it very much. Some of the gunners were also assigned radio work and went off to another school. But in my case I was despatched with others to a Heinkel base where we were shown over the planes and instructed at the gun positions. Then at last we went up in threes with pilot and an instructor; it was my first flight and very thrilling. We learnt the various arcs of fire and within a few days had begun firing live ammunition in the air at real targets towed by old planes, and this was great fun. I must admit it was much more difficult than expected, but after a while like the rest I began to get the hang of it and actually made some hits.

'Our training went on for about two weeks, we were then posted to actual bomber bases where the Heinkels were later models than those we had trained on at gunnery school.'

Johann Schmidt was born in Düsseldorf and like most young men went through the preparatory regimentation of Hitler Youth and Labour Corps training prior to his conscription when he volunteered for the Luftwaffe. From recruit training he expressed a wish to become a pilot which he looked upon as 'an exciting prospect'. After being assessed at Gatow as fit material for aircrew he travelled with twenty other lads to a base just outside the old airship base at Ludwigshafen:

'There we found a variety of aircraft, and after settling into a barrack block we were shown round the base before inspecting some of the planes.

Next day we began our training in the classrooms, and on the field we were shown the controls of some planes, mostly biplanes, including some Heinkel 51 fighters as they then were, and we were very impressed.'

After a few days of ground instruction the new arrivals were assigned teachers and taken aloft for their first flights:

'It was the first time I had left the ground and I was very nervous, but then found it tremendously thrilling. In a couple of days I had been allowed to handle the controls and try some gentle manoeuvres; the plane was a Stosser and I enjoyed the feeling of power I had in being able to fly. But I was a little over-confident and received a warning from the instructor to be careful and not to try and run before I could walk – those were his words.

'The flying training went well for us, though one or two fell out as unsuitable and one lad crashed but survived. We then flew our first solos, which was a big challenge but I passed out as adequate. As my confidence grew I flew farther afield and this was a wonderful experience, and soon we had amassed sufficient hours to face our final tests, which included all sorts of manoeuvres as well as simple take-offs and landings. I passed them all and gained my pilot's badge which was a very great thrill. I remember how we marched off the parade ground singing some Luftwaffe song and feeling on top of the world.

'Then we were assessed again and in my interview I opted to become a bomber pilot, I had no interest in air combat at all. To be in command of a larger plane was my ambition at the time, and this wish was to be granted in full measure.'

Karl-Ludwig Weinfarth was born in the Ruhr at Dortmund, but his family moved to Bavaria and he grew to young manhood nursing a great interest in aviation and especially the military aspect. So following his stint in the Hitler Youth and Labour Corps he was conscripted and chose the Luftwaffe:

'I had some rather grand ideas of becoming an officer, which made my parents laugh, I'm not sure why, perhaps they were surprised by my nerve. I was a very keen youth at the recruit camp and did well, asking at the end of my training to be sent to a flying officer school, and that I was most interested in commanding planes. This was a great joke to them, but I was quite serious though woolly-minded and had no idea how it would work out.

'I was sent off to Berlin-Gatow where they entered me for a pilot's course, but I was not all that keen to actually fly a plane, but said nothing. But to my surprise I did far better than I would have expected if I had had a really set idea of what I wanted to do, and in a short time I had become a star pupil, which despite my earlier brashness embarrassed me because the NCO instructor told the other pupils in front of me to

follow my example. It seemed I had a 'natural' aptitude for controlling a plane, which again came as a surprise to me. I seemed to do the right thing automatically, and did not mind performing aerobatics or anything the instructor desired, so I was one of the first in that course to receive a commendation and pass on to solo flight ahead of the others.

'At the same time my mind was still rather preoccupied with becoming an officer, and when the course was over I again requested to be sent to an officer school, and to my great delight I was accepted. It was all very much a boyish adventure but at that time I believe the Luftwaffe was still short of officers, so I never had to surmount the hurdle of becoming an NCO first but was sent straight off to officer cadet school where we were taught how to handle men, the role of the air force in war, and of course a certain amount of National Socialist indoctrination. I saw Göring and other high officers when they inspected the school, and during speeches they did their best to instil the right spirit of the new Germany and a glorious future in the Luftwaffe. I was very keen and did well and amazed my parents by becoming a Lieutenant after six months training. I laughed at my parents' expressions as they inspected me in my new uniform. I had a brother who was already in the navy; he became an NCO on U-boats and was lost in the Atlantic in 1943. But in the late 1930s I was in great excitement as I returned to the school where we were to receive our postings.'

Otto Jufen was actually Danish inasmuch as he was born in Denmark, his father having a business in Copenhagen; but his parents were firmly German and moved back into their native land to set up home in Hamburg. Following the routine membership and training in the Hitler Youth and Labour Corps, Otto was conscripted into the Luftwaffe in 1937. After recruit training he volunteered for aircrew and following assessment was sent to train as an Observer-bomb-aimer:

'This was very interesting, we had old Dorniers and Heinkels and after training I passed all the tests and became a qualified Observer and was promoted to Sergeant with the possibility of becoming an officer. I was not especially interested in rank; I was quite content as I loved the planes and flying in the nose as I was very interested in navigation and that was an important enough job. But I was persuaded by our CO to enter my name for officer training, and so I went off on a special course of training which included both flying and classroom lectures on the role of an officer in the Luftwaffe on flying duties. While I was at the school, which was in Berlin, I met a young lady and asked her to marry me, but then discovered she was Jewish and under threat; it was a very bad time as I loved her. I had no option but to withdraw from this contact as she was sent away and this greatly affected my view of our system. But I had made my choice and did my best; I passed all the tests and was posted to a regular bomber unit equipped with the latest Heinkels.'

One name that came to the fore in 1940 and has become well-known to Battle of Britain historians since is that of Johannes Fink. A professional soldier, Fink saw a more interesting future in an air force long before Germany had a Nazi government:

'I had my own ideas on the use of air power, but of course until we were given the wherewithal we could do little. I suppose I was one of those military career officers who wish to further themselves, so inevitably when Göring, Milch, Udet and others created the new Luftwaffe I saw it as a golden opportunity, as did others, to promote a career in the way we desired most. I had always taken a great interest in the larger type of aircraft, by which I mean bombers, and had studied the subject.

'So by 1935 we found ourselves with a new air force. It was up to those in command to provide the equipment and work out tactics, which were always to act as an arm of the army. We therefore set out rough guidelines based on firm co-operation with the ground units, and to this end appointed liaison officers who were more or less permanently attached to certain army corps. This was to prove a very good idea when war came. Inevitably, there were those who did not see eye to eye with us in this and who could never conceive of an air force replacing conventional artillery and the old methods. We had no intention of replacing the older arm, only of supplementing them, especially in certain circumstances, and this we were able to do.

'Throughout the later 1930s we carried out manoeuvres with the army and did our best to perfect co-operation with them in such a way that some of our bomber units would always be on call to assist them. These were mainly the new Stuka squadrons, but the great bulk of the Heinkel, Dornier and a few of the new Junkers 88 units were also on standby to carry out behind the line attacks on enemy dumps and concentrations. They were not trained to carry out strategic warfare however in any way, but were merely an extension, shall we say, of the army's power.'

One of the best-known German pilots to emerge in the Second World War but become more famous outside his own country later was Hans-Ulrich Rudel, who gained acclaim as a Stuka pilot on the Russian Front and the very highest decorations, knocking out several hundred Soviet tanks with his Ju 87D model tankbuster armed with twin 37mm cannon. Rudel became known as a convinced Nazi:

'I grew up in the Hitlerian era when relentless indoctrination of youth convinced me and most of my age that our glorious Führer would lead Germany into a great new era that we would indeed inherit from our leadership. Our Empire would last for a thousand years.

'It was in this spirit that I volunteered for the new Luftwaffe and went through the usual recruit training, after which I was assessed as *suitable for pilot training. At that stage I had no particular preferences and was able to enter flight training without preconceived notions as to what direction my ambitions in flying should take. I progressed well and after a few days had flown solo, my instructor telling me that I had a gift of natural ability to control an aircraft. After a few weeks I passed out as qualified and then had to make my choice; my tutors had recommended me for fighters but I felt unsure, yet agreed to go to fighter school to see how I progressed. I was soon aloft in a Heinkel 51 biplane which was fast and delightful to fly. But then one day during an inspection I met a young officer who during conversation told me of a new type of squadron being formed – the dive-bombers. This sounded very interesting and I suppose I had some kind of youthful desire to knock things down, yet was not all that interested in piloting large aircraft. So I enquired of my CO who told me that yes, it was possible to join one of these new units, he would see what could be done. Meanwhile, we transferred to the new Messerschmitt 109 fighter which was a very good plane, but certain aspects of it did not please me. For a start I felt far too cramped in the very small cockpit and the hood did not permit a very good view. It also had vices on take-off which did not make for safety. So after a few flights in these planes I decided to transfer to the Stuka units, as by then I had seen some photographs sent to me by the same officer who had been very friendly and told me his CO was always looking for suitable aircrew. The Stuka of course had a second crew member, the gunner who sat facing rearwards behind the pilot with one or two machine-guns and had nothing to do most of the time; the key man was clearly the pilot, who was to be of a special kind and very fit.*

'In about a month my CO sent for me and with a flourish handed me a letter he had received telling him to forward any suitable volunteers for Stuka service; he said I could leave at once and he would arrange it. He also said that others would be leaving with me, and in fact two more pilots volunteered and we travelled together to our new base where I soon met the same young officer I had known. We were greeted as new brothers-in-arms and a day later were shown over one of the Stukas which was of the earlier type with fat wheel spats (Ju 87a). We were amused by its angular appearance, but as soon as I sat in the cockpit I knew it was the right place for me. I had a marvellous view and it was very roomy. I had soon started up the engine and taxyed round the field. Of course, like all those aircraft of the period without a tricycle undercarriage the view forward was very restricted, but this did not dampen my enthusiasm.

'Within a few days we newcomers had received adequate ground instruction and were ready for our first flight, so we followed the CO round the track and took-off in formation. The idea was that my friend would show us the tricks of dive bomber tactics once we had got the feel of the plane. Of course, it felt very different to the Messerschmitt and Heinkel fighters, it was that much heavier and not

nearly as manoeuvrable. But I was not to be put off and after a few circuits of the field I climbed to about 10,000 feet with the two other pupils behind me and our instructor not far off giving us instructions over the radio.

'After a few moments I pushed the control column forward and the machine plummeted earthwards, and very soon I saw the altimeter fall back to less than 5,000 feet, and prepared to pull out. At that time we had no automatic pull-out mechanism, so everything depended on the pilot's judgement. My speed in falling had been about 300 mph, which was the limit; to dive much faster would have resulted in the wings and wheels being torn off. In a moment the nose began to come up and soon I was again flying on the level; the effort on me physically had been very great. I flew off to one side while my pupil comrades did their dives, and then we watched our instructor demonstrate, and he did not begin his pull-out until a much lower altitude. We watched in amazement as he seemed to be hurtling earthwards in a death-defying dive that spelt suicide. I guessed that he must have gone down to about 1,000 feet before pulling back on the stick to begin hurtling upwards again, so we guessed he must have nerves of steel and a very strong constitution.

'He told us to emulate him but start pulling out at about 3,000 feet, but when I did my dive I held on till 1,500 feet before pulling back on the stick and the plane responded quite violently, surprising me so that I blacked out. We had dive brakes under the wings, but these did not greatly alter our falling speed. My instructor was amazed and not all that pleased that I had disobeyed instructions, and my comrades more prudently pulled out from their own dives at twice my height. On the ground again my instructor reproved me mildly and told me to obey orders:

'"You will be no use to me flattened on the ground, will you?" he said. I had to agree with him.

'We flew day after day, now carrying a gunner in the rear cockpit and practice bombs under the wings which we aimed at a ground target. About this time a terrible rumour swept the base that a number of Stukas had flown into the ground during training or giving a demonstration and we received a severe caution to be extra careful and obey orders. We found out the truth of the rumour but felt we knew what we were doing, though I myself had become much more circumspect in my behaviour and less rebellious as I had no wish to cut short my new career.'

The terrible accident involving a whole unit of Stukas did in fact occur when they were demonstrating the power of the dive-bomber, supposedly before a group of Wehrmacht staff officers who witnessed the planes suddenly appear in their steep dives out of low mist and smash into the earth. The pilots had evidently overlooked or ignored their altimeters and mistaken the mist for cloud.

'In some practice flights we were escorted by Messerschmitt 109s or 110s who made dummy attacks on us to give our gunners some training.

I did not fancy our chances if attacked by such powerful fighters. One man with a machine-gun in the rear cockpit was of little use, while our two wing guns were also useless in combat.'

Rudel went on to complete his training and begin his amazing war career.

Peter Kroller's home was in Magdeburg, and having grown to youth in the Hitler era went through the usual Hitler Youth and Labour Corps training before conscription when he volunteered for the Luftwaffe in 1938; his choice was to become a pilot. In this wish he was thwarted as unsuitable, and so became an Observer (*Beobachter*), which he soon learned would mean being in command of an aircraft, for unlike the RAF the new Luftwaffe deemed the commander of a bomber should be the Observer and navigator. This arrangement pleased Peter and he was soon in training, learning the rudiments of navigation and bomb aiming:

'We went up for the first time in Dornier 17s, which was very thrilling but a little nerve-wracking as the noise was so much greater than I had expected; I stuffed cotton wool into my ears under my helmet after that. But I got used to it and after a while I began to appreciate the unique position of observer stuck in the nose of the plane with magnificent views. The instructors were very patient, spending a lot of time in the air with us and passing on valuable tips and also in the more formal classroom work. After a few weeks we had learnt the basics and began flying as complete crews on manoeuvres, learning to spot targets and aim the bombs.'

Peter spent a few more weeks in this training before passing out as an NCO to be sent to another school to learn man-handling and be given the chance of becoming an officer. The course lasted two weeks:

'I preferred to remain a Top Sergeant for reasons I will not go into here. We were then sent off as trained NCOs to regular squadrons equipped with the Dornier 17s.'

Horst Jentzen was another early recruit (1936) who made flying plane models in the Hitler Youth and with an ambition to pilot bombers. The flying training was both thrilling and nerve-wracking:

'Especially when we saw one of the pupils crash, which had a bad effect on us. The plane was a Heinkel 51 and got into difficulties when its engine cut out and it hit a tree, killing the pilot. We had other types of plane including Arados and old bombers which were very safe to fly, especially the latter. I had my first flight, which was very exciting and I was anxious to take the controls, but when I did the plane bucked all over the sky. But within half an hour I had gained some sort of co-ordination and managed to keep the aircraft on an even keel. The instructor seemed quite pleased with my progress and within a week I

had flown my first solo, which was very satisfying. Our path was not always smooth however, for at times the weather clamped down even after take-off and this made flying very bumpy and at times dangerous. I remember on one occasion when I had flown into some cloud, and when I emerged from it I flipped upside down and went into a spin. But we had received careful instruction in how to recover and by kicking the rudder pedal and pushing the stick forward and increasing speed I soon regained control and landed safely.'

Horst Jentzen passed this stage of his pilot training and went on to bomber school where his first flight in a larger plane he says felt safer but far noisier. But:

'It was all a question of temperament, we felt more comfortable with two engines and a larger cockpit. Soon we sat in the pilot's seat and grew used to controlling two engines instead of one. The Focke-Wulf Weihe was a good plane to fly but we also used the old Junkers 52, but thankfully not the Ju 86. Then we were shown over a Heinkel 111, which was one of the Luftwaffe's latest bombers, and it seemed a very big and reassuring type. We were sorted into parties of four pupils with one instructor and a radioman as crew. We taxyed round the field and took turns to handle the controls before at last we were off and soon making our first solo flights. I had no real problems and soon gained confidence, the Heinkel was easy to fly and responded positively and quickly to the controls. Within a few days we had mastered the rudiments and were allowed to make some cross-country flights to get the feel of the plane and familiarise ourselves with the local area. We then progressed to formation flying, which was not at all easy and required great concentration. But we persevered and not one accident occurred, which pleased our instructors; I know there had been some among the previous batch of trainees and we could see a couple of burnt out wrecks near the airfield.'

By early 1938 Horst had been passed out proficient and posted to a regular bomber unit.

It was never intended that the Luftwaffe's striking forces should operate by day unescorted, there would always be fighters on hand to shepherd them to their targets and back. So it is fair to say that the *jagdstaffeln* fighter squadrons were part and parcel of the tactical air corps and trained as part of an offensive force.

Kurt Henner trained as a fighter pilot after a shaky course on gliding while in the Hitler Youth. But, with persistence and a patient instructor, he managed to get his proficiency certificate but had labour service to do before entering the Luftwaffe. After recruit training and assessment he was judged fit to enter pilot training:

'All went better than expected. I got over my nerves and passed out on biplanes before being sent to an Me 109 training centre. This was

very thrilling and I soon saw myself as a dashing fighter pilot hero, and as I had a girl friend in my home town of Hannover I felt sure she would be impressed by my exploits!

'The training was very thorough and we learnt fast and were soon able to take off in the much faster Messerschmitts and practise constantly. In three months I had passed out as a qualified fighter pilot and went proudly home on leave to show myself off to family and girl friend, who I could see thought the world of me. In truth I was a novice and had much to learn, but getting that far seemed an achievement and I felt proud of myself.'

Peter Winker was a Berliner of 'decent family' with two sisters. As a boy he read books on aircraft and always wanted to fly. He got his wish when he joined the Hitler Youth:

'The gliding was thrilling but could be quite dangerous. I saw two glider mishaps in which both young pilots were seriously hurt. But the thrill of it all and our youth enabled us to carry on. Then I went into the Labour Corps for six months before joining the new Luftwaffe to go through basic training, after which I volunteered to be a pilot. After some stringent selection tests I was accepted for training and went to Berlin-Gatow with a batch of recruits. There we were at once thrown into a period of selective ground training which weeded out some of the lads as unsuitable.

'We saw a lot of old training planes and received some instruction on these before being taken up in more modern types. On my first flight I felt quite sick, but soon got used to it and began to enjoy it. I was allowed to take the controls for a few moments to see if I had any co-ordination and all went well – at least, it did after I learnt to use stick and rudder pedals together. A few more boys had to leave so we were reduced to about a dozen lads. There were of course more pupils ahead of us and many more behind as the training was like a conveyor belt with a constant flow of volunteers. When I went home in my uniform my family were very proud of me, even though I had yet to earn my pilot's badge.'

It was 1938 and Peter and his fellows who passed out basic flying training were then allowed to take on the fast and manoeuvrable Heinkel 51 biplane:

'Some of the lads had accidents but no one was killed. We learned all the tricks of flying including formation, aerobatics and low level and by that time it had almost become second nature to us and was great fun. At last we passed out and received our coveted pilot's badges and were sent to a proper fighter base at Oschersleben. There we saw the Me 109s for the first time and were very impressed, it was a great thrill to be shown over these machines and then to actually sit in the cockpit.'

The pupils received a lot of ground instruction before being permitted to taxi an Me around the field prior to attempting flight. By then its vices, such as they were, had become well-known, it had a tendency to swing on take-off and other faults near ground level not helped by its very narrow track undercarriage.

> 'When it came to my turn I was careful to watch out for its less desirable qualities that we had been warned about and to remember to pull up the wheels. The plane was very fast and got off the ground in no time at all and I was soon circling the field at a few hundred feet and marvelling at it all. It was only a short flight and before landing I opened the hood as the view was very restricted in the Me. When I came down it was a little bumpy but good enough to receive congratulations from the instructor. From then on we practised take-offs and landings daily until we felt we had mastered the thing. We had one fatal crash when one of the lads came in too fast and tried to land instead of going round again; the plane turned over and caught fire and the boy died alone. It was a shocking thing to see, but we knew he had made a silly mistake and resolved never to do such a thing ourselves.'

Those young novice bomber pilots who escaped training on the beast of a Junkers 86 with its temperamental diesel engines were fortunate.

Horst Juventus:

> 'At this time there were still some old Junkers 52s and 86s in service as trainers and we had some at Berlin-Gatow, but only for ground instruction. A number of us received this tuition in 1937 and were then sent off to a new field near Wilhelmshaven where we found not only the same planes in flying condition but also more modern types such as the new Dorniers and Heinkels. It was all very exciting for us and impressive. We had very comfortable barrack rooms and were soon able to inspect the machines and met some service pilots who were to be our instructors in the training wing. I will not forget my first flight in a Junkers 86, which was almost my last. The conversion from flying small biplanes and monoplanes to those great twin-engined bombers was radical. No matter how much talk you received on the ground and in the air it was quite another matter to actually sit in the pilot's seat and take the controls!
>
> 'I took off with two other pupils and the instructor at the controls and we did a few minutes flying around the area with our tutor talking all the time, pointing out the various characteristics of a larger plane etc. He had already gone over the various controls and instruments on the ground. It was my chance to show what I could do, and the machine at once felt like a great elephant to me and I felt panic. We lurched all over the sky, I'm not sure who was most alarmed – myself or the passengers. The instructor yelled at me to straighten up and he increased the throttles and at once I found we were in a steep climb

and over compensated so that we went into a dive! I was now getting quite desperate and I believe my passengers were in some terror. But our instructor was used to such situations developing with new men and at once knocked me out of the seat and took over the controls – much to my great relief.

'The Ju 86 had troublesome diesel engines which were not really a success. On that day we spent a further half-hour in the air and my companions did no better than I did, so all in all it was not a very good day. However, the instructor was a model of patience and when we went up next day things went a little more smoothly. And a week later I looked back on my first flight as laughable and by then had not only achieved a good deal of control over the beast but had also actually landed safely and taken off again.

'But one of my two fellow pupils could not get the hang of it and was transferred to fighters where I believe he did very well. I had no such desire and continued the course, soon moving on to the new Heinkel 111 which at the time was the early version with elliptical wings. This was much easier to fly and I enjoyed it. We would take off, three pupils with an instructor and fly over the sea in a great circuit before returning to the field. I seemed to be doing very well and a month later went home on leave to the delight of my family who thought I was a really dashing hero!

'But when I returned to the base it was to find that one of my fellow pupils had been killed in an accident and another seriously injured, which was very sad. But being young we recovered quickly and it was not all work, in off duty hours we went into the nearest town where the girls and beer were plentiful and we had a lot of fun. We were also inspected during training by higher officers including Göring who was a very laughable figure but popular as he seemed so jovial and brimming with confidence and made us feel important and like heroes.

'After several weeks, during which we continued flying including formation work, we were assessed as competent bomber pilots and following a parade were assigned to our units; I was to go to KG26 (Kampfgeschwader or bomber Wing comprising three gruppe or groups plus a stab or staff unit). Most of the Wings were new as the Luftwaffe was still growing very rapidly and built on a cadre of old hands, professionals from the earlier war and of course the 'civilian' organisations built up by the Nazis.

'We arrived at our unit, which was based on a new field near Dortmund, and there I was given an Observer who would be the plane commander, plus two gunners, one of whom was also a radio operator. We then began to train as a crew with flights to the North Sea and country ranges to practise bombing. There were also classroom lectures on bombing techniques, targets and the forces of our potential enemies, namely Poland, France and England. We knew the Czechs had a very *high technical capability, but their country was now occupied so they no longer counted.'*

The Observer Karl Haulmeier had found his own fascinating niche in his assignment to Dornier bombers:

> *'This was all very exciting and I had a great love of these machines; to be ensconced in the small glazed nose with good comrades behind me doing the other jobs was enough for me.'*

Karl Haulmeier found life 'very agreeable' as he entered into operational training in the same manner as Horst Juventus in KG26, though his period of preparation preceded the latter's. He became a Sergeant in 1937 and it was only then that it was decided to make the Observer the plane commander, which enabled him to gain further promotion to Lieutenant (*Leutnant*):

> *'This was even more agreeable and meant my being sent off on a special training course where we learnt man-handling etc. When I returned to my old base I was given command of a different crew and the whole organisation was changed. We now flew in larger formations and learned new tactics of war flying and before long it became obvious that the international situation was deteriorating alarmingly. Until then I had not taken a great deal of interest in politics, though of course a great deal had been drummed into us in the Hitler Youth, Labour Corps and on the national level. But in the air force we had been too busy training in the profession we loved to have time for politics. I woke up with a jolt to see the true situation and realised that war was possible and that we would be involved.'*

When Hans Gilbert, the Dornier pilot still under training, arrived on a regular unit he found veterans in command who soon made sure the newcomers knew of their fledgling status:

> *'The discipline was fair but strict and we did a great deal of formation flying and bombing exercises and I was assigned to a regular crew and learned to work in a team. The Observer was a fraction older than myself and in command. His name was David which was a little unusual, but he was a fine sort of lad and had an easy way of command and certainly knew his job. Our two gunners were both likeable lads, Karl and Jochen, the latter worked the radio. We had to learn all about the Dornier 17's capabilities as a flying machine and as a bomber, and received lectures on the role of army support. All this took up most of our time as we tried to absorb the lessons, and it dawned on us that we were training for a war which began to look increasingly likely.'*

Georg Kessler had arrived at Wunstorf as a half-trained Heinkel air gunner and attended lectures by the 'chief gunner' after being shown round the base and over the unit's latest bombers:

'He told us that next the day he would personally test each one of us including the radiomen–gunners and we would learn to shoot from all positions – top, floor, and nose, although in the last case that was not really a gunner's post. Sure enough, next morning we were taken up and had to 'shoot' at various small planes which made dummy attacks on us from all angles, with the gunnery chief watching us. The attackers were only training machines, but when later on we exercised with Messerschmitt fighters it was very different, they came in so fast that we only had seconds in which to sight our weapons and let fly before they were gone. In fact, it was far more difficult than shooting at towed targets, as we should have known.

'Then we went on big manoeuvres as complete crews and I met my new comrades including the plane commander. They were very easy to get along with, but as it turned out I was not to be with them long, for soon the groups were reorganised and I found myself with a different crew. Both myself and the radioman–gunner Hans were new, but the Captain–Observer and the pilot were officers and by comparison veterans. One was called Karl, the other, like myself, Georg, we had a fairly informal relationship with them and they treated us like comrades.'

Johann Schmidt also went to the Dortmund base to further his training as a Heinkel pilot, finding both old and new aircraft types on the field. Johann found the Heinkel bomber roomy and his first flights were exciting, the type was easy to fly and he handled the controls with confidence. It was customary for a fellow pupil to handle the throttle controls, allowing the man in the pilot's seat to concentrate on the flying before they changed places. They flew all over Germany and up to the North Sea, the instructor setting the courses:

'So we had no trouble with navigation. After a month we were considered reasonably proficient and at this point some later type Heinkels arrived on the base, together with other crewmen, including an Observer called Lothar who became my commander and friend, and we began to work together. He told me that we would soon continue operational training at another base where we would collect our remaining crew members. And that is what happened, we went off on a long exercise which ended at a base near Lübeck where we collected our two gunners, and found that the radio operator spoke French. We then began to do formation flying and bombing and as pilot I had to fly straight courses over targets which were sometimes near or else could be hundreds of miles away. We learnt about support for the ground troops, the reason for certain types of attack and how to fly good defensive formation. Lastly, we carried out manoeuvres, which included dummy attacks by Messerschmitts and also old Heinkel 51s. After all this training we were declared an operational unit and

inspected by higher officers who told us how proud they were of us and expected great things of us. We were then given the unit number KG27 and someone presented a design for the group which was then painted on the nose of our Heinkels.'

Danish-born Otto Jufen, having passed out as a qualified Observer (and therefore aircraft commander) was posted to one of the new Heinkel bomber groups, KG30, who at the time were based near the island of Sylt. The unit used a plunging black eagle on a tricolour shield as their insignia, the badges painted just behind the heavily glazed noses of their Heinkels, the same motif being used when the group later converted to Junkers 88s under the renowed Werner Baumbach.

Horst Jentzen entered serious war training, piloting a Heinkel bomber in mock attacks, his unit commander himself observing results of their bombing:

'He used to make some stiff comments in some directions and assign us more intensive instruction if the results were bad. Of course, dropping the bombs was not my job but that of the Observer and CO of our plane who was a Sergeant I got to know very well in those days. Named Karl, he was a big fellow from Berlin and kept us amused with his jocular comments in the air. In fact, we often went off the base as a crew in off-duty times and had fun, finding girls who we invited onto the base during an open day. We even had a small party with them in our mess, but it never got out of hand as the base commander appeared and insisted on joining us; I believe he fancied one of the girls.'

Jentzen's crew were posted to the field near Wilhelmshaven to continue their bombing lessons, which included attempting to hit a towed target at sea:

'This was very hard and we did not do very well. Then we did a lot of long distance practice missions across Germany as far as the French border and eastwards as far as Poland, usually escorted by relays of Messerschmitts who attacked us in mock combat to give both sides some practice.'

Karl-Ludwig Weinfarth had been made Lieutenant by the age of twenty, his great ambition apparently fulfilled. Assigned to a bomber wing he now looked forward to commanding a whole formation of bombers in the air: 'I was very proud and felt I was bound to succeed. Such was my confidence!'

He now entered a new phase of training, for until this time he had never piloted a multi-engined aircraft and so went through schooling on old Heinkels and Dorniers. His confidence was justified as he passed all tests with flying colours, so that after two months he was posted to an operational squadron:

'It had just been formed and I was promoted to Oberleutnant (First Lieutenant). I always remember the CO addressing us newcomers who were all young officers and NCOs, he told us we were the cream of the Wehrmacht and in fact the cream of the Luftwaffe. He had high hopes of us and expected us all to do our utmost. From the reports of us he had seen he thought some of us would go far. This sounded very good to me as I felt he had me especially in mind, such was my cockiness.'

Like many other Luftwaffe bomber crews, Weinfarth's carried out many mock war flights across the Reich as far as their neighbours' borders, as well as the customary trips over the North Sea.

'However, I had not reckoned that I would not be in command of an aircraft, it did not seem natural to me that the crew member sitting in the nose with the maps as navigator should be in command. In fact I thought it was madness and had no good reasoning. I also realised that as a mere pilot I would never become a wing or group commander in that kind of situation. I tried to curb my disappointment and looked for ways to improve myself, but this did not seem possible and I saw that my CO's remarks had been misinterpreted. However, I learned later that there were certain cases where a bomber pilot had become so well-known and received promotion that although technically he was not the captain of the aircraft he did in fact execute the greater authority. But in those early days I was young and impatient and wanted to get on with my career, I never saw such matters in the long term, I was much too young. And although the prospect of war did not frighten me I did not realise that combat itself would effect changes. So I was forced to accept the situation and remained a Lieutenant until war came.'

The later famous Stuka pilot Hans Rudel remarks that, with his comrades, he had become 'very expert'. He flew the B model, Ju 87s with revised wheel spats and fitted with small sirens:

'Which produced a screaming sound on diving, purely for effect, listeners on the ground told us the noise had a very unnerving effect on them. We had carried out many manoeuvres with the army, demolishing targets for them with considerable accuracy and after some demonstrations received congratulations from the ground commanders on our work. We felt we had become very proficient and had become a potent weapon of war.'

Meanwhile, the Messerschmitt pilots Kurt Henner and Peter Winkel had progressed in their training to the fun of attacking Luftwaffe bombers in what the RAF came to call 'fighter affiliation' flights. Henner:

'Sometimes they were the old Junkers 86s or even 52s, which we thoroughly enjoyed "attacking". Then we flew with Heinkel and Dornier

*formations and had little trouble in our opinion in "shooting them down"
also. In fact, we felt sorry for the crews who were forced to endure such
things.'*

Of the aspirants described earlier, Wolfgang Schauer, like his con-
temporary and future hero Rudel, discovered there was such a thing
as dive-bomber squadrons, then in embryo form:

> *'It was not a new idea, I discovered it had been copied from the
> Americans and especially from one of their machines which seemed to
> impress our people very much. In short, I applied at once to join these
> new-type squadrons and was soon very involved in training. It was all
> very new and we had much to learn in flying these rather ugly planes,
> as well as in tactics. I'm afraid there were some terrible accidents. I
> remember I saw more than one plane dive straight into the ground
> and it was a very shocking experience for us novices. However, we
> were young and soon recovered our morale and became proficient in
> our job. I passed my assessment tests and we had to take a gunner
> with us in the rear seat, so our training was a little more complicated,
> otherwise it was fairly straightforward.*
>
> *'By the late 1930s our political leaders had become very powerful
> and were making all kinds of threatening noises, though we airmen
> had not been too interested in all this. I myself had completely
> given up politics and lived only for flying. We had many parties
> and no shortage of girl friends, life was rather good and I enjoyed
> myself.'*

Having entered the Luftwaffe 'by the back door' as he puts it, Christian
Rossler again became bored, for he found as an officer he was stuck in
a desk job, only occasionally relieved to make inspections. In short, he
was a chairborne airman, and so amazed his superiors by applying to
become a pilot:

> *'So I went off to elementary flying school and enjoyed it very
> much. I did not encounter any special problems, passed all my tests
> and became a pilot, But, it was the big birds that I wished to fly,
> so I went on to learn how to handle bigger aircraft, starting with
> old-fashioned machines, graduating to Junkers 86s and Dorniers. By
> the end of the course I had qualified and loved flying, wishing I had
> set out as a flyer from the beginning. I was now a qualified bomber
> pilot and when I returned to my unit I was given command of a whole
> wing! This was a big promotion, but my superiors felt I had earned it.
> I at once began to get to know my units and something of the theory
> of aerial bombing. It was a very different world I had entered and I
> tried to master all the problems connected with possible wartime flying
> and the administrative tasks involved. I had landed myself in a very
> big job.'*

Arthur Tieker recalls that he had to pass all sorts of tests before even being accepted for flying training:

'They were very strict at that time, as they wanted to build up an élite force. Eventually, I was allowed to fly with an instructor, but to my surprise I did not do very well. It had all looked so simple as a boy; somehow I just did not seem able to co-ordinate my hands and feet to control the biplane in the air. I was terribly disappointed and tried harder and managed to improve a little. However, at the end of the course my instructor told me I would never be any good as a fighter pilot. I was interviewed by the CO who told me there were vacancies for bomber pilots if I cared to give it a try. It would mean much hard work, but by my reports he thought I might do better in a larger plane. I agreed at once and was soon despatched with other failures to another flying school.

'We saw Heinkels, Dorniers, and a few old Junkers 86s and were soon introduced to the cockpits and then took our first flights with instructors. I found it all very impressive and at once felt more confident, perhaps for psychological reasons. Before long I was seated in a Junkers 86 with an instructor and we took off. I can recall that first flight only too well as it was nearly my last! Despite my confidence I failed to co-ordinate my movements again and nearly crashed into some trees. My instructor was furious and could not understand how anyone could be so clumsy. But it was early in the course and I had another chance and at once took a better view of how to handle a larger aircraft and began to improve; as I did so my confidence improved, this pleased my instructor which in turn made me feel even better.

'Before long I had graduated with most of my fellow pupils onto the Heinkel 111 in its earlier form with the elliptical wings, and this type I took to much more easily than the old Junkers 86 with its fixed undercarriage and I progressed very well. We now had Observer–Navigators as well as gunners flying with us as crews under training, all trying to learn the job with a couple of instructors squeezed in with us. I can tell you it was all very cramped.

'The day came when our flights across Germany included the bombing of dummy targets, and this was more difficult as it meant following a set course for a certain time, with the instructors watching our every move and being very strict. I was glad it was not my job to drop the bombs, as if we missed by a wide margin I would get into trouble.

'At last, after many weeks we were passed as competent and went on leave, following which we were sent to a regular Luftwaffe unit where we found a very friendly, relaxed atmosphere, and soon felt at home.'

Peter Harmel underwent preliminary training in a light plane, passed out successfully and was posted to a fighter base equipped with the speedy Heinkel 51 biplane: 'These were very thrilling aircraft, but after a couple of years I saw the sleek new Messerschmitts and before long we had converted to them.'

By the summer of 1939 these Luftwaffe aircrewmen were typical of thousands who had been as thoroughly trained as possible, short of the lessons which could only be learned in war. They were probably the best trained aircrew in the world, and, whatever British propaganda was to assert later on, few of these Germans were Nazi fanatics. Certainly they believed in their country and probably much of the propaganda that was drummed into them concerning Germany's rights as a self-respecting nation. As airmen, young men in love with the adventure of flying and enjoying the glamour of being in uniform, plus the element of danger, they were little different to their counterparts in the RAF. Like the British lads, they had also entered into that other world of the sky and of course the bond of comradeship found in the armed services.

However, by August 1939 none were ignorant of the deepening crisis in Western Europe, and here the Nazi government made certain its Wehrmacht were well indoctrinated into the 'facts' of Polish atrocities against the German minorities living within its borders. Even though Germans as a whole had no desire for war, the alleged crimes of the Poles should not go unheeded.

Across the North Sea the nation owning an Empire saw things differently, even though most Britons had little or no knowledge of Poland or the fact that it too was not entirely innocent in power politics. They did, however, know enough about the ranting, bullying, lying Nazi dictator called 'Herr Hitler'.

Events built up to a momentum which even the efforts of Prime Minister Chamberlain was unable to control; Herr Hitler was determined to wage his war of conquest in the East. By August the Wehrmacht had deployed the necessary forces in eastern Germany to deal with the Polish 'problem'; the Luftwaffe had built up a force of 3,750 first-line aircraft, of which 1,270 were twin-engined bombers, plus 335 Ju 87 Stuka dive-bombers. The Allies at government level feared a much greater strength and estimated German aircraft production at some 2,000 machines per month, whereas the true figure was barely 800 of all types. And despite all the fantastic estimates of Luftwaffe strength bandied about in pre(and post)-war days, and despite all their secret preparations over the years, once the real air war got underway the Luftwaffe found itself short of planes and pilots.

When Adolf Hitler gave the order for the 'incident' to excuse his war on Poland the Luftwaffe deployed 1,929 warplanes in the East, of which 897 were actually attack planes, that is, bomb carriers. These figures may be compared with the number of planes fielded by Göring to counter any attempted intervention by Britain and France: 2,775 machines, of which 1,182 were bomb carriers. These totals were part of the 'all-up' strength of the Luftwaffe at this time of 4,704 aircraft of all types, the figure including all kinds of miscellaneous units such as the Führer's special flight, units under Göring's personal command and those planes allocated to convey other high commanders. Then there were the transports of the new airborne corps and very many reconnaissance planes, and the little biplane Henschel 123s which were used in the ground attack role in the East.

Despite all their efforts, Göring and his staff were completely under Hitler's sway, and the Führer had ideas only for short-term blitz campaigns to secure living space for his adopted nation in the eastern zones, which was why no long-term planning took place at any military level.

It is, however, necessary to briefly examine how the new and most modern air weapon of its time came into being, the effect this had on its western neighbours, and how Hitler's aviation industry fared in the war.

CHAPTER THREE

QUALITY FIRST

U ntil the Nazis came to power in January 1933 the German aviation industry remained small, thereafter it expanded rapidly.
Thanks to the energetic efforts of General Hermann Göring
and his cronies and direct funding from the new *Reichs Luftministerium*
(Air Ministry). The funding came by direct loans guaranteed by the
government, thus enabling the aircraft firms to commence work on the
new plane contracts awarded by the RLM.

The first requirements were manifold and, since primarily military,
the industry was obliged to follow the lines set down by Göring. He in
turn was influenced by the policy directives laid out by Hitler, who at
this stage of the game was intent on placating his European neighbours
who had been thoroughly alarmed by the twin disclosures of German
conscription and a new air force.

The man with the real brains to ensure a powerful air arm for his
nation contracted the German aviation industry to provide some 4,000
aircraft by September 1935. That man was Erhard Milch. He stipulated
that of those aircraft ordered, 1,863 were to be combat planes. The
German firms had now to grapple with the same problems besetting
foreign companies – principally that of mass production – but with the
difference that in Germany the Führer was becoming more and more
bellicose in his foreign policy, and as he did so he pressured Göring
to hurry along the air power he needed – and this pressure was passed
on to General Milch. Yet by Göring's own schedule the apogee of
German military aviation would not be reached until 1943, whereas
his Führer's aims seemed to be ensuring a war long before that.

By late 1935 German aircraft production had risen from 190 to 300
units per month, and during this period those names which would
become known in every household, even outside Germany, began to
come to the fore: Heinkel, Dornier, Junkers, followed by Henschel,
Arado and Focke-Wulf, these were the firms whose products began to
fill the new Luftwaffe bases across Germany. And though the striking
power of this new air force was, as laid down by Hans von Seeckt,
designed to act as a tactical air force, its use as a weapon of terror
against neighbouring countries was not only suspected by them but
also an idea encouraged by Hitler. It was this fear of bombardment
from the air which led to the appeasement of Hitler in the 1930s, a fear

first engendered in Britain by the Zeppelin and Gotha raids of the First World War, a fear exacerbated by the indiscriminate use of air power by the Japanese in China and then by the Guernica 'incident' created by the Luftwaffe in Spain. As Winston Churchill recorded later in his memoirs: 'Ministers had to imagine the most frightful scenes of ruin and slaughter in London if we quarrelled with the German dictator.'

By the late 1930s, when successive crises overtook the Western allies, provision for deaths by air attack on Britain amounted to hundreds of thousands at least. This was the official view, perhaps fuelled by repeated warnings from Churchill and an exaggerated belief in the power of the Luftwaffe, for even though reasonably accurate estimates were made as to its numbers, a wholly wrong set of conclusions resulted as to the bomb tonnages that the enemy could drop. But while the provision of large numbers of coffins was taken into account very little was done to provide mass shelter for the population in the event of air attack and virtually nothing at all was done to succour the bombed-out.

In fact, by the time von Seeckt vanished from the scene the kind of air force most dreaded by Germany's opponents did not really exist; at least, not in the strategic sense, for the nervous statesmen trying to placate the fiery Nazi dictator had no inkling of *Blitzkrieg* in which the German Luftwaffe, as a tactical air force would play a leading role. The Germans developed a horizontal and dive-bomber striking force designed to act as short and long range artillery to prepare the way for the panzer wedges of the new armoured divisions, tanks used en masse against which no army at the time had an effective defence.

Though preliminary operations by the Luftwaffe as the 'volunteer' Legion Condor in the Spanish Civil War which began in 1936 gave little or no hint of what was to come in German *blitzkrieg* tactics, one facet did give an augur in an important direction; this was the use of tri-motor Junkers 52 transports to fly Moroccan troops from North Africa to help the fascist General Franco combat the largely communist forces. The Junkers 52 had become a common sight at Croydon Airport as operated by the Germans' new airline Lufthansa, which daubed its planes in a colour all too similar to the Nazi Party uniform sometimes accurately likened to an unmentionable shade of brown, the tail fins decorated with the red–white–black of the state swastika emblem. The type had seen some service as a bomber, but was now being relegated to aircrew training – except for this new and highly important role as troop transport, seen in the Spanish war as a pointer to the future.

In the first of a number of 'mischances', the kind of episode to become commonplace in the big war to come, German Heinkels bombed a place called Guernica in Spain, and the opponents of Hitler chalked up the first 'atrocity' of a new Western air war. A fairly straightforward operation by the small Luftwaffe component involving the bombing of a bridge went wrong, a town was struck by bombs and civilians died. The casualties were minimal compared to those caused in China for years by the Japanese air force, but the incident was blown up out of all proportion, brought embarrassment to the German government and added to the fears in Paris and London of an erstwhile enemy who would not hesitate to use terror tactics in war. It is a fact that in this period the Allies saw the French Army as the bulwark against German aggression on land while conjuring up an irrational atmosphere of nightmare concerning the capabilities of the new Luftwaffe.

But it took the so-called 'Munich Crisis' of September 1938 to prompt the British government at least to begin a programme of air raid precautions by issuing gas masks to the civilian population and ordering local authorities to commence the building of air raid shelters in parks and other open spaces. The use of poison gas on the battlefronts of the earlier war had induced fear that a new war would inevitably bring its use by air bombardment. This never happened, and the 'settlement' achieved by Prime Minister Neville Chamberlain at Munich ensured that the proposed public shelters in parks were put on hold, remaining no more than ugly deep trenches for children to play in which soon ran with water when it rained.

Winston Churchill thought that in a war with Germany the Luftwaffe would attempt to burn down London and other British cities, for even this great man with all his inside information had no inkling of the real purpose of Germany's new air arm, however much his fears proved justified in the long run. He saw London's great sprawling docks as 'military targets of the highest possible consequence'; the fact that they were located in the heart of the metropolis was unfortunate for Londoners as the docks remained a prime target for the Luftwaffe through much of the war. The future Prime Minister, despite his admiration for things French including their army, imagined a dire situation in which Britain was separated from its ally and subjected by the Germans to an attempt to test the will and resistance of people and government by violent air attack, with the Nazis trying to gain their way by the destruction of cities and the slaughtering of citizens. But Churchill also believed that if such an assault could be blunted then this kind of method by 'frightfulness' to break British morale would fail.

While these dread preoccupations filled Allied statesmen in these tension-filled years the German aviation industry strove to fulfil the dictats of the Nazi political-military set-up in providing the combat planes needed for a new *blitzkrieg*-style army. The fact that this industry was already well dispersed across Germany was to prove an asset when the Allied bomber campaign began, and even before the war new aircraft factories were designed, built and sited with a view to such attacks. This foresight enabled the German aviation industry to survive even heavy air attacks later on and to actually step up production despite the worst bombing. Despite their technical and craft competence however, it is extraordinary how, in view of mass production methods, this German industry lagged behind in terms of actual numbers of aircraft produced. While not lethargic, the tempo of production continued at only moderate pace until 1944, one researcher has noted that under the incompetent handling of Göring, the Messerschmitt plant continued to work on an almost peacetime 'quality first' basis in a family atmosphere. The Nazi politicians had scoffed at reports of American mass production methods and refused to believe the figures quoted. Not until the 'damned Yankees' appeared in mass in daylight over the Reich did Göring find himself dismissed as economic supremo, his place taken by the extraordinarily gifted 'architect' Albert Speer.

By September 1939 the German aircraft industry was producing 700 machines a month on a one-shift system or the 40-hour week. This tempo was of course in the Germans' case entirely dictated by the course of events and the delusions fostered by Hitler and his government which came about as the Wehrmacht conquered Poland. The atmosphere of euphoria was hugely enhanced by the stunning victories in the West the following year when the Luftwaffe's losses were minimal, and even the considerable setback suffered in the *Kanalkampf* or Battle of Britain did nothing to change the almost leisurely pace of German aircraft production, which had partially returned to making even non-war products after the collapse of France. In fact, even after the war spread into the Mediterranean, the Balkans and then the Soviet Union very little was done to boost production – so that deliveries barely kept pace with losses or even failed to do so. As shown, not until the dire turn of events of 1944 did changes come: Speer introduced the seven-day week of 72 hours with workers earning extra rations for more effort.

It would be wrong of course to denigrate German aviation for the kind of situation which resulted in the mid-war years; like all plane firms who relied on military orders they were dependent on government directives and requirements. Hitler's belief in a short, lightning war resulted in no long-term planning, and as a result the Germans lacked any real central direction and co-ordination in long-term military aviation. By 1941 its two principal 'heavy' bombers were obsolete and incapable of development; yet the firms themselves did produce a great range of designs and even prototypes, most of which were impractical, bizarre, or in a few cases very advanced. Neither Luftwaffe leaders nor their political masters saw the need for a long-range heavy bomber, but the technical inspiration of General Wever thought otherwise and work began on one or two projects – only to be dropped after his death in an air crash. By the time a fresh look at the ideas came it was too late. This too was the fate of the best jet warplane, the Me 262, which with other new designs proved no lack of imagination and technical expertise on the Germans' part.

However, the delivery of 90,000 tons of bombs by the Allies on German aviation industry only succeeded in dispersing it even more across the Greater Reich and beyond; despite enormous difficulties, production was increased and quality maintained.

* * * *

By 1939 the Luftwaffe was organised as follows. At the top of the command chain lay the *Oberkommando der Wehrmacht* (OKW), the Supreme Command of the Armed Forces under Hitler, under which the army, navy and air force were subordinate. Each had its own command, in the case of the air force the *Oberkommando der Luftwaffe* (OKL), which with its parent body the RLM Air Ministry controlled five Air Fleets or *Luftflotten* numbered 1–5. Beneath this tier the organisation was divided into three: Administration, Signals/Flak and Operations. Under the first segment were the *Luftgau* or Air Regions which administered all air bases, dealing with personnel, medical, maintenance, supply and training, while into each was inserted from two to twelve regional airfield commands. At the base of this chain came the actual airfield commands which incorporated the operational units.

The purpose of the German air force was indicated by the allocation of Air Corps (*Fliegerkorps* I, II, III etc), which could be assigned to Air Fleets according to operational requirements – that is, the needs of the army. These Air Corps were split into *Geschwadern* or Groups which were in turn split into *Gruppen* or Wings, and then down to the basic *Staffeln* or Squadrons. The actual number of aircraft in units varied considerably, whether bombers or fighters etc, as well as the number of squadrons in each *Gruppe* which depended on purpose and requirements, from one to ten or even twelve planes per squadron. The whole intention was to provide a flexible and highly mobile air arm tailored to the needs of the ground troops; in other words, the great bulk of the Luftwaffe was under military not political control in time of conflict. And when war came its organisation proved sound.

At the outbreak of war in September 1939 the Luftwaffe was divided into four operational areas of command, each containing an Air Fleet and HQ, thus: 1 (Berlin), 2 (Brunswick), 3 (Munich) and 4 (Vienna). This organisation had transpired following Hitler's policy of expansion and covered the whole of Germany, Austria and Czechoslovakia; both Austria and Czechoslovakia had been absorbed by 1939.

Various modifications came about to the Luftwaffe organisation as the war progressed, so that the original 'Air Divisions' became 'Air Fleets', with two such components often assigned to a particular campaign, as happened in the West. The main tactical unit within the Corps was the *Gruppe*, whose own sub-units had evolved from the experiences of the First World War – the *Feldfliegerabteilungen*, or field support squadrons which had co-operated closely with the German Army, especially in matters of scouting, reconnaissance, air photography and direct observation, reporting via wireless telegraphy. The aspect of tactical spying received special attention in the new Luftwaffe and considerable strength was given to those units assigned such tasks, whether close or long-range reconnaissance. These squadrons were known as the 'Eyes of the Army' (*Das Augen der Armee*), this consideration given far greater weight than in any other air force. In August 1938 the Luftwaffe possessed no fewer than 197 twin-engined aircraft alone which were given the role of strategic reconnaissance, while a further 285 were allowed the tactical role. The chief purpose of the latter units was to photograph enemy airfields, troop and vehicle concentrations and military railheads for the bomber arm to deal with. But an extremely important adjunct for them was immediate battlefield scouting.

But it is with the Luftwaffe striking force with which we are most concerned here, those twin-engined machines designated in that era as 'heavy' in terms of bomb load.

At the time of the Munich Crisis of September 1938 the Luftwaffe's striking power lay in its 1,157 twin-engined bombers, the Heinkels and Dorniers designed to strike at an enemy's rear areas, with 207 Junkers 87 Stukas earmarked as dive-bombers for intervention on the battlefield. Added to these totals were 173 planes marked 'ground attack', usually Henschel 123 biplanes not used in the Western campaigns. A year later these totals had risen to 1,270 bombers, made up of 780 Heinkel 111s, 470 Dornier 17s, and only 20 of the new Junkers 88 'wonder bomber'; the Ju 87 Stuka force had risen in number to 335, though its stablemate the Ju 88, although twin-engined, had also been dubbed a dive-bomber, or *sturzkampfflugzeug* – dive-battle plane. In addition were the reconnaissance squadrons which were mostly equipped with the Dornier 17P and at the army's disposal.

Obviously, the increase in operational combat strength over the year 1938–39 had not been great, due to disappointing production figures caused by re-tooling and re-organising as the German aviation industry geared itself up to a greater production mode – or tried to.

Whatever Göring's well-known boast concerning the inability of an enemy air force to penetrate Reich air space, he and his Luftwaffe chiefs were taking no chances when it came to home defence and did not appear to belittle their opponents' air power. At this time the Germans probably over-estimated the threat, for a figure of 900,000 men is given as the strength of the Luftwaffe's air defence forces (flak, searchlights), a quite fantastic number. The air signals and reporting service numbered a further 100,000 men, while 60,000 men were engaged on airfield construction and other air force building work; 80,000 men provided general maintenance and supply, while 25,000 occupied Air Ministry and HQ staff; 50,000 men were actually connected with flying, the rest of the Luftwaffe's one and a half million men were under training. This figure can be compared with the mere 20,000 or so which comprised its strength in 1935.

During the later 1930s the British Air Ministry allowed itself to be bamboozled by the figures and reassurances given by the then Prime Minister Stanley Baldwin, but by the summer of 1938 the Air Staff, Winston Churchill and French experts were in a good measure of agreement on German air strength, inaccurate though their estimates were. This was partly due to German boastings, bluff and propaganda and all part of Hitler's strategy. In October 1939 the Allies overestimated the Luftwaffe's bomber strength by some 730 machines. By then Hitler had launched his Wehrmacht against Poland in the first blitz campaign in which all the theories propounded over the years of a new kind of air war were successfully put into operation by the Luftwaffe. Most of the Polish air force was destroyed on the ground, those few that took to the air were soon shot down. It is not much of an exaggeration to say that the Luftwaffe not only enabled the German Army to easily overcome its opponent, but specifically win the battle for Warsaw which surrendered following air bombardment. The Polish refusal to give in and their fortifying the area inevitably led to air attacks and civilian casualties – and a new name was added to the Allied propaganda list of German atrocities. Allied propaganda for home and world consumption also painted a dire picture of the German air terror, though for the military there were important lessons to be learned concerning German military tactics.

CHAPTER FOUR

IN A GREY DAWN

A	t dawn on Friday 1 September 1939 the German Wehrmacht began its demonstration of Blitzkrieg warfare. The term 'blitz' would continue to be used thereafter, irrespective of campaign or tactics. The whole concept was a German one, and intended as operations to overcome an enemy force in the shortest possible time and with the least casualties to the attackers by the use of concentrated armour wedges heavily supported by air attack. In fact, in the first blitz war the Luftwaffe did a great deal to enable the ground army to advance, initially by air strikes which pulverised the Polish air force on the ground and also by an 'on call' system of Stuka dive-bombers who eliminated opposition immediately ahead of the advancing troops. Certainly, the German Blitzkrieg on Poland would have taken longer to subjugate that nation had it not been for the Luftwaffe. For the aircrew the short campaign of just over three weeks was akin to manoeuvres, with little for the horizontal bomber crews and fighter escorts to report on return to their bases, targets were routinely bombed and the handful of Polish planes caught in the sky destroyed.

Horst Juventus had come to realise the danger of being a bomber crew during mock attacks by Mes during training, having largely overlooked this factor before. Yet the fighters as escorts always looked reassuring, and the only bugbear came when as pilot of a Heinkel he became tired during long flights, though being young he soon recovered after touch-down. Like his fellows, Juventus only knew of the international situation what his political masters wanted them to hear:

'. . . what we read in the newspapers or heard on the radio. The Poles were behaving badly towards our minorities in the border areas and this could not go on. We thought something ought to be done about it and hoped the English and French would help in mediation. Of course, we learned differently later on, but at that time we had no idea that Hitler was intent on war.

'We were despatched to East Prussia and feared the worst. We had some respect for the Poles who we understood had large armed forces but no really modern air force. I myself felt apprehensive, as I'm sure we all did, but this was mixed with a youthful zest for adventure and the thrill of combat. We had no real idea what to expect, but felt we *would achieve success though have some casualties which was only to be expected in war.*

'Then the day came and we learned that Germany had decided to settle the issue by crushing Poland. We were briefed to fly against a variety of targets, mostly airfields, followed by troop concentrations and then war plants. We took off in a grey dawn and soon flew over the frontier, our Observer and CO giving the course to fly. We saw smoke columns where our Stukas had already attacked targets including some of the Polish airfields. Then we reached our own target, an airfield where some of the Polish aircraft were in the act of taking off. Down went the bombs from our whole formation and the target was soon smothered in smoke and dust and completely obscured, and as we turned for home we saw that we were well escorted by about 60 of our Messerschmitts.

'The days that followed were much the same, we did not see a single Polish fighter and bombed our targets at will, and on some days we flew two or even three raids, these were always against airfields, troops and dumps. We heard that the Poles had retreated and were fortifying their capital Warsaw, so we were briefed to attack their positions in the city. We had no option in this matter as we were bound to support our ground troops so carried out several attacks on known enemy positions. The Poles then gave in, and I must say the suffering they brought to the city and its population was unnecessary. Naturally, it was the German invasion that instigated it all, but the Poles insistence on turning Warsaw into a redoubt was foolish.'

The Dornier Observer Karl Haulmeier remarked of the assault on Poland: 'Ours was not to reason why, we were obliged to believe what we were told.'

Like their comrades in the Heinkel squadrons, the Dornier crews attacked similar targets behind the lines and destroyed most of the Polish air force on the ground, only occasionally encountering flak.

'It was a strange kind of war, and although we were shocked by the British and French declarations of war, the campaign in Poland soon ended.'

Haulmeier flew back to Germany in triumph, his parents looking on him as a model soldier, and hoped he would now find a suitable lady friend, but though he knew several 'not one of them appealed to me enough to form a permanent liaison'.

Hans Gilbert was one Dornier pilot whose unit remained in reserve, stationed at Gütersloh in West Germany until those squadrons of the Wehrmacht attacking Poland returned, at which point one *staffel* joined them so the crews were able to receive accounts of the war first hand. This particular unit had done all that was asked of them and lost only one aircraft through accident.

As a Heinkel air gunner Georg Kessler had looked forward to shooting down some Polish planes, but though they flew daily in the campaign not one enemy tried to intercept them:

> *'I always flew in the top gunner's position and had a magnificent view of the other bombers which was very thrilling. The only problem was that it was rather cramped and I got cold and was uncomfortably aware of our bomb load stowed nearby! We had gone into that war with an expectation of several months of combat losses, but in less than a month it was all over and we were back in Germany celebrating our good fortune and no losses and a good leave which was very agreeable. I was proud of myself even though I had won no medals. I had a nice girl friend named Elisabeth who seemed glad to go out with me and we planned to get married in due course, though my parents were not too happy over the idea and advised me to wait until the war was really over, for much to our disappointment England and France did not give up the struggle.'*

Johann Schmidt married his long-time fiancée during post-training leave, her name was Petra and the couple enjoyed a wonderful honeymoon in the Harz mountains. But their idyll was rudely interrupted by the coming of war when Johann joined his fellow crewmen in a Heinkel squadron, his friend Lothar as an *Oberleutant* and aircraft captain, their two gunners, Emil and Franz were corporals, while he himself was promoted to *Feldwebel* (sergeant). With the rest of the Luftwaffe bomber units, Johann's group began bombing military objectives behind the fighting lines but unusually on one occasion were intercepted by some obsolete Polish fighters which were promptly attacked by the Messerschmitt escorts and driven off, some being shot down.

When the campaign ended Johann's unit returned to its starting point in East Prussia, the men confident the war must now be over and surprised to find the Allies maintaining a front against Germany in the West.

'As for our Führer,' Johann remarks, 'whatever we thought of him, he had achieved some remarkable successes.'

The Heinkel Observer Otto Jufen remained in reserve during the Polish campaign, as did Peter Kroller in the same job. The pilot Horst Jentzen admits that he did not relish going to war at all, and by September 1939 some of the glamour had worn off. But he was committed and obliged to carry on with his job as the Heinkels flew east and took part in daily milk run missions over Poland:

'It was all rather dispassionate, I simply flew the course given, the Observer dropped the bombs, I turned the plane and flew it home again. The flights lasted about one hour and were not especially tiring.'

The crews seemed to have plenty of free time as the war became a routine:

'I had become a wartime bomber pilot with very little effort – or so it seemed. And when it was over we flew back to Germany and were granted leave to our homes; I went to Munich where my family were overjoyed to see me. My sister hugged and kissed me and treated me like a hero, though I did not feel like one at all. But we were very pleased that the war in Poland had ended so soon, and really believed that peace with the Western Allies would now come.'

The Luftwaffe's new weapon – the dive-bomber – faced its first test in Poland. Hans Rudel:

'When the invasion of Poland came we thought nothing could stand up to our blitz tactics. We flew to East Germany and on our first mission were escorted by 109s, I was very excited as we were directed towards Polish troops fortifications ahead of our army and went into our first attack. I saw little winking lights shooting up at us and after adjusting my flight path fired my machine-guns before releasing a large bomb at about 1,000 ft. My gunner called out that we had hit the target fair and square, the bomb had exploded on a Polish fort and demolished it. We reformed our formation and looking back I saw great columns of grey smoke rising into the sky.

'On our next job that same day we roared low over a Polish column and my gunner let fly and used up a lot of ammunition while I dropped the bomb load in horizontal fashion. Next day was the same, there was no shortage of targets as the army demanded our services over and over again. We used to spread our maps over the grass on the advanced base and mark up the enemy positions or columns and never had any trouble finding them. I remember on one afternoon we had climbed to 8,000 ft when someone shouted "Fighters!" and looking round I saw several little specks which proved to be ancient biplanes which were at once shot down in toto by our Mes. We got on with our job, encountering a little flak which was no deterrent, diving down onto a wood said to be full of Polish tanks and artillery and let loose our loads; the whole wood erupted in flame and smoke. And when we landed at base the CO told us that the army had already called up to congratulate us, all they had to do was advance and collect prisoners.

'In no time it seemed our new way of life came to an end, the Poles collapsed, we flew back to central Germany and soon went on leave. Some of us were able to attend a party in Berlin and see the great celebrations. I and a number of my comrades received the Iron Cross, which was very heartening. Then, as the furore died down we realised that the war in the West would go on, so we shrugged our shoulders and got down to more routine training.'

It may be as well at this juncture to bring up one small point that may seem significant to the Luftwaffe aviation 'expert'. Some thirty years ago one or two British aviation historians discovered official German wartime documents which referred to the premier German fighter of the day as the Messerschmitt Bf (*Bayerische Flugzeugwerke* or Bavarian Aircraft Works) 109 (or Me Bf 109); thereafter every self-respecting writer on the subject followed suit as if by rote. In view of the fact that the prefix 'Bf' does not appear to have been used at all in the German media and certainly not by word of mouth and since it makes easier reading the old term will persist here.

For most German fighter pilots the campaign in Poland also proved an anti-climax, very few saw an enemy aircraft in the air. Kurt Henner relates how he and his comrades had been too busy training and enjoying themselves to realise the seriousness of the international situation:

> '*When war came it brought us up with a jolt and for the first time we began to think of the possibility of being killed or wounded. But we were full of confidence as our commanders told us that the Poles were useless as an air force and that our tactics would upset their plans from the start.*
>
> '*Which is exactly what happened. On 1 September we flew over enemy territory for the first time and one of our flights saw some old Polish bombers and shot them all down. This was the only combat our unit was involved in, the rest of that short war was spent escorting our bombers, and as soon as our blitz was over we flew back to Germany and I enjoyed a really fantastic leave. My girl friend looked at me with love and admiration in her eyes, while my father shook my hand and told me how proud they were of me. I felt terribly elated and a hero, even though I had not fired a shot from my guns. Everyone was talking of peace and how the war must surely end now. Yet the Allies showed no sign of it so we were posted nearer the Western Front and began flying patrols on our side of the border.*'

Like his fellows, fighter pilot Peter Winker found the prospect of war both exciting and frightening, but being reassured as to the obsolescence of the Polish air arm by their officers went into action sure of success. Offensive patrols saw not one Polish plane rising to intercept them, and the Messerschmitts began bomber escort duties. But the German pilots did shoot off some ammunition, scouring enemy airfields at low level, finding only a few training planes which they shot up.

> '*We were very disappointed to have no combats in the air before the Poles surrendered. We took part in a big victory fly-past over Warsaw and then flew back to Berlin-Gatow for a short stop before going to a new base in West Germany. We then went on leave and had a good time at home. I had a girl friend and we fell in love, so got engaged though my parents warned me that as the war continued we should not rush into anything. I saw the wisdom of this, my lady friend only with reluctance I believe.*'

Like most other Germans, Peter Harmel felt the Poles needed teaching a lesson, so war became inevitable:

> '*We believed in our leaders and superiority of arms, but were apprehensive that a new bloodbath as in the earlier war might erupt.*

*However, our officers taught us that to strike first and with all arms
would ensure a quick victory, and so we believed them.*

*'We were one of the first squadrons to overfly Polish territory, and
we began to encounter obsolete aircraft and had no trouble destroying
them. But most of their planes were destroyed on the ground and gave
us and our army little or no trouble. I remember when I first shot down
an enemy plane: it was a twin-engined bomber and I set one of its engines
on fire. Two of the crew baled out, the plane then went into a dive and did
not recover. I felt elated and did not think too much about the enemy
airmen I had killed or wounded.'*

The Heinkel pilot Arthur Tieker:

*'In our first war missions we hit the enemy on the ground and succeeded
in destroying most of their planes. Those few that managed to fly were
quickly dealt with by our fighters. We got into the routine of flying
from an advanced airfield near the border, and our attacks were usually
completed within an hour. It all seemed so easy. We took part in the
bombing of Warsaw as the city had been turned into a fortress by the
Poles which made it a legitimate target.'*

Christian Rossler had settled into his new life as a Dornier bomber
commander:

*'I found myself – the former novice priest – flying over enemy territory
at the head of bomber squadrons, intent on killing or damaging our foe
into surrender. I did not have much time to reflect on such things, for it
was a very hectic and exhausting time for all of us. The Polish campaign
was a triumph of arms for the new Wehrmacht.'*

Wolfgang Schauer was one of those pilots who took the dive-bomber
concept into reality:

*'Of course, we swallowed all our own propaganda: when you only
hear what your leaders want you to hear you tend to believe it. Our
newspapers were full of tales concerning atrocities by these foreign
neighbours. We youngsters had absolutely no idea at all that it was all
a scheme by our Führer to coerce and then conquer the neighbouring
peoples to the east of us. So when our army invaded Poland we felt
our cause was just and could not really understand why England and
France declared war on us.*

*'But the die was cast and we were thrown into the thick of it. Our
Stukas were now being tested as a weapon of war, and I must admit it
was a thrilling time for youngsters like us. We revelled in our missions
and never had any problems finding and destroying our targets, which I
must stress were completely military: planes on the ground, supply trains
and troops. There were never at any time orders to attack civilians in any
circumstances. We suffered no losses through enemy action but one or
two accidents which were normal anyway.'*

When Polish resistance collapsed by the end of September the majority of these Luftwaffe aircrews returned to Germany and leave, many of them wearing the red–white–black ribbon of the Iron Cross Second Class on their tunics, heroes welcomed home by families and girl friends. Everyone was relieved the campaign was over and assumed the stunning demonstration of Wehrmacht tactics would convince the French and English that to pursue the war was senseless; even if Germany's enemies failed to call for peace, at least it was thought, they would refrain from attacking in the West. These sentiments have been expressed by Messerschmitt pilot Peter Harmel and reflected the views of all. However, unlike him, most of the Luftwaffe fighter pilots had been disappointed by the lack of opportunity to score in the campaign against Poland, that country's air force had not been geared to modern war; few German pilots saw anything of the enemy in the air. It was different for men like Werner Mölders and Adolf Galland who had already become aces in a minor way through their experiences in the Spanish Civil War, returning to Germany with the Legion Condor, to parade in their strange brown uniforms, bearing the new awards, the Spanish Cross instituted by their own grateful government and under the leadership of a man who would prove most instrumental in proving the theory of tactical air co-operation – General Freiherr von Richthofen.

As for the bomber crews, they had no such feelings of frustration, being of a different mettle and returned to the Reich in satisfaction of a job well done, especially the Stuka men, whose interventions had time and time again enabled the ground troops to advance and certainly speeded an end to the fighting. Yet, however satisfied men and commanders felt over this performance, for the Luftwaffe at least the real test would come not in the greater campaign then being planned by Hitler but in its decisive aftermath – the Battle of Britain, the *Kanalkampf* or Channel Battle as the Germans, curiously, preferred to call it.

For Hitler it had been a cheap victory, yet his army's losses were considerable: for the Luftwaffe, 455 men were killed or missing (including 42 ground crew), with 150 wounded; 285 planes were lost, a further 279 out of action through damage. Polish losses numbered 745.

Above all, the Polish campaign had been the great testing time for the new Wehrmacht, a time for all the theories and tactics formulated through discussion and manoeuvres over the years to be put on trial. As Colonel Johannes Fink confirmed in regard to the bombers' contribution:

'The generals came to see us as a real asset and this was proved in the war against Poland. The enemy had no comparable organisation and were quite unable to defend themselves against our bomber fleets and the campaign was a short one. When it was all over we switched the bulk of our air power to the West.'

CHAPTER FIVE

'NAZI AIR PIRATES'

T he French called it the *'droll de guerre'*, to their ally it was the
'Phoney War', those months after September 1939 when nothing
very much at all seemed to happen on the Western land front.
As pointed out elsewhere, things were rather different at sea and in the
air, where almost every action produced headlines.

Following early RAF incursions into German air space, Göring
directed similar probes by his Luftwaffe across the North Sea, and over
the next few months these small-scale operations were chiefly carried out
by KG26, the Lion Group of Heinkels, with their efforts augmented in
special sorties by the Eagle Group, the new and experimental unit flying
the 'Wonder Bomber', the Junkers 88. These two units carried the bulk
of the early air war to Britain.

England's first air reporting service and defence network had been
hurriedly set up in the earlier war; it proved inadequate but once
reorganised an efficient system of communications enabled the London
Air Defence Area to face up to German attack by aircraft and airships.
Disbanded when the war ended, it was re-started in the 1920s, albeit
in embryo form, as a string of observer posts resulting in the Observer
Corps being formed, namely civilians under the command of an Air
Commodore to eventually number five groups in all. Not until the
emergency of 1939 were eleven more groups authorised, by which
time the reporting organisation was being well meshed into the new
radar system and Anti-Aircraft and Fighter Commands.

However, the enthusiasm and efficiency of these volunteer civilian
observers was hardly matched by the AA defences of the British
Army, which under General Frederick Pile possessed barely 100 guns
to defend the sprawling capital. And these weapons included obsolete
3-inch weapons and crews who included half-trained, part-time soldiers
of the Territorial Army, the 'Terriers' whose main bout of training came
via the fortnight's summer camp each year.

By comparison, it has been estimated that by 1938 the Germans
possessed over twelve times as many flak guns, and all of the most
modern kind. By the time the Battle of Britain got under way the
number of AA guns available in Britain would rise to 1,200, of which
306 were the mobile 3.7-inch type, the remaining heavy batteries being
of the same calibre but on fixed sites, often in public parks or other

open spaces in or near residential areas. Additionally, there were 355 of the heavier 4.5-inch type, 226 old 3-inch, with a further 136 of this last calibre adapted for low shooting. The light AA batteries were equipped with 273 of the Swedish designed 40mm Bofors gun; there were also 140 2-pounders of doubtful value and a mere 38 20mm cannon. By the end of 1940 these main totals would be increased to 1,450 (heavy) and 650 (light), and five months later to 1,687 and 790 respectively. The heavy 4.5s were encased in naval mounts, that is to say, housed in warship type turrets. These guns could hurl a projectile weighing nearly half a hundredweight (56 lb/25.5 kg) to a height of eight miles (42,240 ft) in fifty seconds. The 3.7s fired a smaller shell to a lower height, but had a higher rate of fire, while the 40mm Bofors used clips of five rounds at a maximum rate of 120 shots per minute (though it would be impractical to expect any gun crew to achieve such a performance) to a height of 6,000 ft.

It would take the war itself to bring on the development of vital gun control equipment, and in this radar was to prove invaluable. Until then the pre-war and even later gun crews had to make do with quite inadequate sound locators and back-up from predictors, which though antique by latter day standards proved fairly effective in action. The chief function of the AA gunners was to force enemy aircraft to fly higher and thus hopefully lessen their chances of accurate bombing. Otherwise the use of barrage fire or predicted shooting against single planes did harass and occasionally damage or destroy German aircraft, forcing course changes or even the break up of formations so that the raiders became more vulnerable to fighter attack. In mass raids bomber fleets relied on collective security, the combined weight of fire from many machine-guns in a formation.

As far as London was concerned, AA guns were sighted on the eastern approaches, on the Kent coast, along the Thames Estuary and into the city environs, sometimes as it proved in highly vulnerable areas, such as the Isle of Dogs where during the Blitz one battery was overwhelmed by bombing. By contrast, some gun sites and crews plus their searchlight components were placed in remote areas of East Anglia and elsewhere, in places of near wilderness with little in the way of facilities, the troops living under canvas, so morale suffered.

Unlike the German Führer and his government who looked upon their females as mere child-bearing *hausfraus*, the British authorities had no objection to recruiting women into its armed forces. The enemy would not do this until conscripting them in 1943 when 'Total War' became the cry, though small numbers were accepted as volunteer auxiliaries earlier. By 1941 the British had allowed the first experimental AA units to include women, females of the Auxiliary Territorial Service – popularly known as 'ATS' – were trained on mixed gun and searchlight sites, and then worked in action with great success. The female soldiers braved the hardships on remote sites and did their jobs well, though on the odd occasion that German bombers were hit and struck the ground they tended in some cases to be more affected than their male colleagues.

Balloon Command did not come into existence until May 1938 when the first Auxiliary Balloon Squadron was formed, but by the outbreak of war forty-four squadrons were in being. At first, recruiting was carried out by the Territorial Army and Air Force Associations, with men up to the age of fifty being accepted for training and these included a good proportion of ex-servicemen. But when war came recruiting was stopped and the men were supplied by the RAF; the pre-war volunteers could always be picked out by the 'A' on their jackets.

Although many balloon crews with their winches and charging trailers full of gas cylinders were stationed in quite pleasant surroundings such as parks etc, others were less fortunate and lived like AA troops in remote places or even on a barge on the Thames. The danger during storms to the hydrogen gas cylinders was not a great hazard, though in rough weather such as high winds balloons would be kept on the ground, for undue pressure could snap the tough steel cable securing the balloon to its winch.

Although the chief purpose of the balloon barrage was, like the guns, to deter enemy aircraft from low flight and even divert them from a target, there were occasions when both German and Allied aircraft struck the cables, the planes being damaged and brought to earth. This happened in 1940 during the battle for Le Havre when a German aircraft was brought down by an RAF balloon. And on 13 September a Heinkel collided with a balloon cable over Britain, swung round it, pulling the steel hawser out of its drum on the ground far below and flying off with the wire clinging to it. But the cable then fouled a wire on another balloon site which sent the bomber crashing to the ground.

A balloon cable could slice off an aircraft's wing or part of it, and this did happen to at least one German bomber during the war. German raiders would cross the British coast from 15,000–20,000 ft before making a shallow dive to drop their bombs, but not lower than 10,000 ft because of respect for the balloons. This at least was the belief in wartime, though it often worked out otherwise, for the mass of Britain had no balloon barrage, and occasionally there came an intrepid German aircrew who braved the obstacles to attempt precision attacks. One British aircraft works was protected by a ring of balloons, so one German pilot who became highly decorated and was undoubtedly an ace bomber captain simply dived his Junkers 88 into the open well within the balloon circle, bombed his target and climbed steeply out again. The steep diving attack was practised by Ju 88 crews since the type was classified as a dive-bomber.

The outbreak of war found the British defences against air attack in a state of semi-preparedness, only in fighter defence, radar and ground control was the situation satisfactory.

Since it suited both sides at first to refrain from bombing inland targets and thus killing civilians, the RAF and Luftwaffe bomber crews were under strict instructions to attack only ships at sea or in harbour, and initially this meant warships. Hitler's orders were quite specific on this, he reserved the right to order bombing elsewhere. As a result German bomber crews were obliged to fly long distances in attempting to seek out suitable targets, these at first being the Royal Navy's Home Fleet anchorage and environs at Scapa Flow and around the Firth of Forth. To this end the handful of new Junkers 88 crews were directed, but their efforts met with no great success, despite the haze of propaganda regarding their triumphs from the German side.

Göring's petulance and demands had already resulted in the German Navy or *Kriegsmarine* losing most of its independent air units to the Luftwaffe. Göring insisted on controlling everything that flew, the Navy was thus left with a handful of *Kustenflieger* or coast patrol flyers. However, the 'man at the wheel' was often in Luftwaffe uniform, and some sort of uneasy compromise was reached if only to ensure that the proper identification of ships at sea took place. The Germans used Dornier 18 and 24 flying boats to patrol the North Sea and watch out for British warships, and when such planes were brought down by the enemy, prisoners taken usually included one naval officer.

The RAF had been quick off the mark in despatching a Blenheim to reconnoitre the German naval bases at Wilhelmshaven and Kiel; the Germans soon sent their own spy planes to the Orkneys and Firth, these followed by small forces of bombers, and apart from the 'experimental' Ju 88 unit the only regular bombers made available were those of KG26, the 'Lion' group, whose personnel were mostly ex-Navy, having been transferred *en bloc* into the Luftwaffe following Göring's tussle with the *Kriegsmarine*. The distances involved ensured a heavy fuel load and little in bombs, the Heinkel's cruising speed of 230 mph or less meant a round trip of some eleven hours. As often as not, when the German aircrews arrived in the target vicinity their searches were hampered by bad weather, especially in the winter of 1939–40, which was one of the worst on record. For the Heinkel crews it was sheer tedium, exhausting flights made again and again for little or no result.

Horst Juventus had, like his comrades, returned home in triumph to be feted in the general heady atmosphere of victory and the expected peace which most Germans now saw as inevitable. To their dismay the war continued, Horst being even more sobered when his father warned him that war was a serious business and that he should expect the sort of blood-letting that occurred in the previous war. This dire pronouncement made Horst downcast and was hardly calculated to sustain a flyer's morale, but on returning to the usual cheerful atmosphere of his unit he soon recovered.

'*My own unit returned to north Germany where we were on constant alert and then briefed to take part in attacks across the North Sea; the other sub-units had already been in action but only on a small scale, for the flights were long and arduous and the targets elusive. The orders were to attack only English shipping – especially warships.*

'*I well recall our first flight across the North Sea. We were about a dozen aircraft split into two sections, but we broke into flights of three before reaching England and the coast of Scotland. Once this was in sight we began searching the sea lanes for traffic, as our orders did not take us as far as Scapa and owing to the thick weather we had a lot of trouble even following the coastline at all. In fact, we became separated from the other planes and flew on alone for some time until turning for home. I was disappointed that our flight had been so unproductive, but glad to get back in one piece.*

'*But in the same week we made our first attack on a small steamer off Harwich. At first we saw only a small smoke smudge through the clouds, but on flying nearer we saw the ship which was zig-zagging and even firing a few rounds from a machine-gun on deck. I turned the Heinkel and we roared in low over the ship from the seaward side, both our gunners giving it a lot of fire as the bombs went down. The explosions were all round the ship which, however, did not sink. We then had to fly home and report our ship as damaged.*

'*My plane commander at this time, who was of course the Observer and bomb aimer, was a little older than myself, and also from Berlin. He was newly married with a baby and was always showing us pictures of his family. Both the other crew members were very young and keen and always hoping to see an English Tommy in the sky to get a shot at. Well, they certainly had their fill of that in due course.*

'*As the weather grew worse nearer Christmas we were relieved, and while away two of our machines and crews were lost, assumedly to fighters. They had gone off to attack shipping off the English and Scottish coast and never returned. We knew by then that the RAF had begun coastal patrols, so the work had become much more dangerous. And on our first trip in December following our leave we encountered our first English fighters.*

'*We were trying to get into a favourable position to attack a small merchant ship, had just cut across some cloud and were about to go in and bomb when our top gunner called out "Fighters!". I banked the plane at once as our CO told me to get into the clouds and shake them off. This I managed to do, but just as the cotton wool appeared about us a line of holes appeared along our port wing as we were hit. I never saw or heard that fighter and tried to keep the plane in the clouds, but there were gaps, and every time we were exposed our gunners reported fighters following us. I believe they were Hurricanes, and after a while it became hopeless, so we dropped our bombs in the sea, managed to evade the enemy and fly home.*

'A few days later one of our most popular pilots was lost in such a raid so we began to wonder who would be next. The weather in January 1940 was very bad, but we flew as often as we could, and on our very next flight had another narrow escape.

'I remember telling my crew that I had a feeling we would be in greater danger than usual – and they told me to shut up! I had a flask of hot coffee, but it got cold owing to the very low temperature. The flight was bad and when we reached the coast of north-east England we could see nothing but solid cloud in all directions. We had no option but to descend, and when we finally broke through into clearer air below we immediately saw a small convoy and went after it. I told the gunners to be especially alert as we went into the attack. The CO was at his bomb sight and I lined the plane up at about 2,000 metres and descending. Everything was going smoothly and the CO told me he was attacking the largest ship in the convoy.

'Our bomb doors were opened and just as the bombs left the racks we heard a tremendous racket, our gunners opened fire behind us shouting "Fighters! Fighters!". Then I heard a rattling noise and a lot of small bits flew past me in the cabin. I tried to dive the plane to one side, and then saw a Tommy whizz past us – it was a Spitfire I believe. And then all hell broke loose as more bullets pierced the body of the plane behind me. I crouched down into my seat as far as I could and tried to zoom the plane down almost to sea level and away from the ships who were also shooting at us. Our gunners were calling and I realised the top man was wounded, his name was Franz and he was a very jovial young fellow.

'Then the CO moved past me to see what he could do, and as he did so we were hit again and the starboard engine caught fire. Flames poured out over the wing and I could see we were in serious trouble. But then we hit a squall and were hidden in low cloud from the pursuing enemy, but I had doubts of our reaching home again.

'The CO managed to extricate the top gunner Franz, but he was dead. Then the lower gunner Peter came up and I saw that he had blood over his right arm. The CO bandaged him up and said we'd be lucky to get back as the damaged engine was useless. I had shut it off and feathered the prop. We were down to about 100 metres and I did not think the crate would stay up long enough for us to reach home.

'Yet, by some miracle the Heinkel stayed aloft and after a while the sky cleared a little and by great good luck we encountered a patrol of Me 110s who dived around us and escorted us back until we reached our base where I circled before making a landing where the smoking engine could be dealt with.

'This flight had given us a severe jolt. We had lost our comrade Franz and Peter was wounded and out of action for some weeks; he never returned to us. We enjoyed a few days rest thank God before being given two replacement crewmen and resumed action, but with no great enthusiasm, for although the weather had improved – so had the British defences. We had lost planes weekly and had a lot of new faces in the unit.'

It was then that these Luftwaffe men began to hear rumours of the big offensive impending on the Western Front, yet as spring came and the weather grew warmer they were not re-deployed as expected but remained on their own North Sea 'front'.

These over-sea excursions which proved so draining to KG26 were accompanied by a furious propaganda war, for no matter how 'phoney' the confrontation on the western land front, at sea and in the air action was frequent, and it has to be said that the greater successes were achieved by the Germans despite some of their wilder and unsubstantiated claims.

Corporal Francke was a pilot–engineer seconded to the first Junkers 88 unit which had been experimental but was now pushed into action over the North Sea. Francke dive-bombed the British carrier *Ark Royal* and scored a near miss off its bow, which was first translated into a hit and then a sinking by the German staff and propagandists. Feted, Francke was promoted to Lieutenant and given the Iron Cross on Göring's orders. But within a day or so the British Admiralty had invited journalists to view the still afloat and apparently intact *Ark Royal* safe in its berth.

However, whatever embarrassments the Germans suffered, they could rightly crow over the undisputed sinking by the daring U-boat captain Gunther Prien who slipped U-47 into Scapa to torpedo the old battleship *Royal Oak* at its moorings, with the loss of some 800 lives. The hounding of the German 'pocket battleship' *Graf Spee* and its eventual scuttling off a South American port brought great celebration to Britain in December, but Göring was envious of the German Navy's triumph at Scapa, ever anxious to promote his Luftwaffe as the cream. He had instigated the making of a film – *Feuertaufe* (Baptism of Fire) – as self-glorification following the Luftwaffe's triumph in Poland, and so urged his staff again and again to keep up the pressure on England in the only way his Führer would allow. For, as shown, Hitler had no plans at this time for any kind of blitz bombing of Britain, his offensive in France and the Low Countries would, he believed, achieve the kind of outcome he desired most.

In Britain a vociferous press campaign was directed at the 'Nazi air pirates' who attacked helpless fishermen peacefully going about their business in the North Sea. Churchill himself led the scathing attacks on the morality of such men who could stoop so low, suggesting that it was mere Nazi spite over the loss of their warship *Graf Spee*. These Luftwaffe attacks as described by Horst Juventus received coverage in Germany where Göbbels used first-hand aircrew interviews to bolster claims of heavy damage to British merchant shipping and warships. Questions of what is or is not a military or economic target would only arise much later; it could easily be argued then that fishermen were helping to feed the population who were behind the nation's war effort, food was a commodity of war, and war supplies were legitimate targets for bombers. It is asking much for an aircrew to attempt to discern the exact style and function of a small ship at sea in bad weather, and once the trawlers began to receive machine-gun armament for self-protection they at once became armed ships and ripe for attack anyway. Besides which the Admiralty had taken over a number of trawlers, put Navy crews aboard and sent them off as minesweepers or disguised AA lookout ships in the North Sea. Despite all the claims and counter claims, neither side gained anything very much – apart from experience. For their small successes the Luftwaffe bombers paid dearly; far greater rewards would be gained by use of the deadly magnetic mine, a weapon laid by Heinkel 115 floatplanes close to the British coast and on a couple of occasions by daring destroyer incursions.

In March 1940 the first civilian was killed by German bombs in Britain. This occurred when the single Junkers 88 unit was ordered to attack RAF and naval installations such as airfields and gun emplacements in the Shetlands area near Scapa Flow. Obviously, precise reconnaissance was needed to pinpoint suitable targets as the bombers would not have time to spare in searching for them. It is doubtful if the Luftwaffe provided such intelligence. There were a couple of airfields, one of which was the naval air station at Hatston, later used by Spitfires, plus various AA sites which had been increased through Admiralty nervousness following the Luftwaffe's previous attempts to bomb the Home Fleet.

To return now to the career of Horst Jentzen, who had graduated as a Heinkel bomber pilot and reached a base at Mannheim where he found various types of flying equipment, including a lone Junkers 88. So enamoured was he by the look of this machine that he sought out the pilot who he found was in process of touring various bases before picking up a crew for service with the soon to be christened Eagle Geschwader – KG30. Horst asked this pilot if he could be allowed to fly the Junkers, but was told he would need a lot of ground instruction first. Unabashed, he asked how he could join the Junkers unit, so the pilot rightly told him to go through channels, in other words to see his own commanding officer. This he did, and a few weeks later he received a summons to get his marching orders. By that time his earlier enthusiasm had been partly forgotten, but as soon as he thought of the Junkers his excitement of such a prospect as piloting one returned and he said farewell to his own crewmates, who were somewhat baffled by his desire to leave for another unit. But the visiting pilot had extolled the virtues of the new plane, telling him it was the best and would certainly be built in large numbers. In this he was broadly correct, the Ju 88 proved a very adaptable bomber and even fighter, and was built in greater numbers than any other German bomber (15,000 all told), though it has to be mentioned that its success was due largely not to Junkers but one man whose experience in America enabled him to adapt the techniques of design and production learned to the Luftwaffe's benefit.

When Jentzen arrived at his designated base near Wilhelmshaven he was directed across the field to the Junkers 88 unit where the CO made him welcome:

'*In a short time I had met some of the other crews, mostly pilots. Some were on leave, and I soon learned that it was the only squadron of its kind in existence and still experimental. That is to say, they were still evaluating the plane's capabilities as a bomber and dive-bomber. The CO told me that various plans were afoot to try and attack the British fleet in its anchorage, but it would not be easy owing to the distances involved and the likelihood of heavy defences. He showed me various maps and I could see that the round trip would be quite long. But there were more immediate matters for me to attend to, so I was shown to a barrack room and met new comrades, and the CO's adjutant arranged for me to be assigned to a crew for instruction both on the ground and in the air, and this began next morning.*

'*I was quite excited when I was shown over the plane next day and climbed into the cockpit, which was cramped and this disappointed me; at my first glimpse of the plane at my former base I had failed to appreciate how much smaller it was than the Heinkel. There was just room for the pilot and barely enough space for the Observer to crawl past into the nose, with the two gunners immediately at the pilot's back, one of them to act as radio operator. However, the view was excellent, and when the engines were started up I felt the beast was a powerful one. I had never trained in dive-bombing of course which was the intended prime function of the 88, so as soon as I had mastered the control functions the pilot instructor with me taxyed the plane away for take-off. We two were the only men aboard and I sat on one of the gunner's seats behind him, noting all he did as he explained the correct procedures.*

'*Then we took off and I was amazed at the plane's speed and rate of climb. We had soon flown above the clouds and the views across the sea were magnificent. We did a few turns and then climbed to 20,000 feet and prepared for a dive. I strapped myself firmly into my seat and the plane's nose dipped and we hurtled down towards the sea at a 75° angle. The noise was very considerable, and then the pilot showed me how the dive brakes operated to reduce the speed and make bombing more accurate. When he pulled the plane up again all the blood rushed to my feet and I thought I would lose consciousness, but this feeling soon passed as we climbed up into the clouds again for further instruction.*

'*In half an hour we had landed and once more I marvelled at the plane's performance which seemed to me as good as a fighter. In fact it made our old Heinkels look rather lumbering. Once on the ground I took over the pilot's seat to try the throttles and then taxi round the field to try a take-off. I opened up the engines and we raced along the runway, I felt nervous, but as soon as the tail came up I was able to pull back the control column and the 88 soared into the air with effortless ease. I trimmed for cruising and flew over the sea at about 2,000 feet, and with no problems the instructor invited me to climb to 20,000 feet and try a dive. This time he told me to aim the plane at a little island a little way ahead, and this I did, gradually increasing*

*the angle of dive until we were screaming down at the "target" at 75°.
I was very thrilled and excited and at 8,000 feet started to pull out.
At that time the 88 was not fitted with automatic dive brakes – they
were later, so some effort was needed to get the bomber's nose up, it
needed some muscle power. But this I accomplished without problems,
and as before I experienced some loss of vision as we shot up into the
sky. The instructor then made a few suggestions and I tried the diving
attack again, this time continuing to a lower altitude and instead of
pulling up steeply I flew off horizontally over the sea, my instructor
explaining that in attacking an enemy warship the flak would be far
more dangerous at a few thousand feet, whereas evasive action at low
level could be successful. So I flew back to base where I managed a
good touch-down and felt very pleased with myself.*

*'Next day I made another flight in company with two other machines,
one flown by the CO. We flew as far as Denmark before returning. We
had a lecture on the value of the British Fleet and were shown photographs
of its capital ships. Then I was given a crew who had just arrived on the
base and were as new or nearly so as myself. The Observer was Kurt
who had also trained on Heinkels and like myself was a Sergeant, and
as we both had the same name I called him Porky, as he was rather
thick-set. My two gunners were Peter and Ludwig and we at once
entered training together, both on the ground and in the air, making
many local flights as well as long-distance ones to Denmark and even
further afield, always across the sea. Then the weather turned bad and
all flying was cancelled.'*

Very little flying was in fact done by the airmen over the next months
owing to the terrible winter, with the aircrew even being obliged to help
clear the runways of snow. The flyers found it irksome to remain inactive
and little leave was granted. But as soon as the weather improved the
crews took to the air again and attempted to make up for time lost.

*'We soon meshed together as a unit and I was pleased with my own
crew, this is very important in the air and especially in action. Then
one day, I believe it was in March 1940 we were called together by
the CO and his staff and told that we would now try to attack the
airfields and installations in the area of Scapa Flow and the Orkney
Isles. A large map was unrolled before us and the crews themselves
issued with special ones and the briefing continued. We would cross the
North Sea at sunset in one wave and attack whichever targets presented
themselves. Owing to the distance we had to fly there would not be time
to dilly-dally and make searches, we must identify a target, bomb and
escape before the enemy awoke. We had discovered to our cost that
there were Spitfires and Hurricanes in north Scotland so there was
need for great alertness. Furthermore, there could be no question of
fighter escort; we were on our own. It all seemed like an experiment
to me with success uncertain. But as the CO told us, the experience*

would do a lot of good and lead to better things. To me it sounded like a dubious enterprise.

'We made our preparations, studying the maps and latest weather reports and after a hurried tea assembled in our laden bombers. On a signal we started engines and taxyed one by one onto the runway which was clear of ice and snow. We took off and assembled over the sea at about 5,000 feet in one big formation, which was a little strung out and not at all in copybook style. The sun was in our eyes and it felt warm in the cabin as we set off across the North Sea, yet I soon felt the cold seeping in despite the several layers of warm clothing I wore. We droned on and on and it became rather wearying, but at long last my Observer in the nose called that a dark smudge on the horizon must be land – hopefully Scotland, so the whole formation made a course change to the north-west and we began to spread out into battle echelon.

'Before long we could distinctly see several islands looming on the horizon and our CO and formation leader waggled his wings so we fell back into an even more open, looser formation. In the lead the CO hoped he could spot some suitable targets, but for a start we could see no shipping, and as the islands drew nearer we could see no targets there either. However, we knew there were air bases somewhere in the area, some probably used by the Royal Navy, and also flak emplacements, so everyone kept a sharp lookout.

'Then our leader shot off a flare which signalled "target in sight", and at the same time several searchlights were switched on, though it was far from dark. And someone called "Flak!", but I saw nothing in the way of defensive fire, and then came the signal from our CO – target immediately ahead! This was the sign for our Observer to switch on his bomb control panel. I was busy concentrating on flying the plane, and we were now at only a few hundred feet and it was quite bumpy in the prop wash of the aircraft in front of us. Then Horst called out that our lead planes were banking and all at once I saw sparks flying past our wing and Horst called "Flak!" and at that moment released our bomb load. The plane leapt up and I pulled at the controls to keep us on an even keel. Because of those planes following us our bombs had short delay fuses. Then the gunners called out a clutch of explosions across the island which seemed to be on targets which were flak or airfield installations.

'Our whole formation then turned out to sea again with the searchlights trying to follow us but without much success as we stayed at low level until we were well clear and then climbed to 5,000 feet. It had all been very exciting and over in seconds. My first bombing raid! I was very relieved and we ate chocolate as our tensions eased.

'The long flight back was easier, though we had some anxious moments when one of our engines began making rough noises before resuming its normal note. We touched down in almost total darkness, which was the worst part of the trip, though the runway lights were switched on. Soon

all the crews were in the briefing room and making their reports while the intelligence officers assessed our degree of success. According to the radio communique that night German bombers had successfully attacked RAF, army and naval installations in the Scapa area and returned without loss.'

In this period the Germans gave these raids the full propaganda treatment, even though they were no more than pinpricks, as were the RAF attacks across the sea. Press conferences were called in Berlin, with principal witnesses presented, seated behind tables before large wall diagrams to provide exciting tales for the neutral press. However, it would be wrong to deride the small Luftwaffe raids on this British periphery as a waste of effort. The old battleship *Iron Duke* used for training was struck by a bomb and damaged a second time on 16 March, and the cruiser *Norfolk* was also hit and put out of action for three months. The damage to shore-based military installations is not easy to assess for histories on this early period of Luftwaffe attack usually make a point of ignoring it or giving it scant attention. And the media of the period gave nothing away in that direction; they were not permitted to by wartime censorship and the very remoteness of the Orkney Isles prevented easy access to hard news anyway. There are some one hundred islands comprising the group, and some British propaganda writers, while giving an outline of their history (taken over by Scotland in the fifteenth century from Denmark, population 25,000, 119 women to every 100 men etc), sought to mock and deride the enemy for spending so much time and effort in attacking these little bits of land devoid of military targets. One writer claimed the Germans had wasted twenty bombs and 3,500 gallons of petrol just to damage a window in a Shetlands cottage. 'Just bareness, a few crofters' cottages, that's all' ran one photo caption to assure readers of the truth of the arguments and derision expressed. The same feature writer explained under his headline 'Why the Germans made for the Shetlands' his theory that the enemy saw the area as the northernmost link in the British chain of contraband or blockade control which had worked so successfully in starving the Germans in the earlier war. The enemy were making strenuous efforts, he explained, to prevent such a blockade being set up again. Whether the writer believed such nonsense is not relevant, most people believed such 'authoritative' articles, and in any case it was impossible from a little desk in the city of London to ascertain just what one's own side were up to militarily in such a remote spot.

The Germans by contrast had some excellent information via the reconnaissance photographs taken by men like Horst Jentzen, even though it would seem that these pictures came to hand after the event:

'Soon after that I was despatched with my crew in another plane fitted with cameras to reconnoitre and photograph the same area. This

was a much more interesting task but a dangerous one as a lone plane would certainly attract all the defenders' attentions. We flew at 25,000 feet and it was very cold, and when we reached the target area I made one run from south-east to north-west, then turned the plane to make another from north to south, with all our cameras turning. Then one of our gunners reported two fighters climbing up far below, but they had no chance of catching us. We did a very gradual descent over the sea back to base in safety, and later I was able to see the pictures we took which were marvellous in detail. Our experts were able to pick out all the ships and bases and I felt we had done our job.'

The cameras of the day were good and the Germans' excellent, so with so much spying already done before that attack it is not easy to see why their briefing had been so haphazard. And when Mr James Isbiston met his death when a German bomb destroyed his little cottage the British press naturally caught hold of the propaganda gift while the Air Ministry and Government took it as a signal that the 'no bombs on land' moritorium was off, ordering a reprisal which took the form of a much trumpeted but totally ineffective RAF raid on the German seaplane base at Sylt island, an attack said to have lasted some five hours during which time much destruction was wrought.

But while the Luftwaffe's attacks were often derided, truth in the British fashion did emerge. In the first case the tale of the Shetlands rabbit was made much of. The little creature was said to be the only result of one German raid, and its carcass was later (so the tale went) carefully packaged and dropped with an appropriate note by the RAF over Germany – addressed to Göring. Otherwise, the authorities admitted ships damaged or sunk. Complete details of the ship names, crews' experiences etc being released, and so the enemy were provided with fullest intelligence as to the true result of their raids. This patchy approach to censorship was evident throughout this period. In general, the British daily newspapers reported what they knew in fairly straightforward fashion. It was left to the feature writers in magazines such as *War Weekly* and *War Illustrated*, to name but two, for added colour by way of in-depth stories, which in the case of Heinkel attacks on shipping were typically headlined 'They were the targets of Nazi air murderers', while one of the ex-military men turned columnist referred to the past behaviour of the German Air Force as *'despicable'*. But he then told the tale (hurriedly censored in the dailies), of how a downed German aircrew had rushed to rescue the British pilot who had shot them down before crashing by accident himself.

All of this aerial activity by the Luftwaffe could be construed as directed wholly against the islands off northern Scotland or the ships about there and off England's north-eastern coastline. Yet a chart published at the end of February 1940 discloses '72 Nazi Raids on Britain in Six Months', these indicated in the illustration by close-packed route lines starting incorrectly at the seaplane base at Sylt, the island just off Denmark's coast, and radiating down to the Frisian Isles off northern Germany. The lines indicated the German incursions as spread from the very northernmost tip of the Orkneys right down to Dover. A swastika marked the demise of enemy bombers, there were just three, two south of Edinburgh and one near the East Anglian coast. An Iron Cross denoted bombs dropped on British soil, and of these symbols there was only one, this at the tip of the Orkneys. The diagram had of course appeared before the Luftwaffe's March raids, and split the total incursions as twenty-five bombing raids and forty-seven reconnaissance flights.

In this period the sighting of German raiders by the public excited eye witness accounts, whether the Heinkels raced audaciously at low level over seaside piers off the east coast, or appeared as tiny silvery specks followed by white flak puffs over the Thames Estuary. In some cases the journalists preparing the material must have gained real enjoyment, if the following example taken from one column is authentic:

'Aboot 7.30 this morning me and my chum went for a walk wi' a dog. The dog was chasing a hare. All at once we heard the soond o' an aeroplane. It came frae the sea, flying verra low . . . I says to ma pal: "He's a Jairman." It came so low over the sea I could hae hit it wi' a stone. Then another yin came frae the east – yin o' oor fighters . . . Once ah thought the Jairman was doon. He dived towards the ground and started tae wobble, and then sort o' rose again and went awa' seawards.'

This eye witness account of a 'Nazi' incursion and pursuit by RAF fighters was broadcast over the BBC. Doubtless pilots Juventus and Jentzen would have been amused to know how much entertainment their visits brought the British.

These few months of air war between Britain and Germany were but a few bouts of sparring, the allegation of a 'phoney' war usually means that historians tend to ignore the period. But for those men taking part the duel was anything but phoney. Helmut Ruge was a Heinkel pilot operating from the north German frontier:

'We had specific orders at first not to bomb the land at all, only shipping, and especially warships. But this was very difficult, the weather was always against us. And your fighters were always on the prowl. We lost many comrades. However, we had our successes, though I regret the loss of life.

'One day early in 1940 I and my crew took off to look for ships off the east coast of England. We had a full load of bombs but when we finally arrived in the area the cloud was so thick we could see nothing. So I dived the plane to try and see something, and after emerging from the clouds we saw a small steamer; as our time in action was limited I made an immediate attack. Our bombs fell all round the ship, and although we did some damage it did not sink.

*'As we turned away my top gunner called "Fighters!", and so I at once
opened the throttles and climbed hard for the clouds. But the Spits were
too quick for us, and a long row of holes appeared along our fuselage
and many bullets came into the cabin. I pressed to one side and tried to
outmanoeuvre them. They were all around us and firing continuously. At
last the inevitable happened, we caught fire, both engines were burning
and I shouted to all to take up crash positions and make ready to hit
the sea. This we did, very hard. Somehow I managed to escape from
the debris as the plane went under.'*

Helmut Ruge was lucky, a small boat put out from shore and rescued
him, but his comrades were lost.

A Spitfire pilot who shot down a Heinkel watched in amazement
as his victim tried to touch down on land, the flames streaming from
the German plane and fire spreading along one wing. Although the
undercart was down, as soon as the Heinkel hit the rough ground the
wheels collapsed and the bomber slid along the grass on its belly. Three
figures emerged safely, quickly followed by a fourth, and as the British
pilot circled the scene the Germans stood waving at him; he opened his
hood and returned their greetings before flying off. By then the first
civilians and some policemen were hurrying to the crash. Unfortunately,
this RAF pilot was killed later in an aerial collision.

A rather more bizarre incident occurred in the same period, the
essentials of which actually appeared in early evening newspapers
before the story was killed off by wartime censorship.

Another RAF pilot had watched his Heinkel target go down on land,
the crew emerging safely. Perhaps intent on capturing them personally
and securing their almost undamaged machine, the Britisher attempted
to land his plane nearby, but owing to the undulating nature of the
terrain his fighter flipped over on its back, to the amazement of the four
Luftwaffe airmen watching. The RAF pilot was trapped upside down
in his cockpit, so the Germans raced over to his plane and helped him
to get clear.

Such an act of gallantry on the part of enemy airmen simply did
not fit in with the current tone of vilification against the Luftwaffe 'air
pirates'.

CHAPTER SIX

SPEARHEAD IN THE AIR

T he air fleet commander Hans-Jurgen Stumpff has remarked on Hitler's 'psychological obsession' with the east and how the Allies (principally Britain) upset his plans and intentions.

Göring was to boast of the 'undreamed-of might' of his Luftwaffe which he saw as winning Germany its new territories – the *Grossdeutschen Reich*; but it had been pressure from Hitler which had ensured that a strong air force was ready on time. Following the conquest of western Poland (the Soviets having taken over the other half by prior agreement), the German nation and its leaders felt genuine disappointment when the Allies did not call off their war. Hitler was by far the most aggrieved, for he had further dreams of eastern conquest to fulfil and did not dare to pursue them while British and French forces sat on his western doorstep. Although he believed France to be degenerate and ripe for dissolution, his aim was now to strike the Allied forces in the West such a blow that they would be virtually incapacitated and offer no interference when he again moved eastwards. France could be eliminated by a blitz campaign similar to the war fought so triumphantly against Poland, after which Britain would be isolated and so enfeebled as to be helpless.

The British and French menace to Norway and his iron ore supplies diverted Hitler, causing him to send considerable forces to occupy Denmark and its northern neighbour in which Xth *Fliegerkorps* employed 290 bombers and 40 Stukas in a campaign against the Norwegians who were assisted by newly landed Franco-British forces. Despite several disasters to German arms the Allies were beaten and finally forced to withdraw from Norway in June 1940, by which time the Wehrmacht's great offensive on the Western Front had begun.

The German attack would overrun Holland, Belgium, Luxembourg and *la belle* France, and for this operation the Luftwaffe employed five Air Corps plus one Air Division in the 2nd and 3rd Air Fleets, some 4,000 warplanes of Germany's total strength of 5,000 being sent into action. Of these 1,120 were heavy, long-range bombers, plus 358 dive-bombers. Against this array the RAF in France fielded only two weak groups: the Air Component of the British Expeditionary Force comprised fighters and light bombers to support the five divisions of ground troops, while the so-called 'Advanced Air Striking Force' comprised slow, single-engined Fairey Battles and some twin-engined

Blenheim bombers with a small number of fighters as protection. This latter force was designed to hit at the German rear communication areas and support units. The great weakness of the RAF force is indicated by the allocation of just forty Hurricanes and twenty obsolete Gladiator biplanes.

The French Armée de l'Air comprised about 550 fighters of varying quality and a bomber force hardly worthy of the name, an indifferent ground organisation and lack of first-class airfields. Above all it lacked modern and determined leadership.

On 10 May 1940 the Luftwaffe entered battle once more, operating in exactly the same mode as over Poland and with equal success, despite the setbacks suffered by its airborne troop committment in Holland. The German Air Force had remained very passive on the Western Front since the outbreak of war and the subsequent so-called 'Phoney War' period, but now it used all its available strength to overwhelm the opposition, enabling the ground forces to achieve an amazing but far from cost-free victory that far surpassed all expectations.

Hitler's great spoiling attack, which commenced on 10 May 1940, proved to be a triumph of German arms, with the theories already put into practice in Poland re-proven. Once again Göring's Luftwaffe showed itself able to fulfil everything asked of it and more.

Karl Haulmeier:

'We took off in the early morning of 10 May to bomb enemy airfields. This went on for about three weeks until we were able to move to an abandoned French base near Rheims.'

As a Dornier Observer Haulmeier had enjoyed grand aerial tours of France with the minimal danger. Hans Gilbert was the Dornier pilot left in reserve during the Polish campaign, neither had he operated against England and so first saw action on 10 May:

'It was almost as routine as our training flights, except that we flew in bigger formations and dropped our bombs on enemy concentrations etc. After a few days of this we had seen only one French fighter, which was chased away by our Mes, and we suffered no losses. But then as the campaign progressed we did lose aircraft in the following manner.

'We had taken off one morning when one of our Dorniers developed engine trouble and had to return, but as it landed it slid off the runway and caught fire, but all the crew escaped. This was at a field outside Mannheim, but soon afterwards we moved across the border into a French base, and there we suffered two more losses. One came through a Dornier striking some wreckage on the ground, the other through enemy action in the air. We encountered some French anti-aircraft fire and one of our

Dorniers was damaged but managed to reach base, but was not repairable.'

As an air gunner Georg Kessler flew to a base near Dortmund to commence bombing raids against Allied airfields, and during the first flight saw some French fighters but had no chance to shoot at them before Messerschmitts chased them off.

'Day after day we flew this kind of mission, mostly against airfields but sometimes against troops and vehicles. Then we suffered our first loss when one of our Heinkels was shot down by an enemy fighter; the crew was returned to us soon after. Then we had another loss and this time the crew were killed. We also suffered a couple of losses through accidents and did not immediately receive replacements as we were moved into France and had a hectic time getting organised and recommencing operations.'

The Heinkel Observer Otto Jufen had experienced a few reconnaissance trips over France and neutral Belgium before the big offensive began, and once in action attacked Allied airfields etc and when the British were ejected moved forward to a base near Arras.

Peter Kroller had lost much flying time through the bad winter but managed to take command once more as a Dornier Observer by spring in preparation for the coming offensive. He and his crew took off in the grey dawn of 10 May in a formation of three squadrons, nervous until finding the target under some flak fire, each Observer aiming his own bombs at the target:

'I believe most of our bombs landed on that French airfield and many planes were destroyed on the ground. This kind of mission went on day after day in brilliant weather, and although we grew tired we were thankful it had all been so easy and we saw no enemy aircraft in the air at all, though we heard of other units who suffered attack. We remained unscathed, though we lost two planes in small, silly ground accidents though no one was injured.'

The promotion-mad Karl Weinfarth had seen routine action in Poland, but once back in Germany went straight to his commanding officer to express disatisfaction with his lot, expressing the view that 'there must be some way I can achieve promotion':

'This amazed him so he sent for my file and read through the papers and grasped what kind of young fool I was. He told me there was only one option open to me: there was a war academy course which accepted officers from all three services, so if I was interested he would forward my name. Meanwhile, I must learn to be patient and await events! He dismissed me and was I felt not unsympathetic. So I went away with my head in the clouds and envisaging all kinds of possibilities if I managed to attend the academy in Berlin and emerge as a high officer. I realised I had some way to go, but I let my boyish enthusiasm run away with me and dreamed of commanding air fleets. The truth was that I did not

see myself as flying about continually in aircraft and never had done. Perhaps I had been a commander in some previous life and the itch was getting to me again. I only knew that I had to get out of my present position and as the days went by I became more and more impatient until at last the CO sent for me and told me to pack my bags as I had been accepted as an aspirant by the academy. I rushed off and left the same day, much to the amazement and amusement of my comrades who could not understand me and thought I was rather rash and swell headed – which in fact I suppose I was.'

The course Weinfarth joined in Berlin was designed to select and groom young officer candidates for higher office, to place them in staff appointments – behind desks, which the eager young tyro did not realise. He spent some weeks learning about the theory and art of war in company with student soldiers and sailors including men from very good families:

'I was a fairly ordinary sort of chap I must admit and began to feel out of place among them as they were so terribly serious most of the time, quite different to the comrades I had known at the bomber base and I regrettably came to the conclusion that I had been an idiot. I did not mind scorning myself, I knew though that I still wanted what I had always wanted but had been too blind and impatient to see and achieve. I desired to command a unit in battle, not sit in some stuffy office theorising and dealing with paperwork.'

Weinfarth now realised in his new-found wisdom that he was in an embarrassing position and did not know how to get out of it. It was beneath his dignity to try and fail the course in order to be returned to his unit, so he continued into the examinations and passed with sufficient marks to qualify him to leave the academy as a Captain, with an automatic recommendation for a command post.

'This sounded grand, but I realised it meant a desk job. But I had learnt something, and sure enough was sent to the staff of a bomber Wing, this time Dorniers. The job was an executive one, and obviously suited me – on paper. But I decided that this step had taken me much of the way, I would wait for my chance to press my claim to become a flying commander. The thought excited me and I entered into my new tasks with comrades in good heart.'

His wish to command planes in the air was not to be granted during the French campaign, instead Weinfarth found himself embroiled in a mass of detail work on the executive side until after three changes of base he found himself at the time of the armistice in limbo again.

Hans Rudel, like most other Luftwaffe aircrews, had spent much of the winter in the doldrums until April came and the rumours of an

offensive proved true, the Stuka unit CO informing his crews that they
would be in the van of the attack on the Western Front:

> *'We would be the spearhead in the air, our targets would be the
> enemy forts immediately facing our troops on the flank of the much
> vaunted French Maginot Line.'*

The Stukas took off on the morning of 10 May, the crews noting
many other Luftwaffe aircraft engaged in various missions. Within half
an hour they had crossed the border at 10,000 feet:

> *'The first French flak came up at us so we broke formation and were
> soon over our target. An artillery barrage was in progress below and
> we could see the French forts which were very stoutly constructed in
> steel and concrete and apparently impregnable.*
>
> *'Our Mes hovered overhead and we went into our dives at once,
> screaming down one after the other. I was the third in line and saw
> the heavy bombs fall from those in front and these exploded on or
> very near the largest bunkers. I determined to do better and held my
> dive until the last possible moment so that when I pressed the bomb
> release and the plane pulled up we were under 1,000 feet. The automatic
> pull-out device was set for that level but could be overriden by simply
> disconnecting the thing – which is what I did. As we pulled away and
> I greyed out my gunner yelled in great excitement – we had scored a
> direct hit on the largest bunker, though with what effect we could not
> say. So we flew back to our base where we drank coffee and ate rolls
> while our planes were rearmed and refuelled.'*

On their next flight the Stukas overflew the bunkers at low level at the
army's request and saw French troops who then surrendered at once.

> *'The same day we flew two more missions with great effect. All this
> time our horizontal bombers were attacking the enemy airfields in an
> attempt to knock out their fighters and bombers, and in this they were
> very successful, we saw no hostile planes at all.'*

Rudel soon moved into France with his unit and set up on an
abandoned Allied base and worked feverishly to ready themselves for
further action, achieving this in one hour:

> *'We had by then long practised very effective liaison through a
> command set-up with our army comrades which was largely master-
> minded by General von Richthofen of the VIIIth Air Corps, who was
> our commander, and these arrangements never failed. Whenever the
> soldiers were held up by strong resistance they had but to call us up
> and this they did through a Luftwaffe liaison officer on the spot and
> it always worked. I remember one day we received an urgent call for
> help from some of our troops pinned down and in trouble. We were off*

within half an hour and over the target in twenty minutes and pulverised the enemy troops so that our own side could resume the advance.

'We stayed only a few days on that base before moving on and as we did we saw a lot of the damage caused to enemy columns and many wrecked planes on abandoned bases where our Heinkels and Dorniers had done their job. Our flights went on day after day against only weak opposition. The flak was always light and patchy and gave us no problems. Between missions we lazed on the grass or in a nearby château, ate well and drank French wine. It was a good life but the constant flying did begin to wear us down. I must say that in this period we never at any time received any orders to attack or terrorise civilians, but inevitably there must have been occasions when these poor people were caught up in air attacks on the roads, for all too often the Allied troops were inextricably mixed in with refugees. I absolutely refute all allegations of terror attacks on civilians in that war – at least in the part I experienced. There were none. When civilians lost their lives it was for the reasons given.

'We made two more moves and ended up near Orleans before the armistice came. By then it was obvious the Allied front was split all over the place and the French were in no state to continue the war. The British had fled from Dunkirk and it was all over – or seemed to be. Some Stuka units were sent north to try and stem the British evacuation, but for us it all came to a stop and we could relax and ease ourselves which was a great relief.'

The other Stuka pilot, Wolfgang Schauer, had gone home after the Polish campaign feeling rather exhausted but decorated and greeted by jubilant parents relieved to find him in one piece. Curiously, despite the 'enjoyment' and thrills obtained in his first war experiences, Schauer now began to experience dread at returning to a dive-bomber unit. Although his friends were there, he now decided that kind of work was not his vocation after all:

'It is hard to explain. Perhaps it was the sheer destruction that made me feel differently, but I no longer revelled in the idea of dropping bombs on an enemy. Truly, I was much more interested in pure flying, and the Stuka was never the ideal machine for that!

'I now conceived the idea of transferring to a fighter squadron, and wondered why I had not thought of this sooner. So as soon as I returned to my unit I applied for a transfer to fighters. My colleagues were very surprised, but my application was put through and to my great joy I was accepted and sent back to Germany where I joined a training unit on Messerschmitt 110s. This I took to at once, the plane was far better and flew much faster and I enjoyed the training very much. It was not long before I passed my course and was sent back to France to join an active unit.'

Schauer had forgone the Battle of France, he was about to encounter real air combat and his own fate over the Channel.

Like most of the other bomber pilots, Christian Rossler took part in daily flights in the campaign, suffering few losses and these usually to accidents, even these were rare since he found the Dornier easy and pleasant to fly.

'Once again our arms triumphed and we returned to bases in Germany to be feted as heroes. My parents were very proud of me, despite their religious views. I myself did not consider such matters again, I had too much to live for.'

Arthur Tieker recalls that no sooner were they given fresh target maps than these maps proved obsolete, the army's advance was so rapid.

'We flew daily and had no losses, though some other units did lose planes to Allied fighters, and there were always accidents. In fact we lost two or three bombers that way through pilot error. But by and large we completed all our missions without loss through enemy action until we got to the Dunkirk cauldron, when two of our Heinkels went down to Spits.

'Then the Battle of France was over and we moved into the beautiful French countryside and had a very nice time. The population were not unfriendly and we used to barter for eggs and cheese, giving them cigarettes and good German beer, though I believe as Frenchmen they always preferred wine! We also had a few French girl friends who did not see us as quite the terrible boche they'd heard so much about. As for myself, I felt that the war was as good as won, and I'm sure we all felt the same. I know that as the summer wore on it was good to be alive and to have survived such an epic campaign in one piece.'

Peter Harmel:
'France had collapsed, and England was on the brink, or so we thought, of also going under. We were absolutely astounded at this turn of events and held many celebrations.'

As a commander who had helped to formulate the theory of tactical air warfare, Colonel Johannes Fink had helped direct operations during the campaign, with Richthofen directing the bombers where they were most needed:

'I believe the army's campaign was greatly assisted by the Luftwaffe, which I suppose in operative terms enabled them to achieve a quick, cheap victory even though thousands of lives were lost and not a few of our planes and aircrews also. Even so, the enemy's collapse was amazing, so once again we had proved our theories in practice.'

Indeed, the panzer General Heinz Guderian stated later:
'The Luftwaffe was operating in just the way I thought most favourable for my own assault. I was delighted.'

Yet once again the battle had for the fighter pilots proved an anti-climax, for the aerial combats they had so long trained and hoped for never materialised. There were the occasional combats however, as Kurt Henner recalls:

> *'After some days of dull escort duty some of our unit's Mes were set upon by Hurricanes which seemed to come from nowhere. At the same time more enemy fighters attempted to attack our Heinkels and a real combat developed. We were diving all over the place trying to get at the enemy, but they kept falling away out of sight. I saw one Heinkel turn away smoking and an enemy plane fell away in flames. Then it was all over. That was the only combat we saw in the whole campaign, in no time it seemed the French and British were beaten and we were flying in peaceful skies. The whole business had astounded us as we never, ever imagined the Allies would collapse in such a dramatic fashion. We were highly elated and anxious to go home on leave but not allowed to, only a few of the lads went off to Germany. It seemed as if our leaders were uncertain what would happen next. The great celebrations began in Germany and we felt we had earned something better, but we did not complain as we had rather a fine time in France.'*

Many hundreds of thousands of Germans overran much of France and were suddenly struck into a daze of anti-climax by the Allied collapse, as were their leaders and all at home.

Horst Juventus:

'Many celebrations took place at home, with speeches and parades, most of which we missed. I enjoyed some leave late in June and had a very nice time. My father was quite astounded that things had not gone as he had expected. I soon found a lady friend who told me that the war was over so I could spend some time with her. I was not quite so optimistic, but even so the men in my unit thought the end must be near and hoped England would agree to a peaceful solution.'

Karl Haulmeier: 'I went home in triumph and had a grand time, we all thought the war was over.'

Hans Gilbert says the amazing victory had stunned them all and he began enjoying a very nice time in the French countryside. Air gunner Georg Kessler had not fired a shot in anger: 'We lazed about, and were inspected by some high officers.'

Johann Schmidt enjoyed a wonderful leave at home with his Petra, while Otto Jufen toured the French villages and towns, taking pictures of his comrades. Peter Kroller recalls: '[A] great time which followed when we moved into a new base and began to enjoy the fruits of victory – literally, for there were orchards nearby and we helped ourselves to apples, pears and grapes too. It was a rather fantastic end to our little war and we looked forward to returning home to Germany for a good leave and reunion with our families. Few were granted leave but I was one of the lucky ones and enjoyed myself immensely.'

For Horst Jentzen and his comrades in KG30 the situation had not changed as they continued sorties across the North Sea to Scotland

and north-east England without great result. Stuka pilot Hans Rudel went off with his mates to explore the beautiful French countryside, finding a friendly farmer ready to barter eggs, cheese, and even a pig in exchange for German beer and cigarettes: 'All-in-all we had a grand time.'

For the Stuka crews in particular the 'grand time' was soon to end.

The Me 109 pilot Peter Winker was one of the few to encounter an aerial dogfight in the French campaign. Six French Curtiss fighters (bought from USA) attempted to intercept the bomber formation and were pounced upon by the fighter escorts:

'It was hard to get a shot at any of the Frenchmen as there were so many planes milling about, but at last I did get in a burst but missed. And then they were all gone and it was quiet again. I did see a smoke trail and later learned that one of our Sergeants had knocked down an enemy fighter, so we celebrated.'

To curb their disappointment when no more enemy interceptors appeared over the next few days the Messerschmitt pilots were permitted some ground strafing and since the French Army was collapsing the Germans gaped in amazement at the millions of men standing about waiting to be herded off into captivity.

'We now had a really marvellous time, simply lazing about waiting for orders, we did very little flying. At last I was allowed on leave and had a grand time with my family and lady friend Lotte.'

The exact cost in terms of men and machines for the short campaign is not known; the available figures including these dramatic weeks will be given later. One German historian, in commenting on the widespread bitterness of the British Tommy ('where is the RAF?' etc) gave a very different opinion based on the equally bitter experiences of German aircrew attempting to attack troops and installations at Dunkirk. These airmen had suffered interception and loss through RAF intervention. Most of the small number of RAF planes were lost in suicidal actions against the advancing German columns or destroyed on the ground. In some cases newly arrived Hurricane reinforcements were captured intact by the speedy panzers and motorcycle columns. But at Dunkirk the Luftwaffe bombers were regularly intercepted by Spitfires from England and suffered accordingly – usually out of sight of the British and Allied troops on the ground. Of a dozen Dorniers of KG3, for example, half were knocked down in one encounter, and a similar experience befell another squadron of the same group: 'The enemy fighters pounced on our tightly knit formation like maniacs,' reported a Luftwaffe Major. Against the eight-gun Spits or Hurris, the Dorniers and other German bomber types were virtually helpless, as the hapless Luftwaffe crews now discovered, and this factor must have weighed on them when they learned of new orders soon to come. It had been a case of 'Where were our fighters?' for the Dornier crews.

The French Air Force had ceased to exist; those not destroyed were captured, inspected and in some cases evaluated and even used by the Luftwaffe.

As for the RAF in France, it too no longer existed; the last planes fled back to England on 16 June. For the British the war in the air in this campaign had been a disaster: 959 aircraft of all types had been lost, and a further 66 destroyed in the Norwegian fiasco; of the total 509 were fighters.

Yet for all their undoubted triumphs, the Germans had not succeeded in gaining the bonus some felt they deserved through their mastery of the game: the total destruction of the British Expeditionary Force, which although losing all its heavy and much lighter equipment, including small arms, had in terms of personnel largely escaped to fight another day. Göring had boasted to Hitler: 'Not a man or ship will escape the bombing waves of my Stukas. Give my Luftwaffe a chance. to show what it can do.'

It was perhaps the first time Göring had failed to deliver. The chief reason being that despite his assumption and the great mobility of the Luftwaffe units, insufficient strength was deployed to annihilate the British troops at Dunkirk. The bombing raids were frequent, but it was no air blitz and as shown often blunted by RAF Spitfires, mostly flying from Hornchurch.

Yet despite his failure in this not unimportant matter, the Führer was in such magnanimous mood over the great victory that he began distributing largesse in all directions, creating several marshals but awarding his old comrade Göring the new and specially created title of *Reichsmarschall* in recognition of the magnificent achievements of his glorious Luftwaffe in the campaign just ended. He also gave him the only copy ever made of the supreme class of the Iron Cross – the Grand Cross – which Göring was to lose in an air raid later.

The Luftwaffe had now demonstrated twice in one year a new and indelible lesson in the proper use of tactical air power, such as had never been seen before in modern arms. It was a lesson some took note of, though those in command in the British forces – especially the blimps in the War Office – were slow to heed or even failed to notice. Yet the chiefs of the Luftwaffe, including Göring himself, had not even begun to consider how their powerful instrument might be used in an all-out war against Britain.

CHAPTER SEVEN

'BOMBS ON ENGLAND'

Historians differ in deciding which date to apply as the commencement of the Battle of Britain. The so-called 'month of grace' after the fall of France enabled the RAF to re-group until the skirmishing began around 10 July, though for some writers it is expedient to begin detailing the Luftwaffe's cross-Channel expeditions from the 1st of that month. To the Germans of course there is no question that their offensive began on *Adler Tag* or 'Eagle Day' on 13 August, the day previous having been set but the operation was foiled by bad weather. These same and often leading accounts covering this highly dramatic period in British history may easily give the impression of weeks in calm waters so to speak, with the population and its forces enjoying a grand summer free of German interference. Such a view is reinforced by the reminiscences of German aircrew given in this work, but it is an erroneous one, for the Luftwaffe's activities over Britain never ceased throughout this period. For while it is true that many Luftwaffe airmen did indeed enjoy comparatively idyllic conditions in France and Belgium, others were engaged in operations against Britain. The Phoney War period during which the Luftwaffe paid attention chiefly to Britain's east coast periphery went by, and the German bombers extended their range of activity inland, especially over East Anglia where the citizens on the ground suffered very frequently from alarms and action – and casualties. There is no doubt that the German aircrews did their best to attack military and economic objectives, but unforeseen disasters and accidents occur in war, especially in aerial bombing. At the end of April 1940 a Heinkel carrying three parachute mines was damaged off Harwich and wandered along the coast, possibly lost or its crew disorientated. It then plunged in the darkness of the night into a street in Clacton on the Essex coast, its load exploded to kill the four crew plus two local inhabitants, injure 156 and cause widespread damage to a residential area.

Newspaper comments that road accidents were causing more casualties than the enemy's air force were soon invalidated by events as the Luftwaffe stepped up its probings, reconnaisance and bombing sorties. It had become increasingly hazardous for single raiders to approach the British coastline, while by night the blacked out landscape left few or no clues to assist the less experienced German navigators.

For the majority of Germans the period immediately following the French collapse was filled with relief, and not simply the euphoria following victory over opponents. Even some of the military leaders felt that enough had been achieved, Hitler had pulled Germany up from the gutter, and the once defeated, humiliated and bankrupted nation was now the master of Europe, with every neighbouring state subjected to or prone to assuage the Führer's will (except the British). Germany had proved to the world its renewal, and now was the time to show magnanimity, albeit Nazi style. Britain was isolated, helpless despite its Empire, and whatever utterings poured from the mouth of the cigar wielding Premier in Shakespearean fashion, reality must prevail.

The new British Prime Minister had indeed made some remarkable calls to his people, perhaps partly designed to illustrate national defiance and crush those who preferred some sort of accommodation with Herr Hitler within his own ranks. Churchill had heard the French General Weygand refer to the Battle of France, he now warned the nation that the Battle of Britain was about to begin, asserting that Hitler must turn his whole fury and might on Britain to break the nation – or lose the war; if his country went down under the heel of perverted Nazi science then the world including the United States would sink into the abyss of a new dark age. And:

'Let us therefore brace ourselves to our duties, and so bear ourselves that, if the British Empire and Commonwealth last for a thousand years, men will still say "This was their finest hour."'

It was inspired, stirring stuff, doubtless impressing Dr Göbbels, the Nazi Minister for Propaganda and Public Enlightenment, in a cynical fashion, though in all probability few if any German servicemen heard such speeches. But they certainly heard or soon read their Führer's oration delivered in the *Reichstag* or Nazi parliament on 19 July in which he said:

'If this struggle continues it can only end in the annihilation of one of us. Mr Churchill thinks it will be Germany, I know it will be Britain. I am not the vanquished begging for mercy. I speak as a victor. I see no reason why this war must go on. We would like to avert the sacrifices which must claim millions.'

This was wholly cynical, in part designed to present himself as a generous peacemaker – from his position of strength, for home and foreign consumption. Hitler had but a very slight hope that commonsense would prevail in British ruling circles, that perhaps Churchill would be ousted. If this vague hope was realised, then his back would be clear when he turned his attentions eastwards again.

Britain's rejection of these vague overtures which were delivered in leaflet form over remote parts of the English countryside by German bombers came via the BBC before being officially confirmed by Lord Halifax. The enemy was very disappointed, even baffled. Hitler's reaction was to order his military chiefs to prepare to subjugate

Britain, if necessary by a landing and occupation. The army and navy especially began dusting down its old files and case folders, being reminded as they did so of Napoleon's like plans in an earlier era. In its ignorance, the German Army as a whole looked upon such a venture as either foolhardy or just another river crossing, certainly few German officers appreciated the huge effort and resources needed to effect such an operation. Not so the staffs of the *Kriegsmarine*, who were fully aware of their weakness at sea, especially since the disasters which befell them in the Norwegian campaign, when the brunt of British naval power fell upon them. Such an amphibious operation had never been undertaken before, it was a gigantic experiment and the Germans were obliged to start from scratch. The army and naval staffs began their work, which was difficult and fraught with all kinds of problems. However, the prerequisite was command of the air. The Luftwaffe must do its now accustomed task, and so to this end a wholesale re-grouping and deployment of all available resources began, to be completed by 12 August – Eagle Day.

Horst Juventus:

'When July came we were still at war. We visited Brussels where we found the people cool but not hostile to us. We behaved very correctly, there was no resistance movement yet and no friction occurred, so we were able to enter the bars and hotels and enjoyed ourselves until orders came for us to begin practising formation flying in preparation for attacks across the Channel. This was all very disappointing and not a little amazing, especially when we began to hear rumours of a possible invasion of England. So we began our formation flying which had grown a little rusty, and before long were joining up with large Wings including Dorniers and the spectacle was very impressive. We saw a lot of our fighters which we hoped would escort and protect us across the Channel.

'Then our officers briefed us: we would attack and knock out the RAF airfields just as we had done in Poland. The enemy air force was to be eliminated. It sounded easier than we knew it would be.'

Karl Haulmeier:

'After a few weeks of very pleasant living in France we were ordered to prepare ourselves for an offensive over the Channel, and we moved north to a newly prepared airfield and began learning about our targets which would be shipping in Dover harbour and RAF airfields.'

Wolfgang Schauer:

'Everyone felt we could now really get to grips with the RAF. We were not under confident, though we knew that this fight would not be so easy. In a very few days our unit was sent to a new base nearer the

coast and we began offensive patrols across the Channel. At first we saw
little or nothing of the enemy, but then our Stukas began attacking the
convoys and the RAF were obliged to try and defend them. This is when
the first serious combats began, and although we were not involved in
any big fights we had one or two losses.

'I recall my own first fight. We were escorting some Stukas over the
Channel and were jumped on by several Hurricanes. We broke up and
it was every man for himself. I hauled round and took a quick shot at a
passing Hurricane with my cannon and machine-guns, but missed. My
gunner then had a go at him and saw a few pieces fly off the enemy
plane. We were then attacked by another Hurricane and dived towards
the sea, heading for the French coast with the other fellow hanging on
to our tail; but my gunner discouraged him and he flew away.

'Next day it was the same and we realised we were fighting for our
lives on every flight. When we crossed the Channel we saw Hurricanes
and a few Spitfires and at once got into a much bigger dogfight. I
managed to hit a Hurricane in the tail, but now I realised that our
twin-engined machines were much slower than the nimble Hurricanes
and Spitfires. We had a very hard time escaping back to France.'

Peter Harmel had also moved near the French coast into a base
hurriedly prepared for cross-Channel operations:

'We then began our first patrols over the Channel in our Mes and I
remember seeing the white cliffs of Dover for the first time. I marvelled
at the beautiful countryside and wondered when the RAF would start
defending it. Very soon we were engaged in helping our Stukas attack
the convoys, and then came our first serious combats with the RAF
who fought very well, but we usually got the upper hand over the
slower Hurricanes. I recall the first one I attacked. It was off Dover
and we dived on several of them out of the sun. They did not seem
to see us and were not prepared. I shot one down into the sea and I
regret I did not see the pilot get out. We were very pleased over our
success and made bets as to who of us would first reach a score of ten
over the RAF. And then the fun really began as our bombers began to
attack land targets.'

Arthur Tieker says he and his comrades never believed the 'decadent
British' would go under easily, and at first heard rumours the Stukas
were having an easy time and had put a stop to the Channel
convoys.

'We ourselves had not yet flown against England at all, though of
course other units had from the earliest days of the war.

'We were then ordered to commence operations, with airfields as the
first targets. I recall our first flight across the Channel. It was a beautiful
day with grand visibility and I was enjoying my job with no problems,

when suddenly someone yelled "Fighters!" and I looked round just in time to see a brown and green Hurricane with RAF roundels flash past our unit. But we saw no one hit. Then several more came and one of our bombers went down in smoke into the Channel. Unfortunately, this attack had spoiled our flight to the target and we were foiled completely. We just dropped our bombs into the drink and flew home. I'm not sure what our CO thought of us, but in our excuses we made it sound as if we had been under heavy attack and forced to jettison our bombs.

'However, we were not deterred, but realised the job would be more difficult. Next time we flew across the water we had many fighters escorting us and saw several combats, but came through unscathed. I'm not sure what the target was, I believe it was a harbour and shipping.'

The bomber Wing leader Christian Rossler had commenced a series of practice flights in formation before operations began:

'When we did start it became obvious the days of easy victories were gone. One by one my squadrons began to suffer losses. I saw my first combat against the RAF and one of my wing men had to return to base with smoke pouring from one engine. We tried to bomb harbours and airfields and had some success, but it seemed every time we reached the English coast the Hurricanes were waiting for us. We realised we were fighting a tough enemy with a good organisation. We thought we would win eventually, but how many of us would live to see the day of victory?'

Johannes Fink:

'It is possible that if we had ignored Britain then some sort of compromise could well have resulted before they began sending bombers to attack us. As it was the invasion fleet was assembled and this proved a magnet for RAF bombers who flew over by day and night and caused considerable damage. Meanwhile our bombers had been ranging far and wide over Britain and we were under orders to reorganise our groups for the first full-scale attacks across the Channel. For this operation I was appointed the so-called Kanalkampfführer and took up command residence in an old bus on the French coast near Cap Gris Nez from where through binoculars I could clearly see the English coastline including the large radio tower masts as we thought them to be. In this latter connection it did not take our General Martini (the Luftwaffe Signals chief) long to realise that these were to do with fighter control. In this of course he was only partly correct, we did not realise that direction-finding radar, as it came to be called, was in extensive use. I know that some experiments in this direction had been made on our side and that one or two pieces of apparatus were installed on the German coast. But the enemy's use of it on such

*a scale for fighter control came as a big surprise, in this we were
somewhat behind them.'*

The 'radar battle' is of course a tale in itself and could fill more than
one volume. Suffice to say that the Germans were not really backward in
this huge technological advance, in fact in one direction they were ahead:
the pocket battleship *Graf Spee* went on its final voyage equipped with
a crude masthead radar. Otherwise the sets referred to by Colonel Fink
on the German coast were in the early war months not fully implemented
by an adequate back-up organisation.

Hans Gilbert was despatched in some surprise with his Dornier unit
to a new base near Arras and received their first briefing for the
cross-Channel offensive: 'We were to attack shipping and see what
happened next I suppose.'

This sounds vague and half-hearted, as if no real plan existed for the
assault on Britain, which is hardly the case. Johann Schmidt had enjoyed
a wonderful leave with his Petra, but on his return was dismayed to find
himself and comrades sent north to a new base, with their commanders
exuding great confidence as they briefed them on their missions across
the sea:

'This was the climax of all our training and efforts but we felt it
would not be easy. We did not rush to our machines singing "Bombs
on England" or anything of the kind.'

Otto Jufen also recalls the disappointment felt when the war
continued and they moved north, as did Peter Kroller with his
Dorniers.

'Our idyllic life came to an end and we attended our first briefing, our CO telling us that our task was to eliminate the RAF,
our Mes would deal with any fighters that tried to stop us. This
sounded easy enough, but we did not feel it would be any kind of
walkover.'

To Horst Jentzen the news that Hitler had determined to crush Britain,
if necessary by an invasion, was exciting and rather fantastic:

*'We wondered what part we would play in this, and were then told
to pack up all our gear, man our planes and fly to a base in west
Holland (from west Germany). This it seemed was our moment of
truth, for we would take part in a great air attack on England. We
flew in one strung-out formation and our lead navigator took us to our
new home which was Schiphol and still being cleared of debris including
wrecked planes. In fact, when we arrived we found things in a state of
disorganisation. But order was soon restored and we settled into brick
barracks with regular meals again. It was then late July I believe and
we began to study maps of eastern England showing all known RAF
bases. We also received lectures on the believed strength of the RAF
fighter force and what to expect. Our attacks would be on fighter fields
and any shipping we discovered.'*

Having made great progress in realising his dream, Karl Weinfarth had thrown himself into a life of ease, touring the French countryside with his comrades, and even reaching the coast where they inspected the wreckage of the BEF at Dunkirk.

'Then came the surprising news that the war was far from over, we would move north and attack the British Channel convoys. So we were again thrown into the business of reorganising and at this point I received a further promotion and was made a squadron executive officer. This suited me very well as it was a position of authority and I therefore delegated myself to fly on the first mission with our group over the Channel.'

Hans Rudel's life of pleasure also ended when his Stuka group was posted near the Channel coast, the aircrews learning that their first task was to clear the sea of British shipping:

'We would then move on to attack the RAF on the ground and destroy their fighter force as a prelude to a possible invasion. All this was amazing news and very exciting and we prepared ourselves accordingly. Our reconnaissance planes soon reported small convoys moving eastwards on the English side of the Channel.'

Kurt Henner recalls his fighter base as rather makeshift, with labourers still at work on it, and their first briefing in which the CO informed them that England had declared war on Germany without thought of the consequences which must now come to them, that they had so far escaped the war, even though they had been driven off the continent. 'So far the RAF had evaded us, he said, but now the full weight of the Luftwaffe would be turned on Albion, and the result would be a great victory for us.'

Peter Winker and his comrades wondered how the English could be so stupid in rejecting any idea of peace and how they expected to survive:

'We were told to pack up and move north for an offensive across the Channel, that our bombers would attack the RAF bases, we would protect them and hopefully draw the RAF into combat and destroy them. Meanwhile, our Stukas had begun attacking the Channel convoys. The whole atmosphere was fantastic – electric, in those days. The life we began to lead was very hectic and, as we discovered, very dangerous.'

Since the level of German air activity had not ceased but steadily increased it is impossible to lay down any one date for the start of 'the Battle' as such. For example, the last night of June, into 1 July saw the inhabitants of twenty British counties disturbed by air raid sirens, and one incident perhaps indicative of the difficulties facing the defenders in trying to counter Luftwaffe incursions after dark.

A night-fighter Blenheim of 29 Squadron from Digby in Lincolnshire was directed to intercept one raider, but Pilot Officer Sisman was suddenly blinded by searchlights which fastened on to his aircraft so that he lost control and crashed, the wreck catching fire. It is said that the scene was then bombed by the very raider they had been chasing and the two British crew killed.

Then, in the daylight hours that followed a range of German and British activity developed in which both sides sent planes across the Channel, with Stukas making one of the first attacks on a British convoy. On this day the Luftwaffe lost twelve aircraft, including one Heinkel 59 floatplane bearing red cross markings which was forced down by Spitfires, the crew of three being rescued by a British cruiser. The question of allowing the enemy to operate rescue planes over or on the sea was a thorny one, and the Air Ministry evidently decided that it could not permit Luftwaffe aircrewmen to be rescued by their own side to fight again. In the incident quoted the Heinkel was lost, on a further occasion another Heinkel 59 was beached in England.

'The air war against Britain should never have been started.' This was the opinion of Hans-Jurgen Stumpff, perhaps one of the old school of officers who had been a member on von Seeckt's original *Reichsluftministerium* in Berlin and by 1937 Chief of the Air Staff. It has been said that he was not a contributor to the new army support doctrines.

Stumpff was one of three high-ranking German military visitors to a place of interest barely two miles from this writer's home, for in October 1937 the British invited them to inspect the RAF at Hornchurch, but before it received its first Spitfires; all the Germans saw were Gladiator biplane fighters and even more obsolete equipment. Which is a reminder of another encounter alleged to have taken place the following year when Generals Milch and Udet, leading architects of the new Luftwaffe, were invited to the famous Hendon Air Pageant, apparently being impressed with all they saw. Later they met Winston Churchill, who had of course been closely following developments in aerial matters in Nazi Germany. The following conversation took place between the future war leader and his German guests:

'You're very interested in gliding over in Germany I believe? It's a pity you don't take the engines out of your aircraft and confine yourselves to gliding, since it interests you so much.'

To this Milch retorted: 'We should be glad to do that sir, if the Royal Navy returned to sail!'

When war came Colonel-General Stumpff was appointed commander of Air Fleet V and was responsible for operations from Norway. This force was by far the weakest and took little part in the war against Britain itself. Stumpff's view became that to launch air attacks against Britain was a cardinal error both from the military and political point of view:

'It was one of many Hitler made in his conduct of politics and in his intervention in military operations. In view of the fact that the war in Poland had been won it would have been wiser to turn to our western opponents and say, we are finished there, we will no longer fight you, we will cease all military operations against you. I believe that in that case the French at least would have agreed to a peaceful solution. In that event the British could hardly have continued alone, so peace would, I believe, have been possible. Hitler for his obvious reasons chose the opposite course so we as military servants of the state complied with our orders, which in any case were to plan and conduct operations in support of our army. That we did this in accordance with our tactical doctrines is well-known and history will in the further future record them as a typical efficient way to conduct a war of movement, even though in the process I regret to say civilian lives were lost.

'Once the French threw in the towel we were faced with a difficult and quite unexpected situation, for despite our Führer's grandiose pronouncements that the French were too decadent to resist a modern onslaught none of us really expected them to collapse in the way that they did, and this was of course a grand boost for Hitler as the population swung even more behind him.'

Stumpff was a career soldier, and like others had transferred from the army, and become familiar with the ideas expounded by the British military writers General Fuller and Liddell Hart. Like his fellows he was also well acquainted with the theories on air warfare as put forward by the Italian General Douhet:

'But a strategic air arm was not in accord with our ideas, we did not see bombing behind the lines as conducive to the theories of modern war. We had ideas based on the scientific application of an "all arms" battle which if concentrated enough would ensure the collapse of the enemy and enable a rapid exploitation by armoured forces. In this concept we were of the opinion that a strong air arm was an essential ingredient. We did not believe that strategic bombing would achieve the object stated for it by the theorists named. I do not believe that anyone in the German military embraced that kind of doctrine, although there were a very few such as General Wever who desired to develop a long-range bomber. But this was going beyond our needs, our view only envisaged a blitzkrieg war, as it came to be known, which did not in any way involve the civilian population. Later on of course we learned that the Allies had other ideas and managed to develop the strategic bomber to its furthest limits and do very great damage, but the price to civilians was far too high and in that I believe the Allies overstepped the mark.'

These views are very interesting and certainly relevant considering what was to follow in the air war as conducted by both sides, and there is no reason to doubt that they were indeed German military doctrine at the time and are no mere hindsight. Stumpff, as one of the leading German commanders, an ex-leader of Air Staff and certainly, despite suggestions to the contrary, one of the formulators of the close air support doctrine, stuck to the view that if man must make war then the German method was the best. Few civilians who suffered from air attack would disagree with him, and it was not his fault if the Luftwaffe came to be used in a less discrimatory fashion.

'Once Hitler had conquered France he seemed to stand all powerful while we with our triumphant tactical air force were nonplussed and taken aback. I can assure you that for days on end everything came to a complete standstill in France simply because we were unable to think beyond the results that had just happened. This gave the men a good rest and as things turned out they were going to need it.'

Stumpff comments on Hitler's vague peace overtures and suggests that if German forces had then withdrawn from the countries overrun, Churchill and his supporters would have had the rug pulled from under them so to speak, forced by world opinion and especially American, to sue for peace:

'This would have suited those like myself who had not the slightest desire to make war on Britain or indeed on the eastern nations either. Even a military careerist prefers peace at times. We had set our theories and proved them and that was that. Many of the German commanders including myself had visited Britain and from this and other ways greatly respected them for their great achievements and saw no sense in attacking them. Of course Hitler shared these sentiments but could not believe England would leave him alone when he set off on his eastern ventures. He wanted to humiliate France and he did so by leaving an occupying army and by imposing bad terms on them which grew worse in effect by various harsh measures and oppression.

'But once Hitler saw that Britain would not play, he wanted to smash them, or at least force them into quiescence by military operations for which we were not ready; we had neither the knowledge or competency to carry them out. The Luftwaffe was purely a tactical weapon and although it had performed brilliantly in "behind the lines" operations, to fly over the Channel and find military and economic objectives soon disclosed a strategic intent beyond its reach. But once the orders were handed out by Göring and his staff we had to carry them out, though as I said to my own staff at the time, "This will not work, it will cost us lives and machines". But we got on with it, and a great deal of reorganising and regrouping had to take place before the attack could begin.'

Later on Winston Churchill was to quote over 1,550 bombers and 1,300 fighters as being assembled by the Luftwaffe for the cross-Channel attack, this probably being an exaggeration and over simplification. In fact no precise figures are available since not only do sources on this question vary, but also the Germans themselves were to some degree hazy owing to the constantly fluctuating situation and movements in progress and the tardiness of some units in making proper returns. The safest assumption is that there were about 1,200 bombers, of which only half were serviceable or combat-ready. Add to this 280 dive-bombers, again with one third or more unable to fly.

Up to 1 July the Western campaign from 10 May had cost the Luftwaffe 635 bombers – their greater losses were about to begin. The RAF had by late June lost over 386 Hurricanes and 67 Spitfires: 100 fighters had been lost trying to protect the troops at Dunkirk where 80 pilots had gone missing, and 320 pilots in all had been lost in the three weeks since 10 May, 115 being known to be prisoners of the enemy. June was the worst month: only 331 Hurricanes and Spitfires were available, the other 135 fighters being obsolete or twin-engined Blenheim 1s. But the pause as the bewildered Germans sorted out their ideas and units enabled Air Marshal Dowding to build up his fighter force and by early July, Fighter Command could field some 590 fighters with 1,200 pilots, even though overall the squadrons were woefully short of men with experience to take on the German veterans and, to an extent, the better trained mass of *jagdflieger*.

As Stumpff has claimed, the early attempts by Stukas to close off the British shipping lane through the Channel succeeded, a few ships were sunk and the Admiralty was forced to withdraw its warships from the area. But the RAF was reacting and soon set up standing patrols of Hurricanes to intercept the dive-bombers. The attempt by the Luftwaffe to use horizontal bombers – usually Dorniers – to bomb shipping was a failure so these units were soon switched to attacking airfields.

The newly created (Air) Field Marshals of the Luftwaffe set themselves up in comfortable headquarters. Hugo Sperrle with his Air Fleet III staff was situated at St Denis in Paris; Sperrle was said to be fond of the good life. Albert Kesselring, sometimes known as 'Laughing Albert', was located in Brussels to control Air Fleet II. Stumpff, however, had to be content with a billet in Kristiansund in Norway; he had only a small command of 115 bombers and, as shown, had little stomach for what he had been ordered to do and because of the distances involved had no great scope for action anyway. Cousin of the late famous Red Baron, General Wolfram von Richthofen placed his Stukas in the Cherbourg peninsula, while the short-range Messerschmitt 109 and 110 longer-range fighters were grouped mainly in the Calais area where existing airfields were improved and satellites built. From there the experts would operate, men like Adolf Galland and Werner Mölders.

Dramatic and fascinating though the day-to-day accounts of the Battle are, the conflict will be presented here only through German eyes, and to do this additional witnesses will be introduced whose experiences in these weeks became etched indelibly into their minds. But, to begin, the recollections of those airmen already quoted.

Hans Juventus:

'The first attack was a complete fiasco in the middle of August as the weather ruined everything.'

Colonel Fink was the commander in the air who experienced this blundering start, and of this he comments that it was spoilt by bad weather and a communications problem. Fink had taken off at the head of his Dornier Wing and for some reason failed to receive a recall signal. Even a Messerschmitt 110 unit trying to turn the bombers back were misunderstood, so the bomber bomber Wing droned on in thick weather, slightly bemused by events, unaware that the grand Eagle Day opening of 12 August had been called off for 24 hours at least. After dubious results Fink rushed to telephone his HQ on landing to demand explanations as to why no other Wings had joined him, to learn the truth and resign himself to fresh courage for the following day:

'But next day all went well and the first attacks were made against RAF airfields in south-east England, with varied results. The RAF was slow to react when we attacked the Channel convoys with Stukas, but then instituted patrols and things became a lot livelier. The time would come when the Stukas would have to give up, but not yet. The attacks on the airfields were the prime requisite, for we had to so damage the RAF that it would be unable to interfere in any cross-Channel landing.'

In fact, unlike the RAF, the Luftwaffe was not well served by its intelligence branch, despite the plethora of reconnaissance machines available to it. At least two recce flights were made per day by the enemy, but for some reason the results were misinterpreted or vital points missed, so that the bomber units were directed to the wrong airfields in England containing not fighters but trainers and miscellaneous types of aircraft. Even when the right targets were reached, if struck the results were boastfully declared by Göring as proof that the fields in question were out of action, and their fighter complement destroyed. In this fashion over the coming weeks the *Reichsmarschall* would, in his mind, eliminate the RAF.

Karl Haulmeier settled himself into the nose of his Dornier in the morning of 13 August:

'We took off in brilliant sunshine and at last set course across the sea. It was a magnificent sight to see our bomber Wings stepped up into the blue and beyond them the fighters escorting us. There is no doubt we felt very confident and in high morale. We crossed the sea and encountered a little flak over Dover but saw no ships worth our attention so flew on inland towards the airfields of Biggin Hill and Malling. We changed course and then received the first warnings of fighter attack and became very alert. Another squadron came under fire as several Hurricanes zoomed through our formation, but we received no damage. I saw one Dornier smoking and gradually falling away. First blow to the enemy!'

Georg Kessler had an itchy trigger finger as a Heinkel gunner anxious to get to grips with the enemy, yet prior to the 'big day' in August had already flown a few probing flights across the Channel and not seen an enemy plane, only a little flak off the Kent coast:

'The weather was usually very good and we were enjoying ourselves. When our first serious raid took place we were approached by a few enemy aircraft but our Mes drove them off. The bombs went down on some airfield and we turned for home and that was that. It was all very much an anti-climax. I know our Dorniers and Stukas had been in action over the Channel, but that was not our operation.

'Then the raids were stepped up and as usual I had a grandstand view of the proceedings. It was magnificent to see the great formation swinging into position below me and the sunshine, with all the green and yellow of France below us. Then the sea crept by beneath us and that too was enjoyable. Then we heard warning shouts as enemy aircraft were sighted and I gaped about in all directions, trying to spot them. Suddenly there was a rasping noise and two dark shapes flashed down through our formation before I had a chance to even swing my machine-gun. Then more enemy planes appeared at a greater distance and I saw them to be Hurricanes and they came in from behind, but I was unable to sight on them owing to some of our Heinkels being in the line of fire. But other gunners opened fire as two of the Hurricanes came in with wings flashing with the fire from their eight machine-guns. The tracers circled down and then they were gone. It all happened so very quickly and we flew on without apparent damage, bombed our target and turned for home. Nothing else happened that morning and we reached base safely.

'But by mid-afternoon we were off again on the same course and crossed the Kent coast where we were soon intercepted by enemy aircraft which I saw as silver specks above and to one side of us. Our Mes were on guard, but soon it was confusion up there and it became impossible to tell friend from foe. Then I heard a louder noise and saw several dark shapes coming up below and heard warnings of attack. This time they were Spitfires and they came up in low passes, shooting at our bellies before breaking away. I was not in a position to shoot back and once more felt frustrated as the enemy aircraft dropped from sight. I then saw two of our Heinkels in trouble: one had smoke pouring from an engine and it fell behind, while the other climbed up above us and turned back.

'But we bombed our target and the whole group curved back towards the Channel. As we reached the sea, however, we were again attacked by the enemy who came in from two sides and at last I was able to shoot off a few rounds at a Spitfire which whipped across from port to starboard but at such speed it was impossible to catch him. I found I was sweating, but we had suffered no hits and we reached base safely.

'Within a few days the pace had hotted up and we were flying three times a day, weather permitting, and it was usually fine. The day's routine was always the same. We rose from our cots at about seven o'clock, washed, had some breakfast in the squadron mess, then went to the briefing which was usually in the open air or in a hut if wet.

*By eleven we had taken off, an hour later we were over England –
and invariably under attack. The flak grew more troublesome and
the fighters more bold. Our Me 110s proved to be fairly useless and
they soon disappeared from these operations. In one raid over Kent I
watched for some time as two of these types made attempts to shoot
down a Hurricane and missed. The Tommy then turned on the nearest
one and shot him into the sea. He then went after the other and I lost
sight of them. Then I had a good view of a Heinkel in another unit
behind us which caught fire after an attack and blew up. This was
a new experience as after the flash there was nothing to be seen but
small pieces which soon vanished from sight.*

    *'In one late afternoon attack we had turned in over north Kent towards
Biggin (Hill) when a host of enemy aircraft hit us and a great battle
developed. Our formation was split up and we were diving for the coast
with several enemy planes on our tail. I broke into a sweat as the first
Hurricane came in. I tried to keep my nerve and wait until he got
closer, but then I saw the flashes from his wings and a stream of tracer
bullets went into our tail and along the fuselage. I pressed the trigger
and fired at him but it was too late as he had already swept past us.
Then another Hurricane came in and as our pilot banked the Heinkel I
got a chance to shoot at him just as he fired at us. Our bullets crossed,
but mine were from a single gun against eight streams of lead coming
towards me pattering about our fuselage. It was terrifying as I felt so
helpless. Once again I tried to keep my nerve and fired as much as I
could without knocking pieces off our tail. I believe I obtained a hit
but the enemy fighter banked away and vanished.*

    'This was our worst experience to date.'

Johann Schmidt says he piloted his Heinkel across the Channel on
a sunny August day 'with some apprehension and in great alertness',
though like his comrades he found the opening days of the battle
not too bad, with only one or two skirmishes and little in the way
of losses:

    *'I believe much of my old confidence returned but it was to be
rudely shattered before long, for in a few days the Tommies began
more serious and more co-ordinated attacks on us and we lost our
first Heinkel. This is the loss that sticks most in my mind as I knew
the lads concerned who were a good bunch who had joined the unit
when we did.*

    *'We had flown across the Channel and crossed the coast near Margate
I believe when we were attacked by Hurricanes and Spitfires who kept
the escorts busy. Several Hurricanes came at us from all sides and the
machine-guns began rattling. I was very nervous and sank down into
my seat although our captain kept very cool and sat looking at his
map as if nothing was happening at all. A few holes appeared in one
of our wings, but we remained undamaged to any degree and flew on.*

Then more enemy planes appeared and two Heinkels went down, one of them with my friends. One wing was badly damaged and caught fire and they began baling out, but the Heinkel turned over on its back and I lost sight of it. I doubt if the pilot got out. Then as we neared our target we were under fire from both fighters and flak and once again I tried to shrivel up in my seat.

'The bombs went down and we banked away for the coast and all was quiet for the rest of the trip. Our losses were not replaced at once but some new faces appeared in our mess about a month later. They were like we had been at first, excited and full of confidence and I remember one lad asking me on the field what it was like. He said: "Are the Tommies any good? Can we shoot them down without trouble?"

'Our gunners grinned at him and said nothing, so he did not know what to think. But I told him to take along some extra socks and he took my meaning.'

The Heinkel Observer and plane commander Otto Jufen enjoyed a grand view of the English coastline as their formation began their first sortie in earnest:

'In some respects we felt we were on holiday and on tour! This was I believe because at that point we were not too seriously taken up with the idea of attacking England or trying to knock them out of the war; that came later. At the start we had not got over the euphoric feeling of the great victory over France and the kind of life we had been living of late, so when we took off to fly to England we were not exactly in a warlike mood, though we were on the alert for RAF fighter attack.

'I lay or crouched in the nose of the plane which we had christened Anton. The sun was warm and the noise of our engines made me feel quite sleepy. We had quite a pleasant flight and I remember checking my map and the airfields marked on it which were targets of opportunity and of course a priority. Somewhere overhead were our escort fighters and we felt well protected. We flew north and then west and crossed the coast. I lay on my belly and admired the wonderful landscape laid out below. In fact I became so engrossed in tracing all the little roads and houses I almost forgot what we were there for.

'But at last our formation leader had led us to our target and the bombs were readied. I lay over the Lofte bombsight and adjusted everything as I saw the enemy airfield below. The bombs went down from all our Heinkels and we turned for home. Then I heard a shout and I believe some enemy fighters were seen and made a pass but I saw nothing.

'Back at our base we lazed in the sun and it all seemed rather peaceful until we had to fly off again the same day. On that flight we became somewhat separated from our comrades when a host of RAF fighters attacked us and all hell broke loose. Our Mes were everywhere, but

some of the Tommies broke through and in this assault we suffered some damage to one of our engines, but it did not catch fire. Yet we were slowed down and left behind the rest of the group, so our pilot tried to fly lower and merge with the landscape. By now my somewhat idyllic view of the proceedings had been rudely shattered and for the first time I was really afraid of dying.

'But somehow we escaped and were actually escorted back to our side of the Channel by some Mes, so we had a lucky escape.

'Next day we flew in another bomber and this time when we met the Tommies over Kent we saw nothing of them at close hand as our escorts drove them off. But as we cruised back over the coast after bombing an airfield we were well bracketed by flak and some of our planes were damaged. That evening our radio was full of bombastic news of our great assault on the RAF and how it would only be a matter of time before they ceased to exist. We had our doubts about that and next morning took off into the blue again carrying our usual load of high explosive bombs, crossing the south coast near Dover, heading for an inland airfield. At the same time other formations of Heinkels, Dorniers and a few Junkers 88s were flying other courses, hoping to split the defence.

'In less than twenty minutes our target was in sight and we closed up our formation, but as our bomb doors were opened someone called out "Fighters!", and as our bombs fell away the Tommies attacked, and this time we could not see our own fighters although we knew they were there somewhere. I saw a Hurricane flash past and grabbed the machine-gun in our nose and let fly – but too late. Then two more Hurricanes flashed through from above, much too fast for our gunners to sight on them. The formation began wobbling about as one Heinkel caught fire and then dropped back with two or three men baling out. The bomber fell behind out of sight and then more Hurricanes hit us and now our gunners were firing all the time. Another Heinkel caught fire, tipped over on its back and dived straight down, no parachutes appeared.

'By now I was sweating profusely and thankful when we reached the coast with some Mes buzzing round us. When we flew again that afternoon we went up into the North Sea and turned in over the coast of north Kent but once again the RAF caught us; they were always there waiting for us and we now realised they had a very good ground organisation. This time we had some Me 110s nearby as well as 109s, but the former proved a failure as when attacked they went into defensive circles and so were of no help to us at all and soon had to be withdrawn.

'Then a few days later one of my fellow officers and a good friend went missing and I believe was killed. I think he was piloting a Heinkel ahead of us and I had no idea what happened as confusion broke out during an air battle and I was trying to man the nose machine-gun *against some Spitfires, and when we landed he had gone. Then another group of our friends went down and we learned that they had become prisoners of war and were uninjured.'*

Kurt Henner had commenced Channel patrols with his comrades in their Me 109 fighters, sometimes sweeping low just off the English coastline and 'admiring the beautiful landscape', but seeing nothing of the RAF. The fighters did escort some Stukas who dive-bombed a British convoy – hitting nothing, their next job was to escort Heinkels and Dorniers:

'We saw no enemy planes but all this was to change rapidly. I well recall my first glimpse of an RAF fighter over England. We had escorted a large group of Heinkels, and after they bombed an airfield I saw fleeting shapes diving down and all at once we were in combat, with everyone shouting out warnings. I stayed with one of my comrades and tried to catch two Hurricanes which had just attacked the bombers, but they disappeared, so we looked around and saw a lone Spitfire attacking a Heinkel. I managed to get in a burst before he dived away with my comrade after him. They vanished before I could follow and my fuel state was not too good so I tagged onto another Me and we flew back across the Channel together, he waggled his wings and went off to another base. When we had all landed on our field we found that no one had shot down anything, which was very disappointing.

'Next day we were off again and this time the results were more satisfying. As soon as we flew over Kent the enemy appeared and we were soon engaged in a dogfight and split up. There were bombers catching fire and parachutes descending. I was hit in the fuselage by bullets and as I dived away a Spit went past at high speed so I pulled back and chased him. I stuck to his tail though he wallowed all over the place and at last I had him in my sights long enough to get in a good burst and he fell onto his back on fire and the pilot baled out.

'I was very elated and intent on finding a second victim but my fuel state prevented me so I flew back to base in triumph. We had shot down six of the enemy, or so we claimed. My own victory was a certainty as I had seen the enemy pilot fall out of his blazing plane. We drank toasts to the victors and my ground crew painted a victory bar on the rudder of my Emil, as we called the Me 109e.

'Next morning the weather was not so good but improved later, so after lunch we took off to meet some Dorniers and Heinkels over the French coast and cross the Channel once more. This time we had progressed well over Kent before the RAF appeared and we soon split up to combat them. I had a glimpse of a flash as a bomber blew up into pieces and then I was diving after a Hurricane which tried to escape at lower level. I clung to him and caught him fair and square with a long burst of fire and he burned at once. The Hurricane went straight down and I did not see the pilot get out.

'When I looked round I could see no planes at all, which seemed very strange. But then I caught sight of the bombers heading for the sea, so I gave chase and found they were still under attack. I saw a Spitfire with a smoking engine so tried to finish him off, but the pilot turned inland and I did not have enough fuel left to chase him.'

Kurt Henner's stint in the battle was about to come to an end:

'About two days after that I had my last combat. We took off as usual to rendezvous with the bombers at about 15,000 feet over the French coast. We came up on either side of them, with more Mes and a few 110s above and below. I remember thinking what a wonderful day it was and how warm in the cockpit, hot in fact, when someone shouted "Spitfires! Spits!" And then we saw a lot of the enemy planes curving in from inland, opened our formation and prepared to meet them.

'Suddenly some Hurricanes dived down through us and began firing at the bombers and all hell broke loose as some of us tried to catch them, while others faced the Spits who were by then diving on us. I saw several planes catch fire and some parachutes, and as the Spits came through us firing all the way I made to pursue one, firing in deflection. But then I found I had another Spit on my tail so I dived vertically, feeling sure my superior speed would enable me to escape. But then several loud bangs and thuds vibrated the body of my plane somewhere behind me and some bullets struck the engine in front of me and smoke began to appear. I was very frightened and tried to sideslip but went into a spin as if I was losing control of the fighter.

'I lost track of the Spit, the pilot probably thought I was finished. Then I saw small flames licking out from the engine cowling in front of me and it felt very hot in the cockpit and the propeller began behaving very strangely, as if it was about to stop. The plane was vibrating badly and I thought it could blow up at any minute. I tried to see if I could reach the coast, but suddenly a great gush of smoke burst out into the cockpit followed by flickering flame and I was very frightened and knew I had to get out of it and fast.

'So I undid my straps, jettisoned the hood and started to climb out of my seat. At that moment there was a bang and I found myself propelled right out of the cockpit and into a terrific slipstream. I felt a great fear yet relief as I felt the cold air rushing past me and caught a glimpse of my plane falling away in flames and making a terrible rasping noise. I also saw the sea, but realised I would probably fall over land so pulled the handle and in a moment my 'chute opened with a crack and a terrific jerk and I felt a great peace. I knew the war was over for me, but I didn't care. All thoughts of heroic action had vanished – all I cared about was that I was alive and it felt wonderful.

'When this euphoric feeling passed I took stock and found that I was not far from a road and saw people and one or two vehicles. The ground came up quite fast and I landed heavily near a hedge in a green field

28 October 1939: a Heinkel 111 of KG26 lies near the village of Humbie, 12 miles south-east of Edinburgh.

BOVE: 'Herr Niehoff' in the hands of the cottish police.

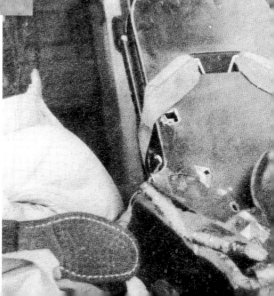

IGHT: The bullet-holed pilot's seat and iscarded flying boots tell a grim story.

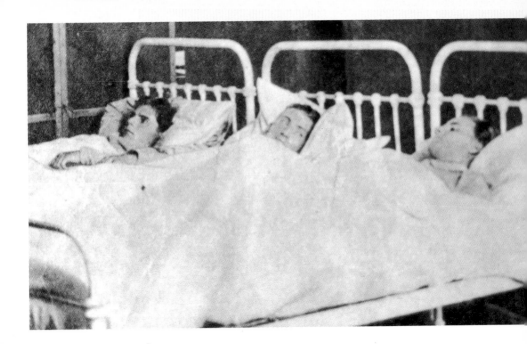

Early days in the air war.
ABOVE: Surviving German
aircrew well tended in hospital.

Full military honours were
afforded the fallen.

All changed when the 'Nazi air pirates' began attacking North Sea fishing boats, some of which were under Royal Navy control as minesweepers and advance warning vessels.

RIGHT AND BELOW: Fullest facilities were provided for *Luftwaffe* propaganda cameramen. The 'hot seat' in the gunner's place in a Stuka would seem suicidal.

Marshal Sperrle commanded the 3rd Air Fleet.

Hans Rudel – Stuka ace.

Marshal Kesselring with Göring and General Loezer on the Channel coast.

ighter aces Adolf Galland and Helmut Wick (killed November 1940).

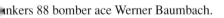

nkers 88 bomber ace Werner Baumbach.

Stukas allegedly strafing an AA camp in West Sussex in August 1940.

This Stuka lost its undercart when it crashed off the Selsey Road, Sussex, 16 August 1940.

Death dive of another Stuka
ear Chichester.

Citizens and troops
approach the debris
with caution.

Boosted by Nazi propaganda as a new type of 'destroyer' plane, the Messerschmitt 110 soon proved more of a liability in the Channel battle. The Adjutant of ZG/76 prepares for take-off.

An Me110 of 1/ZG76 shot down at Lenham in Kent.

where I lay in a heap for a while, not caring, just relieved to have got down in one piece.

'Then an amazing thing happened. I saw the face of a little girl staring at me through the hedge, and as I grinned at her I heard shouts and vehicles and in a moment I was surrounded by soldiers with rifles and bayonets. They helped me out of my harness and searched me and spoke to me in English which I did not understand. Then a policeman came to help them and we all walked out of the field through a gate where some people were watching me and I saw the little girl. Then an army truck arrived and I was put into the back, guarded by three young soldiers who stared at me and grinned. One of them gave me a cigarette, but I was a non-smoker and refused.

'We soon reached their camp where I was taken before their NCOs and an officer who wrote my name and rank in a book before they took me away to another room where I was given a cup of tea and a cake. Then it was a cell for me until about two hours later an RAF officer with some military policemen came for me and took me to London where I was interrogated very politely and shown various photographs of Luftwaffe men, none of whom I recognised. I spent three nights in that place and two more at Cockfosters before being taken to a PoW camp in the north in very nice countryside. My emotions were mixed. On the one hand I had survived, on the other I longed to be with my old comrades and, of course, my family. These wishes were not granted: I never saw my friends again as most were killed or went missing in the war, and I did not rejoin my family until 1947.'

No German airman who began that great but dangerous adventure in the summer of 1940 will ever forget their first views of the enemy land. Peter Winker was one of these as he and his friends zoomed out over the coast of France early in the Battle:

'I will never forget my first glimpses of England. We had climbed up over our base near Calais and across the water could see the white cliffs stretching for miles. And then the Heinkels and Dorniers came into view and it was all very impressive. We climbed higher and higher until we were thousands of feet above the bombers, the whole grand formation making for England and Kent.

'I saw a few ships off Dover and then the first white puffs of flak below us which were near the leading Heinkels, but we all flew on quite serenely. The sun was hot and it became rather uncomfortable in the small cockpit and soon I had a headache. But then we opened up our formation and began to scan the sky for some RAF reaction as the bombers headed for their bases. But we saw not a sign of opposition apart from the occasional flak bursts. Then the bombers reached their target and the bombs began to fall, but I was too busy scanning the sky to watch results.

'Then the action began. One moment all was serene, then I heard shouts over my headphones – "Fighters! Enemy fighters!", and below I

*saw small shapes darting through the bombers. They were Hurricanes
and we at once dived down to try and catch them, but unfortunately
they had already hit two bombers before we got anywhere near them.
One Heinkel caught fire and fell away and another was smoking badly.
We continued our dives and I saw a Hurricane fleeing earthwards but
it was too late. Then I saw another Hurricane to starboard and decided
to go after him, but he pulled away and I was left with empty sky to
shoot at. It was amazing how one moment the sky had been full of
planes and empty the next. I looked around in amazement and could
not see a single plane – ours or theirs!*

'*Then I saw silvery specks to the south and tried to catch up with them
and at last discovered they were Dorniers and at once found myself in
company with some of our Mes. So we recrossed the Channel in some
disappointment. Our first combat with the RAF had been a let-down as
it had all happened so very much faster than we had expected. Back at
base we had discussions on what had happened and decided we must do
better next time as no one had claimed a single victory, though at least
two of our bombers had been lost.*

'*From that time on we flew every single day, only the worst weather
stopped us. Our next combat came after we had taken off to escort about
fifty bombers across the Channel. This time the RAF were waiting for us
and as soon as we crossed the English coast the combats began. There
were Hurricanes and Spitfires everywhere it seemed, with many of the
enemy attacking the bombers. I had a quick glimpse of a Hurricane as
it collided with a Dornier, an amazing sight with bits and pieces falling
earthwards with a dash of flame and not a parachute to be seen. We
found ourselves mixing in with Spitfires and every man was fighting
for his life and carrying out all sorts of aerobatics to escape tracer
fire. I dived to escape myself and then climbed up again and saw a
Spitfire in front of me and squeezed the firing button. I saw pieces fall
away from his wing and then he vanished, so I looked around for more
targets and saw a lone Hurricane attacking a Heinkel which was trying
to reach the sea and fly home. I closed in on the Tommy and fired and
at once his engine blew up in a gout of flame, and as I followed it to one
side the fighter went over onto its back and the pilot fell out. I saw his
'chute open and felt thankful as the Hurricane was a mass of flames.*

'*By that time my fuel state was low so I headed for home; that was
always the problem – our time over England was very limited. When
I landed I saw my ground crew and told them I had been lucky and
they were excited. I soon joined my squadron comrades and we all
went to the bar to celebrate our victories. We claimed six of the RAF
planes destroyed and several damaged. Our intelligence people were
very satisfied, but then we heard that the bomber CO was less so as
we had failed to prevent the enemy from intercepting them. It was
obviously a big problem for us and impossible to stop some of the
Hurricanes and Spitfires getting through.*

'On the next flight my own machine was damaged and I barely made it back to base. I had flown over the Channel with my comrades and reached Kent with the bombers, but just as they bombed a lot of RAF fighters dropped on us and we were thrown into the confusion of combat. It was quite a scrap and I had no time to watch what was happening to the bombers as there was flak and Hurricanes and Spitfires everywhere. I twisted and turned as we tried to escape enemy fire and get them in our sights and then I felt a hammering on the body of my Me and kicked the rudder bar to fall away, then pushed the stick forward violently to escape. I glimpsed a Hurricane whizzing over my head and felt annoyed that I had been caught. Then as I dived I began to wonder how badly I had been damaged but could feel nothing wrong with my plane. However, when I pulled up again going towards the sea I felt a lot of vibration and the plane felt sluggish and I knew something was wrong. But I was still flying though down to a thousand feet or so and at that height I felt very vulnerable. Then I saw a flash of flak below and tried to juggle the plane into evasive action until I was clear and over the sea and I did manage to get back to my base.

'On landing I found several holes in the rear fuselage and tail which was why the plane was sluggish. I was rather shaken that I had been caught and resolved to do better. A few days of inclement weather restricted our flying but then we were off again and this time I was resolved to be more alert. Sure enough we entered a big air battle over west Kent after the bombers had attacked an airfield and this time I saw several planes going down in flames or smoking, with parachutes billowing. I fought hard, having several opportunities to fire my guns, but was frustrated as all proved indecisive and not one enemy plane went down before me which was very disappointing.

'I arrived back at base covered in sweat and not in a good frame of mind. The RAF boys were very tough opponents, even so we felt we could win, given the opportunity to prove our worth. We knew by then that the enemy had a very good ground warning system as they always seemed to be waiting for us or showed up very quickly at the right place. We heard that fantastic claims were being made by them for Germans destroyed and we knew also that our own side were making extraordinary claims; neither seemed to be correct. Despite all our strict training in this matter, in the mad whirl of air combat it was very hard to be 100 per cent certain of an enemy aircraft totally destroyed or not. As to our own losses, again when it was every man for himself no one had time to watch machines crash. Of course, being young we wanted to score well and some very big tallies were made by the top aces on our side who were very good indeed, even though some were themselves shot down in due course. We realised that most fighter pilots on both sides were only average, but if each only managed to knock down one or two of the enemy then we were doing our job.

'Then two of our boys went missing, not the first, but these were like *twins, not related but inseparable friends and both uncannily went down on the same day. No one ever knew what happened to them, they simply never returned and were posted missing, believed killed. We never heard anything of them again so assumed they had gone into the Channel.'*

The hitherto deadly Stukas had been among the very first Luftwaffe bombers to commence the cross-Channel assault, and like the Me 110s be withdrawn soon after. Hans Rudel:

'We took off and saw our escort of 110s and 109s above us and began to enjoy the wonderful views. From my cockpit at 10,000 feet I could see the whole length of the Channel, or most of it. It was very warm, so I opened the hood and waved to my nearest comrades. We felt very confident and quite happy in our tasks. Soon our formation leader waggled his wings and looking down I saw some tiny model ships below us. We went into line ahead formation and went into our dives, leaving an adequate gap between each Stuka. The noise was great as our sirens came into play but we were used to this. And then I saw the first great geysers of water exploding near some of the ships. Only a destroyer fired rather ineffectively at us. I waited until I had a fat steamer in my sights and pulled out at under 1,000 feet and released my bomb. My gunner yelled that we had scored a very near miss which must have damaged the ship's plating at least. We had never trained to attack ships, which, as moving targets that zig-zagged, were always hard to hit anyway. We saw no sign of enemy aircraft and flew back to base where we claimed one ship hit and several damaged. This was only the beginning.

'We took off again later to attack the same convoy and this time we definitely saw one ship go up in smoke. But that was the last trouble-free attack we made on the Channel front and the start of our demise in that battle.

'The very next day we flew across the Channel again to attack not shipping but airfields and radio installations on the English coast in two formations. We went to the airfields at Thorney [Island] and Ford and did a good job but came under fighter attack. I managed to escape but saw some Stukas smoking and a really big air battle in progress.

'It was the end of the Stuka myth on the Western Front.'

The defeat of the Stukas had begun on 15 August when seven were shot down and others damaged attacking shipping off Portland; in further attacks on RAF, naval airfields and radar stations on 16 and 18 August the Luftwaffe lost a further twenty-one dive-bombers. Rudel and his comrades had achieved temporary success, damaging radar sites, the base at Thorney Island, knocking out planes and hangars and causing casualties at Tangmere. Rudel:

'Some fierce air combats resulted. On one afternoon we were stepped up in grand formation and well escorted by our fighters when Hurricanes and Spitfires fell on us just as we were about to dive. In the confusion that

followed I saw Stukas containing some of my best friends going down in flames. Bombs were jettisoned and combats took place all over the sky. Several Mes joined the fray and I saw parachutes descending. I had no chance to attack anything since we were fighting for our lives and at a great disadvantage from the enemy fighters which hemmed us in on all sides. My gunner Hans was firing continuously and I tried to dive the Stuka almost to sea level and escape back to France. We succeeded, but I was one of the few to escape, with bullet holes all over my plane. Three of my dearest pilot friends and their gunners were missing, as were others I knew less well. It was a disastrous day for us and the inquests did not need to probe to discover the Stuka was useless as a fighting machine against real opposition. As a result of this black day in August 1940 we were withdrawn from combat and did not fly any more missions for some time.'

Indeed, the commander of the Luftwaffe's VIIIth Air Corps was moved to record in his diary that his Stukas had had their feathers well and truly plucked. Rudel's last actions on the 'England Front' would take place later in the year.

Horst Juventus had not taken part of course in the largely cancelled Eagle Day date of 12 August, recording it as 'a fiasco', but took off in better weather the next day:

'I had to admit that it was very thrilling to see so many German bombers arranged in the sky together. We knew our fighters were about as we crossed the sea in our Heinkels to attack airfields in Kent. We had just crossed the coast when I heard the first shouted reports of enemy fighters. I looked around but saw nothing, but suddenly shapes darted through our formation and I glimpsed two Hurricanes and our guns fired at them – but too late. This was our first mass action over England. And then came more shouts and two of our bombers left the formation smoking. The flights were now wavering as the enemy attacks came in, and I wondered if our own fighters were doing any good. Then a lot of cloud appeared and we changed course and saw the target airfield ahead. The bombs went down without interference, but as we turned away there came more shouted warnings and I saw a lot of little shapes coming down at us from above. It was very unnerving to sit there and wait for the bullets to come flying.

'This time no one was hit, the Tommies went hurtling through our formation and then a lot of white flak bursts appeared around us but did no harm. Then we were back over the sea and felt safe. It had been quite a hectic half-hour or so over enemy territory. I had no idea how many bombers we had lost, but obviously we were in for no easy time but felt we would achieve our object.

'From then on we flew every day that weather allowed, the targets were much the same but sometimes included ships in harbour. There was a terrible combat one day when I saw two of our bombers collide after

one was hit. There was a flash of flame and then just bits of wreckage floating down, which was very demoralising. We saw no parachutes open. That day I also saw two enemy fighters go down, with one pilot escaping by parachute.

'*On our next flight a flak splinter knocked out one of our engines and we had to leave the formation in a hurry as it caught fire. I dived the plane for the Channel and luckily we saw no enemy aircraft. Next day we took up a different plane, but this one was awful as it would not climb properly and we lagged behind. I wanted to turn back, but our captain insisted on going on, even though we were well behind the main formation. I thought he was mad, but he took no notice.*

'*Sure enough, we were soon set upon over the English coast by two Spitfires who damaged our rudder and wings and I had to dive towards the sea where we dropped our bombs. The whole flight was a waste as I told our captain who, although a friend, had shown poor judgement. I'm sorry to say he did not survive the war, but this was after he had left our unit.*

'*Just after that we had a lot of arguments about fighter escort as we were not being properly protected, or at least the fighter boys were doing their best but not stopping the Tommies from getting at us. We felt we were very vulnerable and had lost a number of planes before Göring ordered the fighters to make closer escort, which of course greatly hampered their freedom of manoeuvre and was not really the answer. The Stukas had proved a failure and were withdrawn before September, as were the Me 110s, which needed protection themselves even though they achieved some successes.*

'*On one flight we lost three bombers in a very short space of time and most of the crewmen died. The first was hit by ships' flak over the Channel and turned away smoking but crashed back at base. The second was hit by a Hurricane over the coast and blew up with a sound we heard above the roar of our engines. Just a quick flash – then nothing at all – as if the plane and crew had simply vanished. We were very shaken by that.*

'*We flew on and bombed an airfield in Kent, but after turning away we were attacked by Hurricanes from all sides. I saw two of them go down as the Mes caught them, but another Heinkel was hit and went down very steeply as if the pilot had been killed. Our lower gunner saw it strike the ground.*'

The Dornier Observer Karl Haulmeier had by now also become thoroughly embroiled in the attack on England, and following one of his early trips when the unit bombed an airfield in Kent heard the customary warnings of enemy fighters but saw nothing at all until quite suddenly a bomber erupted in flames and smoke:

'*Then things got hotter as the Tommies came in from all sides, but our Mes came in at them and we reached the Channel in safety. Back at base we agreed that our enemy was a tough foe, but we had plenty of confidence that we would knock out his airfields one by one.'*

Haulmeier recalls that from then on they knew what to expect; the Heinkel crews flew higher, up over the North Sea, then headed west into Kentish air space, and found and bombed an airfield – Biggin Hill, Hawkinge, or Detling:

'It was rather magnificent to lie in the nose of a Dornier with a grandstand view of it all. I felt no fear as it all went so smoothly. Of course, it all changed over the following weeks, but at first we had no idea what lay ahead and our morale was high. We expected losses, it was inevitable, but were confident that our Mes could drive off most of the enemy fighters. That day we regained our base with no losses.'

Next day Haulmeier flew off again, the Dornier formation splitting into two groups after they crossed the English coast at Margate to seek out different airfield targets.

'This time we were attacked at once and a bomber went down with an engine smoking and out of action. The Tommies then came in continuously, despite the protection of our fighters and there were combats all around us. We took a few bullet holes and our two gunners were in action all the time. As a result of all this we missed our target so turned south and bombed the harbour at Dover. On the way out we were again set upon by Spitfires and I saw one of these shot down into the sea by our Mes. When we reached base we found two of our crews missing, which was sobering enough.

'Towards the end of August we flew a larger raid with many squadrons taking part, our target was the usual RAF fields and we were closely escorted by our fighters who had received some bullying remarks from Göring. They were of course in difficulties, for by the time they broke away to intercept attackers it was too late – the birds had flown. On this raid we lost many planes. I saw one Dornier on fire and it flicked over onto its back, one crewman baled out, but no more followed. As it fell away in flames a large piece of wing fell off. Then I saw a Heinkel go sailing past with both engines on fire and it narrowly missed one of our Dorniers. Two men baled out and then I lost sight of it.

'By the time we reached our target area we had been under attack for half an hour, and I wondered if we could survive – things had become very hot. But the Tommies vanished and we succeeded in bombing and turning south. Yet they appeared again and the combats restarted. I saw two enemy planes going down and the pilots taking to their parachutes. These scenes would have been very impressive were they not marred by the great danger. One Dornier went astray, obviously in trouble, two men baled out and it dived towards the sea.

'Then we ourselves came under attack from ahead, which was especially terrifying. It needed all our nerve to keep going, we could

*not turn away for fear of striking other bombers alongside us. One
Dornier was struck by two enemy fighters which came flashing through
with all our guns firing at them. Then we were over the sea where the
attacks continued and more planes went down. I saw a Hurricane falling
over like a leaf in the wind, its tail came off and the pilot fell out, but his
'chute only partly opened so he fell to his death. Then an Me 110 sailed
past covered in flames before it blew apart in a cloud of debris.*

*'By the time we landed we were in a great sweat and very relieved
to get down in one piece. Three of our Wing were lost and I believe as a
result of this day an order came down that in future only one officer was
to be assigned to each crew, so a certain amount of juggling took place
among the bomber groups. Most of the aircrew were NCOs: young men
who were ageing rapidly in the strain of war.'*

The big raid referred to was probably that of 15 August when the
Luftwaffe made its biggest attempt so far to destroy the RAF bases,
flying about two thousand sorties and losing nearly fifty aircraft. As
usual the Germans were let down by their intelligence, attacking airfields
which had no operational significance for Fighter Command such as
Croydon, which, being in the Greater London area, was a target
forbidden by Hitler; the intended target had been Kenley. A Dornier
group which intended to bomb Biggin Hill attacked West Malling, of
far less significance to the RAF. Also on this day Stumpff's Vth Air
Fleet was activated to fly across the North Sea and attack RAF fields
in north-east England, their intelligence again assuming that the RAF
fighter units were all committed in the south. This proved a disastrous
experiment to the Luftwaffe since the raid cost them 20 per cent losses,
though one unit of Junkers 88s of KG30 managed to hit RAF Driffield in
Yorkshire, destroying ten bombers on the ground. On this day the RAF
put up over 900 sorties, suffering 42 planes destroyed or damaged.

Hans Gilbert had piloted his own Dornier 17z in one of the first
formations to strike across the Channel. Their first trip was on a
beautiful morning he recalls, and their leader took them to Dover where
they turned west, spotting a small convoy which they attacked. It was
part of the Germans' pre-invasion strategy to close off the Channel to
British shipping, but to attempt this with 'horizontal' bombers was futile.
Nevertheless, the Dorniers bombed, doing no damage whatsoever as far
as Gilbert could see, but causing a few splashes. Next day the experiment
was repeated, and the bombers were well escorted by Messerschmitts, but
Gilbert could see little below, being too busy on his formation flying.

Gilbert and his comrades had heard about the notion of a landing in
England – 'quite a feat if they could pull it off' – and their change to new
tactics: they would destroy the RAF bases. When the first probing flight
took place over Kent, as reported elsewhere, little happened, though
some RAF defenders put in an appearance and one of Gilbert's gunners
reported a smoking bomber behind them. They felt comparatively safe,

being well within a large formation. But even the German aircrew must have felt bemused when the much heralded 'Eagle Day' passed with nothing spectacular happening, which was how Gilbert saw it. Not until the schedule really got underway, with constant flights across the Channel and over Kent, did things begin to boil:

'Although we were confident of the outcome we could see the desired result would not come easily. I saw the first Dornier go down in flames after that, which was distressing but the kind of sight we would get used to. I enjoyed flying the Dornier and until then it had not been difficult for me and I had had no problems. But my days as a member of the group were numbered, though in August I had no idea that the daily routine was to be so rudely interrupted. You see, it had become just that. Obviously, the danger was increasing, yet as I sat in my seat in the sunshine all that went on outside seemed slightly unreal, as if of no immediate concern.

'We had been flying over the Channel for about ten days when the attacks on us became much fiercer and we became directly involved. Several Hurricanes and Spitfires zipped through our group firing and some Dorniers were hit. Our own machine suffered holes in the wings, which shook me and I realised at last the great danger we were in. But the damage was not serious and we flew on. I had the machine under full control and we dropped our bombs as planned. I believe the target was the airfield at Hawkinge, although at times I had little idea which as they all looked the same over Kent and our Observer did the bombing.

'That morning after we flew home we inspected our plane and found sixty holes all told, all in the wings, fortunately all repairable. But when we flew in the afternoon we took a different plane, and this was to be our last battle, though we did not guess that as we climbed above the clouds into the blue.

'We crossed the coast in formation at 12,000 feet with our escorts above us. The sea looked like green glass and before us stretched the patchwork green of England and I wondered if I would ever get the chance of a closer look. It was hard to imagine the people down there as enemies. We saw nothing but green fields and woods and little towns and villages and it all looked very peaceful and attractive. The sun was very, very warm in our cabin, and were it not for the roar of our engines it would have been a very pleasant sojourn. Then we crossed the enemy coast and the first flak came up, but it did not bother us. We had come in over the eastern part of Kent heading for the same RAF airfields when suddenly our gunners yelled "Fighters!" and I heard machine-guns firing. The smell from the guns penetrated my oxygen mask and I felt frightened and looked this way and that and at once saw a Spitfire which looked quite big as it was so close to us and seemed to have erupted from nowhere.

'Then there was a roar and rattle and all kinds of bits flew past me – glass from the cabin roof and pieces of metal debris. It all happened in a flash and caught me by surprise so that I sat stunned for a few seconds until the Observer shouted that we were really hit. Then I saw that our left wing was on fire and felt a great wind coming into the cabin through the holes in the roof. I juggled the controls, but the left engine had stopped but did not catch fire. I tried to feather the propeller but it kept on turning. The other planes in our flight avoided us and we felt we could no longer keep up with the formation.

'I was very frightened, but at least none of us were injured. I decided to try and reach base and the captain said we could jettison the bombs in the sea. But we lost height very rapidly and were a long way from the south coast of England and I had no wish to crash off the coast of Kent in the North Sea. But then to my great surprise the whole left wing caught fire and we were in serious trouble. I managed to turn the Dornier to the left before all control was lost and the captain ordered us to abandon the aircraft.

'I had no option than to remain in my seat while the other lads leapt out through the lower hatch. The captain wished me good luck and to get out before the wing broke off. Then he vanished and I was alone in the blazing bomber as the ground began to spin below so I managed to unfasten my seat straps, get down onto the floor and reach the hatch. I saw the green fields going round and round and after some trouble got my head out of the hole. The noise and wind was very great and I felt terrified as I seemed stuck and unable to move. Then suddenly I was free and falling and everything went very quiet for a moment until I heard a tremendous noise and pieces of the plane went flying past me. I recovered enough to pull the cord and the parachute opened with a tremendous jerk and I found myself floating in tremendous peace and relief. I was completely stunned by it all as it had happened in less than five minutes.

'Then I dared to look down past my feet and saw the green fields of England and realised I was about to become a prisoner of war. There was a small road and near it two little houses and I saw some people running, and a man on a bicycle, and I laughed and wondered what sort of reception I would get.

'I came down in a cornfield, and it was very pleasant just to lie there in the sun for a few moments in great relief that I was alive and in one piece. Then I remembered my comrades and sat up, but could see no other parachutes and wondered if they had survived. I decided they must have come down before me. And then as I stood up and removed my harness I heard shouts and some people came across the field from a little lane, all civilians. I recall them distinctly: there were two women in dresses who stood staring at me, and a man in shirtsleeves and flat cap who also did not know what to do I gather. Then came a man on a bicycle who was also in shirtsleeves but he had a rifle over his shoulder.

He looked much more determined as he laid down his bicycle, unslung his rifle and advanced towards me calling out something. I could not understand him but guessed he wanted me to surrender, so I put up my hands and smiled at him. It was all rather amazing and I remember thinking that only an hour or so before I had been in France with no thought of actually visiting England in such a manner. I felt so relieved however and I believe the reaction of my experience overcame me so that I half fainted and dropped to the ground.

'When I recovered my senses these people were all over me and helped me to sit up and with their help I stood up again and removed my flying helmet and threw off my harness. They were all talking as they led me out of the field and I was relieved that they showed no hostility towards me at all. Then, as we reached the road I heard a vehicle and saw a policemen with a steel helmet on a bicycle. But the vehicle was a truckload of soldiers carrying rifles and they took charge. I think the policeman was a little disappointed as he had hoped to capture me himself. As it was the soldiers under their Sergeant took me to their truck after searching me and removing the papers and photographs from my tunic. They were grinning and very correct and one of them offered me a cigarette and called me Fritz, which made me laugh.

'I sat in the back of the covered truck and we drove off for a mile or so until we reached their camp where I was taken before an officer in a hut. I believe it was a flak unit but I'm not sure. The officer left me under guard and soon returned with a younger Lieutenant and gave me a cup of tea, but I refused a cigarette. The young officer then tried to question me in quite good German while the CO took down my replies. I gave my name which they wrote down and that was all. The two officers then left and I was watched very closely by two soldiers with rifles and bayonets and after a while taken to a mess hall and given a meal of meat, potatoes and greens with some bread and butter. I was not too hungry and could not eat much though the food was good. Then I was taken outside to another truck and put inside with two stern-faced men who looked like military policemen.'

We will return later to Gilbert's further experiences as a PoW. Meanwhile, the ambitious young officer Karl-Ludwig Weinfarth had, as soon as the attack on Britain was announced, hurried to familiarise himself with the controls of a Dornier bomber, forsaking his tedious administrative duties, for at long last it seemed he was about to achieve his greatest ambition – to lead a bomber Wing into action:

'We flew off and I must say I enjoyed it immensely, but results in our attack were inconclusive and continued to be over the next days.'

It appears that Weinfarth is referring to pre-Eagle Day probing sorties, for he next describes the real battle which began in August to knock out the RAF bases.

'It was our dear Führer's intention to invade England, or at least put on some sort of show in that direction. Fresh preparations were made and after a false start Eagle Day began and we flew to England in good spirits and looking forward to the adventure. I must admit I was feeling over confident.'

Weinfarth recalls that despite one or two alarms nothing much occurred in their first two or three raids, but his boyish enthusiasm was about to be cruelly dented:

'We were then seriously hindered by RAF fighters and I was one of the first to be put out of action. We had flown over the Kent coast and were attacked by Hurricanes which came out of the sun behind us. Our Mes were caught napping and before they could intervene the damage was done. I heard shouts and a rattling noise behind me and felt a sharp pain in my arm and another in my leg and cried out. My captain – as he technically was – leapt up to assist me and saw blood gushing out of my right lower arm and flying boot. He at once opened up our first-aid box and began bandaging me while I tried to retain control of the plane which was wobbling from side to side. We managed to stay in formation but I could not then carry on owing to the great pain in my leg, so the captain helped me out of my seat while holding the control wheel, then he climbed into my place. This manoeuvre was not achieved without difficulty. I slumped down onto the cabin floor which had blood all over it. Then we reached our target but with the Observer piloting it fell to the radio–operator–gunner to pull the lever to release our bombs.

'We managed to get back to base without further mishap. We had been holed all along our fuselage and the radio operator had had a narrow escape. But I had been thoroughly disabled and had to be assisted from the Dornier after our captain made a very shaky landing. All my great enthusiasm had fallen away, I was only interested in sleeping in hospital, for by then I had lost a lot of blood and was soon under ether and being operated on.

'Later, when I was conscious, the doctor told me that the nerves of my arm were severed and my leg would be useless for some time to come.'

It was the end of Weinfarth's career as a flying leader, for when recovered sufficiently he was put back into administration.

Wolfgang Schauer's decision to switch from Stuka dive-bombers to Messerschmitt 110s may have merely postponed his own day of reckoning against the RAF. Soon after their first encounters against the much speedier Hurricanes and Spitfires the crews of his unit took to debating not only the best tactics to employ, but also whether they should be trying to combat the RAF fighters at all:

'The term "destroyers" as applied to our 110s seemed a little ludicrous as the faster enemy planes were chasing us all over the sky. But we were

ordered to continue and even fly over England, and were promised that the bombers would soon destroy the enemy's airfields. Well, they certainly tried and had some success, but as escorts to them we were not much use any more. Indeed, we soon had whole squadrons of 109s helping us along like lame ducks, and I began to wish I had joined them instead. Meanwhile, my old Stuka comrades had taken heavy losses and many of my friends were missing. We began to wonder if it would be wiser to call off the Kanalkampf and call it a stalemate.

'Then came the terrible day when our squadron was decimated and I made my last flight of the war. It had become obvious that as a combat aircraft against the RAF our Me 110s were useless. True, we had shot down some Hurricanes and even Spits when we caught them unawares or in a bad position, but generally they flew rings round us, and it was only a matter of time before we were destroyed.

'On that day in August I took off with my trusty gunner Franz in the rear cockpit. He was a mere 18-year-old from Bavaria and a very brave boy. He knew the score but as always was cheerful and ready for the fight.

'We flew across the Channel again, over some large formations of our own Heinkels, and were then attacked by many Spitfires and Hurricanes, and it was every man for himself. In no time planes were falling and parachutes descending. We flew like madmen, trying to stay alive. Suddenly I saw two Hurricanes on our tail and twisted my plane into the wildest gyrations to try and escape. But it was no use, my poor Franz was riddled with bullets and the Me caught fire. I could see that I would have to bale out.

'I threw off the cockpit hood and managed to get out, and as I fell away from the blazing plane the petrol tanks blew up and I was burnt by the hot blast. But I fell clear of the debris and managed to open my parachute, eventually coming down in the sea where I was picked up after a while by a British steamer. That was the end of my war.'

Peter Harmel found he and his comrades were 'flying, flying, flying every day' in the Messerschmitt fighters:

'We grew very tired, and though we had many successes the RAF boys were shooting down many of our bombers and we did not seem able to stop them. Also, we were having losses ourselves, and although we scored many victories we became worried as real success seemed to elude us.

'One day we had gone up to escort our bombers over Kent but were intercepted by Spitfires who gave us a very hard time, especially as we did not have the fuel to stay over England very long. I nearly had my cockpit shattered by bullets and barely escaped with my life. When I landed back at base I was shaking all over. We did not see how we could win a total victory, even though our morale was still good. Our leaders urged us to be more aggressive and protect the bombers, but it

was impossible. I saw many of our big planes go down and very many young men die in them with no chance of escape.'

Arthur Tieker sat behind the wheel of his Heinkel, marvelling at the great formations of Luftwaffe bombers arrayed about him:

'They were stepped up into the blue sky. Day after day we took off across the Channel and the losses grew on both sides. Very often we succeeded in bombing our targets, but we were always attacked before or after and more and more of my friends went missing or crashed back at base. I can assure you we were all very afraid on these raids, but in the heat of battle we were too busy to think about it. I remember seeing one of my old friends from the old days of training who was shot down close to me: his bomber exploded and almost took us with him. We dived low over the sea, dropped our bombs and fled for home.

'One day we were over Kent with very many aircraft around us including our own fighters who had a terrible job, but did their best. I saw several Spitfires attacking and some Hurricanes came straight at us from the front. I yelled "Look out!" as the bullets began to fly. And then one of the Hurricanes collided with a Heinkel and both aircraft were broken to pieces, with bodies flying everywhere.

'On another occasion I saw two of our bombers on fire, the crews were baling out into the sea, and as one of the planes went down it hit one of the crewmen in his 'chute and carried him to his death. The other bomber remained in the air for a few moments with no one aboard, but on fire, and it eventually dived into the sea off Dover.

'By now we were exhausted, and we wondered how much longer it could last.'

Christian Rossler:

'It went on for week after week and we had to get in many replacement crews. I had a difficult time as a leader, for the organisation had to be maintained.

'This was not easy with our falling morale. On one flight we were nearly rammed by a Hurricane and I was very frightened, as we all were. The air battles grew more ferocious and our successes in bombing less. Then came the day when we were sent against London itself, and I felt we were in for our biggest battle, for surely the enemy would throw in everything to stop us?'

CHAPTER EIGHT

'TOO MANY FACES HAD GONE MISSING'

T wo weeks after Eagle Day it must have become obvious to even the most ardent Nazis (and there were some) in the Luftwaffe and at Göring's HQ that the objectives set were not being achieved. At least, judging by the daily reports gathered from the returning aircrews, the RAF was far from beaten and was still inflicting considerable losses on the Luftwaffe which could not be sustained for much longer. Later on Göring would complain rather petulantly that the enemy air force had the advantage of a radar control system, as if his men had been operating under unfair rules. Yet the Germans never realised how much they had eroded the strength of their opponents: the 'near run thing' was a fact.

It has been recorded that the commander of Air Fleet V, Hans-Jurgen Stumpff, had made his opinions clear at the outset ('This will not work'), but states that once Göring had handed out his orders the staffs were obliged to try and carry them out. Stumpff recalls that the attempt to close off the Channel largely succeeded when it should not have done, for the Stukas, though proven good in battlefield operations, were soon decimated by the RAF, but not before they had done some damage and perhaps prematurely alarmed the British and especially the Royal Navy into severely limiting all Channel shipping movements. As Stumpff also observes, the 'horizontal' bombers were quite unsuited to anti-shipping work, 'and at that time we had no torpedo squadrons to speak of'.

> *The main object then became the RAF as soon as we heard of Hitler's crazy scheme to invade England, and I recall my remarks when I heard of this. I said to my staff "He's mad to even think of such a thing". From then on I felt we were only going through the motions even though certain preparations were put in hand.'*

The Luftwaffe's bomber squadrons were launched to destroy the RAF bases and draw the enemy fighters into combat where they could be cut down by the German fighters.

> *'Even though we were complete novices at amphibious operations we knew full well that the RAF would intervene and upset operations.*

Apart from which the Royal Navy was a very big menace and we had no confidence whatever in either our Luftwaffe or the Kriegsmarine in being able to prevent it from crushing the invasion fleet.

'My own position as well as that of my fellow commanders was an absurd and invidious one for we had little faith or enthusiasm for the operations from the start. The bombers commenced operations and very soon began to suffer losses, the aircrew were either killed or went into British PoW camps, which was very unsatisfactory. Even those who landed in the sea were too often picked up by the enemy. All our intelligence estimates as to results proved illusory, data as to RAF dispositions was faulty from the start and based on pre-war information or air reconnaissance which failed to disclose the true picture which led to the wrong airfields being attacked. This led to costs to us when the wrong aircraft were destroyed on the ground – not the RAF fighters.

'The importance of radar in the enemy's defences was not appreciated until too late, and here again our weakness and lack of suitable units to cope with a strategic air war became apparent. I myself stood on the clifftops at Cap Gris Nez and other places on many a day and watched our air fleets go over on their missions, only to see them return time after time in disarray. It was quite disheartening and so very unnecessary. Then Göring had the gall to complain because his ill-founded plan was not working through our incompetence and cowardice on the part of the brave young fighter pilots. But we carried on without achieving any worthwhile results until in an absurd turnabout the whole idea of a cross-Channel invasion was diverted by the attack on London which came about as a result of Hitler's emotions and not through any reasoned logic. From then on the air war against Britain deteriorated into a meaningless, pointless series of raids which achieved little or nothing despite all the bombastic Nazi propaganda. I have to say that in those days we in the command echelons had a far more realistic appreciation of the situation and knew perfectly well how foolish were the lies over the radio. Anyone who flew over a great city like London and viewed the amount of damage in a certain area could deduce that little was being achieved. Yet it went on night after night until at last the Führer's latest gamble came up and most of the bombers were sent to the East where a high proportion of the crews lost their lives in an insane war.'

Even allowing for the fact that all the above remarks were made with hindsight, there is no reason to doubt that men like Stumpff were at odds with the Nazi leadership over not only the way they conducted war but also the reasons for it happening at all.

The Dornier leader Johannes Fink had also soon learned of the true nature of the task facing his men:

'The first combats over England had shown that the RAF was well disciplined and controlled but at times a little slow when caught by our Mes. Then the first losses occurred among the bomber units and

began to climb steadily thereafter. It was impossible for the escorts to be everywhere at once. Even though we believed our fighters superior to the enemy's, they were unable to prevent bomber losses. Reconnaissance photos showed damage to a number of RAF fields and it seemed that we were achieving success. Yet the interceptions continued against our formations, they did not lessen, so obviously we were going wrong.

'I remember a visit by Göring and his entourage. He stood on the clifftop overlooking the Channel and gazed through binoculars at England, shaking his head and grinning, telling us that they would be beaten. He had been on hand when Eagle Day was launched and often came to watch "the fun" as he called it. As an old fighter CO he thought he knew it all, but really he had very little knowledge when it came to directing operations; he assumed that once he had given the general directions his orders would be carried out. He grew increasingly angry over losses and eventually upbraided the poor fighter pilots and their leaders such as Galland who were doing their best.

'I often visited the units to speak personally to the returned aircrews in order to get first-hand impressions and it was always the same story – Spitfires and Hurricanes everywhere and lost friends who I knew would be missed in the messes. But they pressed on with great courage and were told by their leaders that the RAF was almost finished as a fighting force. The problem was that all my own efforts had been directed towards a very different kind of warfare as explained, we were not intended for such a role. To fly across a sea, even one as narrow as the Channel, in the face of determined opposition and then come up against more flak and fighters inland in order to find comparatively small targets took a lot of courage in daylight. These young men had seen much success over Poland and France, but the cross-Channel battle was very different. I saw too many sombre faces when I visited the bases and knew that we could not go on like that. When I spoke to Göring I reported on the difficulties and although he listened he was not very sympathetic. I knew his own position only too well, for he had made out a case to Hitler that the Luftwaffe was all-powerful and would soon overcome the opposition, and when this did not happen he turned on us, but even more on the fighter commanders. It was very unfair on these men as I knew them personally and realised they were fighting for their lives every time they flew over England and many of them paying the supreme sacrifice.'

Combat flying, especially at height on oxygen on a near daily basis becomes very wearing, even on fit young men, and the nervous strain in actual danger or the threat of it is an additional drain on the mental and physical make-up. The German aircrews were being called upon to fly two or three missions on most days.

As Horst Juventus states, 'We grew very tired but there was no let-up.'

Karl Haulmeier recalls that during all these weeks of continuous combat operations the crews were given no leave from their bases and grew very tired.

'I was in a better position than many since my job was less arduous. Even so, the nervous strain was very considerable and we all began to show the strain. Crashes became more frequent, but we were forced to carry on.'

The crews were woken soon after dawn, and after ablutions, breakfast on porridge and coffee, with perhaps bread rolls or, if lucky, eggs obtained by barter from a local French farmer. Then came a briefing of about thirty minutes which included a general discussion. The crews could then relax until take-off time, which was usually about ten o'clock, with at least one more raid to fly after lunch.

'Some days the weather would be too bad to formate, in which case single planes would be sent off to look for shipping or targets of opportunity. But it became obvious that we were not getting the results we needed.'

Johann Schmidt states:

'We became worn out. I saw too many of our boys go down to the ferocious fighter attacks, and plenty of Tommies also. I remember one of our Heinkels that caught fire over Kent, the wheels dropped down and it went into a glide but blew up in a flash, scattering bits and pieces over the countryside. One formation leader was hit by flak and dropped away, but collided with another bomber and both went down. Sometimes terrible things happened which were shocking to see and affected our morale. I remember several parachutes in the sky before us after a combat and we flew straight into them, it was impossible to start manoeuvring because of the tight formation we were in, at least not sufficient to avoid one or two of them. I had a brief glimpse of the look on one airman's face as he hung in his 'chute just before the plane next to us hit him – or at least dragged his 'chute along with it so that he was hauled over the machine and killed. It was a crazy accident.

'Then, at the end of August, my turn came. By then I was half prepared for it, for so many planes had gone down. I had imagined what might happen and thought of my comrades trying to escape while I tried to keep the plane on an even keel. Or would we simply vanish in a flash? Or be trapped in a burning crate? All these nightmare thoughts used to occur to me as I lay in my cot at night and sometimes I had bad dreams about it. The actual event was almost an anti-climax.

'We had bombed one of the RAF fields and turned south and were then attacked by enemy aircraft who pounced on us from above. In their first pass they hit us in the wings and we saw fuel escaping despite our self-sealing tanks. I thought "This is the end – that wing will catch fire at any moment." So I prepared myself for the worst. Yet amazingly the flow of fuel stopped, but something was wrong as the Heinkel would not

respond well to the controls, so I guessed we had suffered damage to the control wires. We had by then fallen out of formation and were then attacked again by enemy fighters. Two Hurricanes came at us again and again, and in these attacks our top gunner Emil was killed. The wing now began smoking badly so I decided we could not reach the coast, but the captain said we should try. But then an engine on the damaged side gave up and we were really in trouble. The Hurricanes seemed to have run out of ammunition and gone away, but then a Spitfire appeared, and he too seemed to be out of bullets as he flew alongside us, pointed downwards, gave us the "thumbs down" and flew off.

'We were still over land but losing height and I looked for somewhere to get down and saw some fairly flat fields with no buildings near them so tried to steer the bomber towards them. This proved hard as the machine was not responding well, but eventually we were lined up and my two comrades took up crash positions well behind me. I braced myself, tried to get the flaps fully down, and then we were brushing along the tops of corn and into a green field which had poles stuck into it as obstacles (against glider landings). One of these took off a wingtip, otherwise the Heinkel stayed in one piece and skidded to a halt.

'I undid my straps and my two comrades helped to remove poor Emil's body and we scrambled clear of the wreck. In no time at all we were surrounded by soldiers, so we handed over our pistols and other possessions, which were taken from us, and then marched off to a little lane where a truck was waiting. We lifted Emil into the truck and climbed in with some of the soldiers while other troops went to guard the plane. It was a shattering experience and I felt sick.

'In a little while we reached an army camp where we were locked into a small room until being told to remove our flying clothing and were then taken one by one to an office where we were interrogated, this proving useless as none of the British spoke German. Later we were given a welcome cup of tea before some military policemen took us to London where great surprises awaited us – good cooked meals, comfortable beds and friendly talks with sympathetic RAF officers, who I believe listened in to our conversations when we were together and learnt a few things that way. Otherwise we told them nothing but were very surprised at the friendly treatment and I have no doubt that it persuaded some German aircrew to talk freely. All in all, it was a time of recovery from our ordeal and for what lay ahead in the years of captivity.'

Despite their lapses and mistakes the Luftwaffe commanders knew that their opponents, the RAF fighter pilots, were forced to break off sorties to re-arm and re-fuel, it therefore became their intention to try and catch the enemy planes on the ground.

Otto Jufen:

'Early in September, after we had been in continuous action for almost a month and growing tired, we went off to try and catch the RAF on the

ground. This would it was hoped be accomplished by mounting several attacks in succession. We were in the second wave which went in very soon after the first, and flew towards Biggin Hill, which we were told was one of the chief RAF fighter bases, while other groups went to Croydon and Hornchurch, and I believe the Stukas had another go at Tangmere with some Ju 88s.

'As soon as we crossed the coast we saw other German bombers on the way home, and judging by their formations they had been in a scrap. So we were specially alert but saw nothing of the enemy and hoped that our tactics had worked. Our Mes were in sight and flying even closer following Göring's new orders. And then we saw our target – Biggin Hill. We could see various planes on the ground but were unable to see if any were fighters. But we seemed to have achieved complete surprise as our bombs went down without interference and carpeted the airfield. This was a great success, and apart from a few warnings and some flak as we re-crossed the English coast we remained unscathed.

'But the very next day when we tried to repeat these tactics over Kenley and Detling we were caught out properly and suffered losses and this is when we became victims ourselves.

'We were well on our way over England when we saw contrails above and when these vanished we knew our visitors were coming at us and soon the RAF machines were in combat with our escorts, while other enemy planes attacked the bombers. Our gunners did a lot of shooting, but it was no use, one Hurricane fastened on our tail and shot off all his ammunition and we were riddled. Both our engines were hit and one caught fire; the controls were damaged and I could see the crate was about to go out of control so I called on the gunners to get out at once. I then struggled up out of the nose to help our pilot who was covered in blood from some wound and in a faint. Other Heinkels were flying past and trying to avoid us as we were a dead duck.

'Both our gunners disappeared through the cabin floor and suddenly I saw the eyes of my dear comrade pilot – he was dead. I forced myself to leave him, crawling to the hatch just as the bomber began to fall out of control to the left and the whole of the wing caught fire. There was a lurch and a terrible noise like rending metal and at that moment I hurled myself through the open hatch in a state of terror and fell clear.

'But the Heinkel seemed to stick close to me and I seemed to be falling right beneath it with sparks and bits of molten metal accompanying me as I went. I was terrified and wanted to do something, but I did not want my 'chute to open and be caught up by the burning plane. Then suddenly the Heinkel banked away from me, its engines making a terrible howling noise with flames all over the wing. So I pulled my cord and the small 'chute came out of the bag, to be quickly followed by the main parachute and I was jerked upright and saw the bomber falling away from me. It was an amazing scene. The coast was not far away and I could see a few little boats on the beach and even people

here and there as I floated down in great relief but shocked as I thought of my dead comrade still in the blazing bomber which I saw go straight into the sea with a roar and great splash.

'I almost wept when I thought of my dead friend's parents who he had shown me pictures of. Then after a few moments I realised I was coming down in some green fields, which I believe was west Kent as I later learned. The ground came rapidly nearer and I saw people and some vehicles making their way in my direction. Then as I hit the ground I saw some soldiers with rifles coming across the field, and I collapsed in a heap. I hurt my leg in landing and had to sit for as while as the Tommies took away my helmet and pistol and helped me out of my parachute harness.

'Then a truck came and a car with two policemen, but it was the soldiers who took me away in their vehicle to a camp where a telephone call was put through to the RAF I believe. I was given an egg sandwich and a cup of tea and began to recover. When the RAF came they took me to one of their own camps, not an airfield, and an officer asked me some questions in quite good German, but I only gave him my name and rank. My leg was examined, but it was only a sprained ankle. Then some army policemen came with a truck and took me to London, and it was there that I again met my two gunners – but not until I had been given "the treatment".

'A tall officer with three stripes on his sleeve invited me into his comfortable office where he talked to me of his home of all things which I believe he said was in Enfield, Middlesex. He then asked me about my own home and family, what I thought of the war, so I told him we had not done badly so far. That was all. He said, yes, we certainly had things all our own way, but now things were changing and although Britain would suffer a few more defeats they would win in the end.

'Then he took me outside and we strolled round the garden before going back inside for some tea and biscuits. It was all amazingly informal and I began to feel more like a visitor, a member of his family. He then gave me a great shock. He handed me an album of snapshot photographs of German airmen who had been shot down over England, and there were rather a lot of them. I believe they were copies of those taken at PoW camps or even at this mansion for identification purposes. But to see all those faces including a few I recognised was quite a shock and doubtless intended to be. I'm sure he watched my reactions very closely. Then I was marched out to a larger room where the reunion took place with my comrades. They were very sad when I told them of our pilot's death, but we were relieved to be alive and had quite an animated conversation concerning the moments before we baled out. Little did we realise that the room was bugged and our hosts listened in to all we said. I'm sure they learned a few things as we did mention various names of other officers, plus a few opinions among ourselves.

'After a while, during the evening we were taken to a small dining room where a meal of meat, vegetables and bread and butter and tea was served, which was all very good. There were other German airmen in the room we did not recognise, including a fighter pilot who kept making signs to us, but we had no idea what he meant and only later learnt that he was trying to warn us not to talk! There were two soldiers acting as guards and of course we also learnt later that room was also probably "wired for sound".

'We slept on cots in the larger room, and next morning MPs took us away in a truck to a large station where we boarded a train and after some hours reached our PoW camp, which at that time was a large mansion, though later we transferred to a camp surrounded by wire. Everything was in order there and life was not too bad, and after a year we were allowed out in work parties on the land which was a godsend.'

Many of Otto Jufen's fellow prisoners were transferred to Canada in 1942, including the notorious 'one that got away' – Franz von Werra – who succeeded in escaping from a train in the depths of winter, crossing a river and emerging in due course in official German diplomatic hands in the USA. Eventually he was smuggled out to South America and thence back to the Reich where his revelations concerning the extraordinary wiles of British intelligence and interrogation methods caused upheaval in German Wehrmacht circles and led to an overhaul – to British detriment. Von Werra's book on his experiences with the British was suppressed by the Nazi Propaganda Minister, Dr Göbbels, as almost pro-British and the fighter pilot vanished on a flight in his Messerchmitt 109 over the North Sea. His tale was well told in the British film starring Hardy Kruger.

But Otto Jufen managed to stay in Britain, making good use of the camp library to study English and various other subjects. Further comment from him regarding the German 'Great Escape' plot of December 1944 will appear later.

Following his capture, Hans Gilbert was himself transported by truck to London, escorted by the usual posse of MPs, remarking that he was very interested to see all the fine scenery en route. When they arrived in London at 'a large mansion' – actually No 8 Kensington Palace Gardens, otherwise officially known as the London District Prisoner-of-War Cage – Gilbert was taken to a room containing only a small table and chair. Soon, an RAF officer entered and in good German invited him to a larger room where a Sergeant served tea and biscuits for two.

'I made the most of it, unusual as it seemed. It was still afternoon I believe and the officer who I believe was a Flight Lieutenant chatted away in German about this and that, the war in general, how I had survived the crash and did I have any requests or wish to write home etc. So I said I was in one piece and would doubtless be able to let my

family know that I was safe. He said it would be arranged and that I was not to worry. He also told me that my comrades were also safe, so this was a great relief for me. Then he asked me what we hoped to achieve and I did not know what to say in reply as I was sure he knew we had been bombing their fields and trying to put them out of action. So I said nothing and he smiled and said they were well aware what we hoped to gain and that so far we had failed.

"'You've seen for yourself, our fighters are still giving you a hammering, aren't they?" But I said nothing. "Your losses have climbed and will continue to," he said, "so you don't stand any chance of success, no matter how well you did in France. This is England, we can take better care of ourselves, you know. We have ways of dealing with bomber attack that you can't imagine."

'I wondered what on earth he was talking about. The operations had all seemed fairly straightforward to me – we attacked and they defended. Naturally, we expected to lose a few planes, but so did they. I was convinced our Me pilots were better, but as to results I had to admit I was not sure how much we had succeeded. Then he invited me to look out of the window, so I put down my cup to cross the room and look out as he did. There were very many balloons in the sky. I was not sure what point he was making, but when we sat down again he said: "We have weapons that will always prevent your own side from ever gaining the upper hand. We have a very superior organisation."

'He then proceeded to give me a little lecture on our air force, which was surprisingly accurate and even included various names of commanders and unit personalities that I knew were factual, so I was very impressed. He could see my interest so he then went on to speak of my own Dornier unit in such a way that astounded me, it was as if he himself was a member of our group and could speak of it from first-hand knowledge. All this was delivered in a very casual manner, and then he said: "You see, we know mostly everything that's worth knowing about your unit and all the rest, so there is little we can learn from you which is why I'm not pressing you. Would you like some more tea?"

'The interview came to an end and I wondered what he had gained. But then he said: "I've got a lot more clients waiting to speak to me so I must leave you for a while. Just let me know if there's anything you want."

'The guard then took me to a larger room where I was overjoyed to meet my captain so we had something of a reunion. He told me he had come down in a pond, which was why he was dressed in British battledress while his uniform was cleaned. He too had been seen by an officer and "taken tea" but said nothing beyond the usual courtesies, so we were able to compare notes and found that our experiences at the mansion were almost identical. Then two guards came, one carried a tray containing two meals and mugs of tea. So we ate the cooked food, which was very agreeable, better than our own in France. We were in good condition and my comrade wondered if we should try

to escape. But there seemed to be too many guards, so we decided to await developments, In any case, what was the point my CO said, we would soon be liberated by our invading army, and anyway, how could we cross the Channel?

'Little did we know that everything we said was overheard by our captors! They had little microphones hidden in cunning places and we never dreamt that such a thing could happen. Not that it made any difference, for soon after that the guards came with the same RAF officer and we learned that we would be taken to a PoW camp but would have to spend one more night there. So we were taken upstairs to a large room where, to our surprise, we found more of our comrades already ensconced with comfortable cots, so we had yet another reunion. My captain received his own uniform back and changed his clothes and we sat about talking over our experiences and once more never realised that all was overheard and taken down by the clever British.

'We had suffered a traumatic change of circumstances and went to bed, not to sleep easily, but running over the events of the day with new comrades including two fighter pilots who had arrived the day before. They had been demanding to be removed to a proper PoW camp, but were in good spirits. The other two aircrew were from a Heinkel which had blown up, killing their two comrades, so these two men were a little subdued. Naturally, we wondered about our two gunners, but these arrived later in the camp we were taken to next day by a long train journey to the north of England.

'That camp was very well organised and by then segregated into compounds for Luftwaffe, Navy and a few soldiers. The food was quite adequate. It was to be my home for two years until I was shipped to Canada.'

The Dornier 17 Observer and aircraft commander Peter Kroller was one of those few who had been involved in the fiasco start to the Luftwaffe's grand assault which misfired through bad weather and a breakdown in communications on 12 August. His plane with others had become split from part of their formation by thick cloud, and when they finally landed at their bases recriminations flew. But all had gone well when the attempt was renewed the following day and the Dorniers achieved their objective, bombed and made for home, despite some combats which cost another unit two bombers. Kroller and his friends were in good spirits, they had come through their first combat mission over England. But on the very next flight they were attacked 'from all sides' by Hurricanes and Spitfires. All at once Kroller's earphones were filled with shouts, the raucous sound of aircraft engines racing, machine-guns firing and then the shock of seeing a Heinkel enveloped in flames as it fell to earth.

'It was frightening to see, a great machine like that being destroyed and our hearts were beating as we approached our target. The enemy

attacks continued and I saw a Dornier falling away with an engine smoking badly. Then we too came under attack and our gunners were in action. I heard the rattle of bullets penetrating our fuselage and wings. This was very frightening and put me off my job.'

However, the Dorniers flew on but had missed their prime target, the usual RAF airfield, so changed course until they reached an alternative base which they bombed, being unable to observe results well owing to flak. On the way home they again came under attack and two more bombers went down.

'Back at base all was excitement as the planes returned, one was missing from our unit and never heard of again. After telling our stories to intelligence we had a meal and a nap, but it was hard to sleep as we were in such a state of nerves after the day's events.'

The next day's action was even more heated for Kroller, the bombers and their escorts being set upon as soon as they reached the Kentish coast. Kroller remarks how strange it was to see so much going on outside his cabin yet hear nothing but the roar of his own two engines and of course the rattle of their own machine-guns, which was almost constant. Only when a fighter zipped past close did the higher pitched whine of another aircraft reach his ears. But then came a very accurate flak barrage which caused the Dornier formation to start wavering as some pilots in their nervousness tried to take evasive action. They had bombed and reached the coast once more and were again hit by British fighters.

'I could smell the powder in our cabin as our gunners fired at a Hurricane which came in close, and suddenly I saw one of these fighters falling past in flames, which was very spectacular. It passed out of sight and I did not see the pilot get out. The noise of that plane whizzing past remains with me to this day.'

Even then they were not in the clear – though the Germans had assumed so – for they were suddenly hit yet again, with enemy fighters on all sides which split up the Dornier formation so that some bombers tried to dive nearer sea level while others zoomed off in all directions. Kroller was in fear of his life, but somehow they reached the safety of French airspace where on landing they found planes damaged and two missing. It had been Kroller's 'hottest' trip to date – but the worse had yet to come. Late in August the group had set out as usual across the sea to attack an RAF airfield, flying at 15,000 feet towards Dover where flak drove them onto a more easterly course before they moved north and then west over Kent. The crews expected attack at any moment – and it came – a host of Spitfires and Hurricanes which soon provoked a ding-dong battle. The formation leader changed course which prompted two Dornier pilots to collide and fall to earth in a great bout of flame.

'*This was a sickening sight but I had no time to watch the outcome with so much else going on around us. In a moment it was all over. I was trying to adjust my bombsight as the target came into view. Suddenly there was a tremendous racket behind me and shouts and looking round I saw our pilot Franz slumped back in his seat with blood all over him. There were splinters of glass all over the cabin floor and I at once moved up to try and help one of our gunners move the pilot out of his seat. We were terrified as the plane began to fall away to the right.*

'*After a struggle we managed to get Franz out of the way but he was quite dead. The plane was going down so I got into his seat and took over the controls. I had only received a minimum of flying training in case of emergency, I was not a qualified pilot. I pulled back on the control column and pushed the rudder pedals and opened up the throttles and could see that most of our Dorniers were well above us nearing the coast. We seemed to be alone and I knew that at any moment enemy planes would see us and give us hell. So I turned the plane south-east and tried to get every bit of speed out of the engines. As far as I could see the plane was still virtually undamaged and we stood every chance of reaching our base – providing the enemy left us alone. In fact, we saw no more Hurricanes or Spitfires and on reaching the sea picked up an escort of two Mes who flew at our wingtips.*

'*I was in a state of some shock, my friend Franz lay dead beside me on the cabin floor. The cabin was quite cramped and he was huddled there with one of our gunners bent over him in dazed shock. Then we crossed the French coast and I saw our base and began circling over it as I prepared myself for an attempted landing. Fortunately the Dornier was easy to fly and I managed to put the plane down without difficulty. When we stopped, ground crewmen ran to us and soon Franz was lying on the grass and we all fell out of the plane and sat about for some minutes trying to recover. Then a truck came which took us to our flight HQ where we made our report before having a stiff drink of schnapps followed by coffee. We could not eat a thing so went to bed, but were unable to sleep.*'

Peter Kroller and his crew waited two days for a new pilot, he was called Ludwig but did not last long:

'*He crashed during a practice flight before we had a chance to fly with him and died in hospital soon afterwards. Our CO commiserated with us and told us we would now be sent as replacements to other crews which was very disconcerting. My two gunners went off to another unit and I never saw them again, I joined another crew as plane commander, but did not care for these lads as I had done my old comrades, though we flew as a team and took part in the first big attack on London on 7 September.'*

Horst Jentzen, having transferred his allegiance to the new Junkers 88 squadron, was one of the few aircrew to experience action with the new bomber in this period, taking part in the early probing attacks, flying across the North Sea to dive-bomb shipping off Kent, with inconclusive results. Jentzen recalls that their command still looked on the Junkers 88 crews as 'some sort of élite', to be used with care.

'But soon after we had made a few more flights after the big start in August in what the British came to call the "Battle of Britain" and we the "Kanalkampf", everything came to a sudden stop.

'We had attacked a warship of destroyer type without observed result because of the very heavy and accurate flak. This was off the Kent coast, and as we flew off at low altitude we were picked up by Spitfires. At that moment our planes were rather vulnerable, having just bombed and become rather scattered and not yet regained formation.

'I heard the sudden shout "Fighters!" and at once began jinking the plane from side to side and almost at once the top gunner opened fire and I heard a terrific racket as bullets sliced across the body of our plane and hit the wings, some slugs hitting the port engine which began smoking at once. I tried to reach cloud cover but we were too low and they were too far away. Then I saw a Hurricane zoom past and another came on our tail and our gunner was shooting at him. Once more I heard the rattle of bullets and all hell broke loose as splinters flew about me. My gunner cried out in terrible pain and something hit me in the right leg. The port engine caught fire and we were in serious trouble, but hoped we might just reach our base in Holland. But the plane lost height rapidly and when Horst our captain came up from the nose his face was aghast at the mess in the cabin. There was blood flowing from my leg and the gunner had fallen down, apparently dead. Horst tried to lift him up, just as the Junkers lurched suddenly. I stopped the port engine which had caught fire, flames streaming back over the wing.

'It all happened very quickly. Our right wingtip hit the sea and everything turned over in a terrible crashing noise and I found myself flying through the air with large pieces of the cockpit still around me. Then I hit the water and felt a lot of pain in my right leg. I went right under and swallowed some salt water and this sobered me up for a moment, I felt like giving in. I said to myself – "It's all over".

'But to my surprise I found myself bobbing up on the surface of the sea so inflated my lifejacket, which worked perfectly. I was in some pain and felt as if my leg was on fire. I called out and looked around in case any of the lads were near but could only see smoke and debris. I could hardly believe I had survived. There was not a

plane to be seen and suddenly I felt sick and horrible as I realised my predicament. I felt I would succumb to the sea as although the day was warm the water felt very cold. I tried to flail my arms but the effort was too much for me. I tried to kick out with my one good leg, but it seemed too heavy and cold. So I began to give up hope and thought of my family at home in Munich and how they would cry, especially my sister who loved me so much and I cried with the misery of it all.

'But this feeling soon passed. I told myself not to be an idiot. My comrades had died in action, those things happened in war, it was to be expected. I had by some miracle survived and I must try to stay alive as long as possible. But I could see no hope of rescue.

'I don't know how long I floated there, trying to keep my limbs in movement but increasingly numbed and unable to progress in any direction. Then I heard a plane, and looking up saw a Messerschmitt fly over, not too fast, and as if perhaps the pilot was looking for survivors – at least, that is what I hoped. I tried to wave, but the effort was too much for me and I was forced to just float there in the swell and hope that by some miracle he would see me. Unknown to me, the debris from my plane was still afloat, which saved me, for seeing this the pilot flew round for a closer inspection and saw me, making a very low pass and waving at me several times, and I hoped was calling for rescuers over his radio. He then waggled his wings and flew off, obviously short of fuel. I thought, "Even if rescuers are on the way, I won't last much longer."

'It was perhaps an hour at least before I heard another plane, and this time it was another Me with a Dornier seaplane and after a few moments they found me. The Dornier landed on the sea and taxied slowly towards me, they had to drag me aboard as I could no longer move my limbs. I was placed on a bunk and given a drink of schnapps but vomited and passed out. When I came to, the plane was taxying into its base and I was soon whisked to hospital.

'Owing to my experience and severely wounded leg I never flew again and spent the rest of the war in a desk job.'

Fighter pilot Peter Winker recalls that by the end of August he and his surviving comrades were feeling very tired:

'Too many faces had gone missing and the replacements were inadequate. I recall one lad who was very blond and handsome and just from training. He was full of pepper, red-hot stuff and raring to go but was shot down on his first mission. One of our experienced NCOs had told him to stay close and do nothing, but as soon as the combat began he went off on his own at once and was not seen again. I believe he was shot down over London but probably hit nothing so that was a total waste.

'Another boy I recall I had known in training at Berlin-Gatow in the early days, we used to enjoy a drink together and had met on leave and

had a meal in Berlin. He had survived all the fights we had had, but one day flew back with his fighter damaged, I believe his engine was badly damaged. I had already landed and watched his plane coming in, though I did not know it was him. Just as the Me was about to touch down the engine seized and the plane fell to the ground and broke into pieces. We ran across the field and found him still in the cockpit, which was just one large lump of twisted metal. He had been killed instantly.

'By September we knew we were in serious difficulty, the battle was not being won and no invasion of England was possible. Yet we knew we had destroyed a lot of RAF planes and their pilots. We used to listen in to the German and British news bulletins and could detect the lies in both! But Göring was very annoyed that our fighters were failing the bombers, though we were doing our utmost to protect them. When he ordered us to stay close to the bombers we were finished. There was no way we could help in such a situation. It meant that we could only react too late when the RAF came into attack, by which time the damage was done. We would catch a sudden glimpse of camouflaged shapes hurtling through the bomber formations and the Heinkels and Dorniers catching fire, at which point we would try to intercept the attackers – but much too late. It was all very demoralising for us.

'Then our staffel CO went missing himself. He was very experienced and a grand type of lad. We never knew what happened to him. It was often the case that we would hear later through the Red Cross that missing pilots were prisoners of war, but sometimes nothing, which was very sad. We had by then come to learn the true meaning of war and our morale suffered.'

The chance bombing of an outer London suburb prompted the British Bomber Command to launch a pinprick response on Berlin, which in turn appeared to give Hitler the excuse to rage and switch his own bombers to London. Although the diversion took the RAF defences by surprise, it proved a godsend for the British, for the hard-pressed RAF bases were given a breathing space and in fact never came close to being erased again. The Germans never knew how close they had come to defeating the British or how their Führer (not for the last time) had reversed their fortunes, harsh though the price now became for British civilians.

Peter Winker:

'When the target suddenly became London a whole new atmosphere prevailed as some felt sure a big decision would come about on 7 September when we flew in a large formation across Kent and amazingly saw not one enemy aircraft until the bombs went down. I looked down on the large city and saw the Thames winding silver in the sunshine and then the bombs bursting all over the dock areas. And as our planes turned away someone shouted "Fighters!" and at once we saw a lot of Hurricanes and Spitfires turning in to attack us.

'Our formation spread out and all hell broke loose as the bombers

*fled for home and we were left fighting for our lives with our fuel states
very low indeed. In fact, we saw no chance to contemplate combat for
that reason. We had only one thought – to dive for the coast and reach
home before our tanks ran dry. I saw a number of combats in progress,
mostly bombers in trouble, but we could do nothing to help. I also saw
two RAF machines going down in flames and one Messerschmitt. The
Me 110s had of course long shot their bolt. I recall seeing one formation
of these planes over the Channel which had been decimated, the survivors
trying to escape Hurricanes. On that occasion we were able to intervene
and drive off the attackers. But the 110s were so vulnerable they were
withdrawn.'*

Horst Juventus:

*'In early September we heard the amazing news that we would take
part in a two- or three-prong attack on London, I believe it was called
Operation Loge (the Luftwaffe's target name for London). We flew
across Kent and then towards the Thames and arrived just as the
Dorniers were dropping their bombs. To our amazement we had not
seen a single RAF fighter and all the planes bombed the London docks.
A great column of smoke rose up and we turned away, but had not
gone far when the RAF caught up with us and all hell broke loose
again. There were planes scooting about in all directions, some falling
in flames and parachutes opening. I saw bits of wreckage and smoke
trails and suddenly it was quiet again.'*

However, to the German crews' amazement and disgust, on regaining
their bases they were told to be ready to take off again in the evening
to make a night attack on London.

*'We were not really trained in night flying, I was very much a novice
and therefore apprehensive.'*

To Karl Haulmeier, Göring's idea to lure the RAF into one last decisive
battle by attacking London seemed a gamble. Familiar photographs
show some of Haulmeier's Dornier group flying up the Thames and
then over West Ham in East London:

*'I noted a great many hits on the exact target area before we turned
away. Then we were struck by enemy fighters . . . I saw planes going
down including some of our Dorniers, bits of aircraft going down too
as well as slowly descending parachutes. By the time we reached the sea
again we were in some disarray and dispersed. But we had achieved our
objective and that evening our own propaganda broadcasts were full of
stories about blazing London.'*

The Heinkel gunner Georg Kessler reckoned that by then he had
witnessed some twenty German bombers go down. As for the big raid
on 7 September:

'*I recall it so clearly as I felt we were flying into the lion's mouth! As we neared the great sprawling city some flak came up and we saw the balloons below but not a single enemy fighter, which surprised us greatly. We thought they must be setting a trap for us. Then we were over our target the docks and the bombs went down, and as we banked gently away I saw great clouds of smoke starting to rise from our target and I distinctly remember thinking, "We've stirred them up, they'll hit us for sure."*'

Yet Kessler survived the combat which broke out moments later but was surprised and frightened when told by their CO that their job was now to keep the London fires burning, 'All we had to do was fly to the Thames and there would be burning London waiting for us!'

Johannes Fink:

'*Hitler and Göring seized on the excuse of a minor British attack on Berlin – itself a reprisal – to order us to hit London. Some believed it would force the RAF into a huge battle against our superior Mes which would finally break them. Well, we all know the result, great damage was done to a very small segment of London and the war economy of Great Britain, but we suffered heavily for it and within a week or so had to call it all off. My bomber Wings were being bled white, too many had vanished, burnt alive, shot into the Channel or gone into British PoW camps, and we could not continue. Yet the idea of London burning so took hold that we were ordered to continue the attacks by night and this proved another great strain because few of the crews, apart from a new pathfinder unit (KG100), had had any real night training. And as the weeks went by so increasingly bad weather brought more and more crashes at home bases.*'

Horst Juventus took off again after a rest and meal on that momentous day, reaching the Thames just after eight o'clock:

'*We could see the great fire of London and it was quite a sight to see. It was horribly fascinating and we were like moths drawn to the flames as we crawled up river, seeing other bombers before and behind us, not in formation but a long train. It was impossible to miss the target for the docks were still blazing. I thought of the brave firemen down below and how frightened they must be to be put into such a situation, trying to put out those great fires with bombs falling around them.*'

As many East Londoners could testify, numerous Germans missed their target, for high explosive and incendiary bombs were scattered across West and East Ham and even further afield. As for the firemen, hundreds were drafted in from outside areas to combat the vast conflagrations, largely highly combustible foodstuffs and other goods unloaded onto dockside wharves and in warehouses.

'*We dropped our bombs and turned away carefully, watching out for other bombers. It was a sight I will never forget. I know Hitler made*

*many threats, and some he carried out. This was one of them, great
fires burning in the world's greatest city. I felt we were taking part in
an historic event, it was impossible not to be impressed by all this, even
though we were in danger.'*

Karl Haulmeier records the view of burning London as 'an awe
inspiring sight . . . we dropped our bombs into the orange-red glow
below, unhindered by flak or fighters'.

Georg Kessler says: 'We saw the great fires from way off . . . it was a
simple matter to drop our eggs into the flames below which were quite
a spectacular sight . . . it was an experience I'll never forget.'

Just one of the several conflagrations raging below the Germans
would have brought front page headlines in peacetime. Peter Kroller
had sighted his Dornier's bomb load on the East London targets (the
docks, Woolwich Arsenal, Beckton Gas Works, etc) and suffered some
terrors when they were assaulted by RAF fighters on the way home,
with planes going down and parachutes in the sky:

> *'We reached our base in a state of nerves and sweat and thankful
> to get down alive. There was a great deal of crowing on our side over
> the great fires in London and the propaganda services were going full
> blast. To our astonishment we were told to have an early meal and
> prepare to fly again to London before dark . . . we could see the fires
> of London long before we reached the mouth of the Thames. We gazed
> down in awe at the great fires and dropped our bombs into them – part
> h.e., part incendiary . . . when we reached our base again it was pitch
> dark and in this period many accidents occurred as the crews were not
> trained in night operations.'*

The Londoners' ordeal had begun, the dream of the Chief of the
German Imperial Naval Staff in 1914 had become a reality. The capital
suffered fifty-seven consecutive night attacks which brought about most
of the casualties in the Blitz, even though the worst individual raids
had yet to come. The cessation of daylight raiding about to take place
enabled the Luftwaffe to widen its range of night bombing to include
most other British cities over the coming months. But first Göring tried
one more fling by daylight, the biggest raid of them all. Peter Kroller
took part in this:

> *'On 15 September we joined a very big formation which stretched
> for miles across the Channel and was a fantastic sight, we had
> never seen so many planes in the air at once and were quite
> excited and wondered what would happen when we met the RAF
> over England.'*

Kessler:

> *'I will never forget the sight of all those hundreds of planes in the
> blue around us, stepped up in waves for mile after mile.'*

side the cockpit of a Dornier 17. They wear
fejackets for the cross-Channel sortie.

Dornier bomb-aimer at his *Lotfe* bombsight
nd (right) a bomber releases its cargo of
0kg (110lb) bombs.

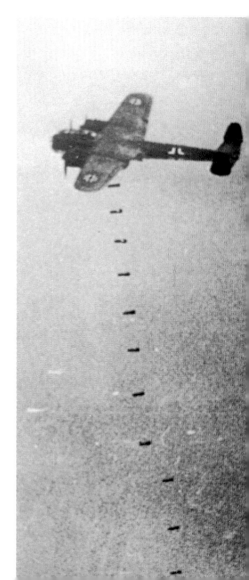

Theo Osterkamp (left).

Werner Moelders.

BELOW: RAF officers inspect the wreck of a Heinkel.

nwounded *Luftwaffe* aircrew escorted away from a burning Heinkel shot down at Burmarsh in
ent, 11 September 1940.

ABOVE: Intercepted over Middlesex, this Me110 came down off the Ridge, Hastings 25 September 1940, Oberleutnant Nelson and Feldwebel Weyergang being killed. *(Andy Saunders*

A rare snapshot from the ground of a Heinke flying low over East Anglia.

Feldwebel Weyergang's grave in Hastings cemetery.

Two New Zealand soldiers ride with an Me109 of 1/JG52.

Local citizens of Thornton Heath in Surrey pose with 'their' Heinkel, which carried the insignia of an unidentified unit.

The pilot of this Messerschmitt vanished after it was shot down over the Thames Estuary on 24 August 1940.

ABOVE: A Royal Artilleryman inspects the engine of a Dornier 17.

BELOW: Unusual litter on the beach at Lydd in Kent; this is an Me109 of 7/JG54.

Descending parachutists became a common
sight over Kent in 1940.

ABOVE RIGHT: Fire officer Pat Short releases
the body of Me110 pilot Ernst Mollekamp
after he baled out too low over Eastbourne.

BELOW: Luftwaffe NCO crewmen from a
Dornier based near Antwerp which crashed
on Folkestone beach on 31 August.

The classic, much-used photograph of a
Heinkel crossing the U-bend of the Thames
over Stepney, 7 September 1940.

German propaganda artist's fanciful view
of Thames reflections in the sky over
burning London, 1940.

Haulmeier:

'The sight of all those Luftwaffe planes was amazing as we crossed the coast of England in one giant phalanx, escorted by a great number of fighters, well over one thousand planes I believe.'

Juventus:

'When the 15th came we were told that a final great decisive blow would be struck at London and that the RAF was so decimated it would no longer be able to stop us. Well, we were tired but took off and formed up and it was quite a fantastic sight, the biggest formation we had ever seen, stretching over many miles of sky, all bobbing up and down in the blue sky with a lot of white cloud below us as we crossed the coast and flew across Kent.'

The still powerful and far from beaten RAF fighter pilots were also awed by the extraordinary sight of this great Luftwaffe show, but soon tore into them, as our witnesses experienced. Juventus:

'A terrible surprise awaited us as a great chorus of shouts erupted – "Fighters! Fighters!" – everywhere! We had never seen so many. So this was the air force our Luftwaffe had decimated!'

Haulmeier:

'As soon as we crossed the enemy coast we were attacked by large numbers of RAF fighters and this came as a great shock as we had been assured that the RAF was on its last legs.'

Kessler:

'There was a lot of cloud that day and despite what we had been told many more enemy aircraft came up to challenge us.'

Kroller:

'Things did not go as hoped, there was a good deal of cloud and very many enemy planes hit us. We had heard stories that the RAF was finished and some fantastic claims of machines lost by both sides, but on that day we knew without doubt that the enemy was still in great strength and very much in business. There were lots of combats all around us and our formations were broken up. Things went wrong and some bombers were left without escort. I saw two Heinkels go down as well as three Hurricanes and Spitfires. Then a lone Me came to us and escorted us home. The whole thing became a fiasco, we lost all cohesion. Our formation leader vanished and the units were left to fend for themselves in sorry fashion. As we crossed out over the coast I saw lots of Heinkels, Dorniers and even some few Junkers 88s flying singly, with combats still going on. Some of these planes crashed into the sea, while more were destroyed on landing at their bases. It really was a shambles, but we ourselves landed unscathed and at once a lot of

de-briefing took place. We had lost two bombers, one through a collision I believe. The crews were tired out, dispirited and, being burned out, could not possibly continue.'

Horst Juventus had seen a Dornier falling like a leaf with a wing missing; then a Hurricane flew past without its pilot before dropping away. Next he saw two Heinkels collide and remain locked together until falling in pieces:

'The noise was such that we could hear the bangs above the noise of our engines. We stood no chance of reaching our targets as the formations were too disrupted, and although our Mes fought like demons they could not deal with all the enemy planes, there were too many of them. Our own flight managed to stay together and we dropped our bombs on we hoped an airfield which might have been Biggin Hill. Then we made our escape, luckily without being attacked at all. It was quite a fantastic experience to see so many hundreds of planes all mixing up together, and then the sky was almost empty, and we flew off home.

'There was an inquest and it was decided that the daylight sorties must be curtailed because, coupled with the night raids, it was taking too much out of our units who had lost heavily. I myself felt drained, but we had to fly on, night after night, against London.'

Karl Haulmeier's Dornier Wing was broken up in the great mêlée:

'I saw planes going down continuously with parachutes all over the sky. We came under heavy attack and were forced to disperse to escape. The bombs went down over the Thames and countryside and I heard a loud rattling as our gunners went into action. Glancing round I saw holes appearing all along our fuselage and buried my head in my hands. We were attacked again and again and my pilot dived the Dornier almost to sea level as we reached the coast. We somehow escaped and reached our base, completely riddled by bullets and very shaken by the experience. That was virtually the end of the daylight air war. Now began a new chapter which although safer was to prove a great strain on us all.'

In that great battle the first plane that gunner Georg Kessler saw go down was a Hurricane, shot up by a Messerschmitt, the next was a Dornier minus a wing quickly followed by a flaming Heinkel, and lots of parachutes:

'I don't know where all the hundreds of bombs went that day, I know many were jettisoned in the Thames or over Kent. I saw another Heinkel on fire and its crew baling out before it fell away in a dive. Then we dived away over Kent and the other planes with us became separated in cloud so we were on our own. White mist came around us and then we were in the clear over the Kentish landscape and when I looked around for attackers I saw none until we reached the coast where there seemed to be Hurricanes and Spitfires all over the place looking for victims. We

went at top speed for the Channel and I believe that's where we got rid of our bombs, with so many enemy planes about it was not safe to hang on to them. Yet we escaped and this was a surprise to us. After landing we found three of our crews missing and at the de-briefing we gave our impressions to the listening officers, clearly we had suffered a defeat and I heard later that Göring was very angry.'

Kessler states that the change to night operations was much more tiring and of course completely altered their life patterns:

'The invasion was off but Hitler desired to subjugate England by U-boat and Luftwaffe attacks. And so we went on, over the Channel, often by moonlight which was good, to view the glowing fires in London, then home for a quick meal and sleep. It became a peculiar occupation, night work. For those crews ordered to carry out two sorties per night it was especially tiring.'

By mid-September and the grand fiasco (for the Luftwaffe) of the 15th, which was thereafter to become known to the British as Battle of Britain Day, the Me 109 pilot Peter Winker had 'scored a mere three victories', with two possibles. His last two triumphs were over Spitfires, the first losing its tail and the pilot failing to escape, while the second RAF flyer took to his parachute as his plane began smoking. On the 15th Winker flew high above the vast array of bombers, crossing Kent and heading for London, which was cloud covered. Then the RAF fighters fell on them from all sides:

'We were amazed and tried to meet them. In no time the huge armada began to break up into smaller formations and I saw bombs being jettisoned all over the place. Then I ran into a big fight with planes wheeling all round me, some were hit and went down. I got my sights on a Spit but missed and then saw a Hurricane and dived after him and tried to cling to him, but he weaved this way and that until at last his tail was knocked off by my fire and he fell like a spinning leaf and the pilot did not emerge. Then I had a narrow escape as two Spits fastened on to me so I dived away as fast as the crate would go, weaving this way and that until a cloud swallowed me up, and when I emerged I was not far from the coast. I saw no one below me but all sorts of planes heading for home. I was bathed in sweat.

'The raid had started out as a grand show but ended in fiasco. By then the bombers had started their night blitz and everything changed. Within a few days we learnt that the bomber crews were too worn out to continue flying by day also, so their efforts were confined to night operations.'

September 15 also saw the collapse of Christian Rossler's career as a Luftwaffe bomber pilot. His was one of the 1,200 German planes that crossed the Channel, intent on striking a final death blow at the British capital, the great phalanx comprising an almost equal number of fighters and bombers, a mile and a half high, stepped up from 14,000–20,000 feet and smothering some 800 square miles of sky.

'We soon reached the Thames under fire from flak, then masses of RAF fighters dived through to attack us. There were constant cries of "Look out – fighters!" and my gunners were firing continuously, plane after plane went down in smoke or flames or simply blew up. It seemed hopeless to continue – but how to escape? Our bomber Wing was completely broken up, the Dorniers were scattered and trying to reach the Channel and home, dropping their bombs everywhere to gain speed while the Hurricanes and Spitfires pursued us relentlessly.

'Then came the moment of our own destruction. I was diving the machine towards a big cloud when a Hurricane swooped on us, firing its eight machine-guns. My gunners were killed at once, I heard their awful cries over the intercom as the bullets cut us to pieces. My cockpit and everything in it was smashed to pieces and the plane began to go right out of control. Pieces flew about and I was hit in several places. There was blood over me and I felt very frightened and alone and faint. My Observer was dead and I managed to scramble past him to open the nose hatch and fell out head first – just as the plane began to break up completely. I was lucky not to be struck by a large piece of wing which came hurtling past me.

'I opened my parachute and after some minutes hit the sea off the French coast and was very quickly rescued by a German motorboat. But I was never able to fly again.'

By then Peter Harmel had scored six victories; he would not score again:

'On that last day, our biggest, I felt very weary and hoped that by flying so high we would see our opponents first and be able to jump them. Well, we did see many RAF fighters and dived to attack them as planned. But as we did so more of the enemy swept down on the bombers and then we had to fight for our lives and were unable to assist. The battles were all over the sky, and right down to low level. I believed I hit two enemy fighters, but then I was hit myself.'

Worn down by so many days of continuous flying and combat the nerves and stamina of both British and German aircrews were nearing breaking point. No longer in top form, the Germans' former edge through experience had been worn away. Harmel expected one side or the other to crack up.

'I had dived down, but decided I had insufficient fuel left to continue in the battle, and intended flying home. Then something hit me behind the cockpit, I felt a pain in my shoulder and knew I was hit. My machine caught fire and dived straight for the ground. I had to get out at once *or be killed. I tried to keep calm, but felt very frightened. I managed to undo my straps, released the hood and pushed upwards and went straight out. Some of my clothing caught fire but the flames went out before I opened my parachute.*

'The noise of battle faded away, though I could still hear the drone of planes. When I looked down I saw the English countryside, and realised I was about to become a prisoner-of-war.'

That historic day also saw the last war flight of Arthur Tieker, though no presentiment of disaster came to him as he and his three crewmates settled themselves into their places, no more than the usual pre-flight nerves and inevitable apprehension after witnessing so many of their fellows disappear. Ever since that first flight to England when things had not gone according to plan their morale had slipped lower and lower.

'The English did not seem to have been decimated enough to give up and the flak was ever stronger. We reached the Thames and very many fighters dived straight through the flak bursts to get at us. Our Mes were into them at once but could not catch them all. It became a mad whirl of diving, turning aircraft, with the bombers trying to get through to the targets.

'I was hit by a flying splinter and the Observer took over the pilot's seat. We could not go on as we had lost an engine, so we dropped our bombs in the Thames and dived away to a lower level to escape. We hoped we had made a safe getaway. I was resting while a gunner bandaged my arm, but suddenly the other gunner yelled "Fighters!" and the Observer turned the machine desperately to avoid them. But it was no good, we were riddled with bullets and soon a whole wing was ablaze. It was too low to jump out and we knew the end had come.

'We crouched down on the floor of the plane as it hit the sea. We were at once hit by flying debris and everything went black. I had managed to inflate my lifejacket just before we hit the water, and after a bad moment I shot to the surface of the sea and found I could just stay afloat. I saw one of my comrades not far away, and in a little while a British boat came and rescued us.'

Despite the fantastic British claim of 185 enemy planes destroyed, only 34 bombers were actually written-off in the Luftwaffe returns. But the number of bombers fit for action had been reduced by a quarter owing to those damaged.

On September 16, Göring summoned his field commanders, berating them and railing against the failure of the fighter force, rather than engaging in realistic assessment, smarting in failure, especially in view of his bombastic promises to Hitler. Later, Colonel Koller, on the staff of Air Fleet III, stated: 'The *Reichsmarschall* never forgave us for not having defeated England.'

CHAPTER NINE

'COVENTRATED'

The Germans did not, however, accept defeat in the battle against Britain by air, rather they saw it as a 'stand-off', the fight would go on with new tactics. There was no escaping the fact, however, that the first and prime requisite for an invasion of Britain had not been achieved, the RAF was not only in command of its own airspace but challenged the enemy over the Channel. All the pessimism and fears of the *Kriegsmarine* were realised, for, apart from viewing the German Army command as entirely unrealistic in its appraisal of such a sea crossing, the German naval chiefs had by their own previous studies come to the conclusion that such an operation was not feasible, if only because of their own weakness. The Luftwaffe had clearly failed, which meant that all the great effort in preparing an invasion fleet of vessels suitable to transport the German troops, horses and other impedimenta across the unpredictable Channel had been in vain. Much disruption to inland waterway traffic on the north-west continent had been caused by the round-up of commercial barges, tugs and assorted small ships by the hundred, many of which lay wrecked or matchwood through RAF bomber attacks on the 'invasion ports' of Boulogne, Le Havre, Calais etc. These raids had been carried out almost daily by Bomber Command and at heavy cost, mostly in Blenheims, the heavier squadrons operating by night. These assaults alone had caused more doubts among the German planners and undoubtedly much relief was felt when the whole scheme (Operation *Sealion*) was postponed, most of the assembled shipping being dispersed or returned to civilian owners.

The last of the mass daylight raids on Britain had ceased, but small formations, usually of fighter bombers, began harassing the RAF, while single bombers made many sorties by day of only nuisance value to supplement the larger scale efforts by night which became routine. The night attack losses in the Luftwaffe to RAF interventions and flak were negligible, though as indicated the accident rate rose, which was inevitable. The reduced actions by day were reflected in the losses from all causes on both sides in the days immediately following 15 September, as shown in the table overleaf.

DATE	RAF	LUFTWAFFE
16 September	4	18
17 September	13	17
18 September	20	20
19 September	1	20

Accidents occurred daily to both air forces during training on units and flight testing; the Luftwaffe's losses on the last date mentioned included six, while the RAF's only loss was a Hurricane which forced landed due to engine failure following a convoy patrol.

Horst Juventus was now set to become a veteran bomber pilot and would survive the war, and after months of routine flying to London his captain and navigator routed their Heinkel to other British cities such as Plymouth, Portsmouth, Birmingham and Manchester as the German command pulled out its target maps and military geographia on every locality of size as far afield as Glasgow and Belfast.

'We were often assisted by a new pathfinder unit who flew via radio beams and showed us the way by lighting flares and using incendiaries. The attack on Coventry was one raid and from our point of view a great success as we knew that many war factories were hit and put out of action.'

This was true. A number were small but vital contractors who had turned from making car components to machines of war including plane parts and were situated in small streets radiating from the city centre. The whole area and much around was gutted by fire and high explosive and inevitably many civilians were killed and injured since the streets containing the factories also contained many houses, many of them old. The roads were narrow so fires spread rapidly. The name Coventry was now to be repeated over and over again thereafter as an example of Nazi wantonness, and at the time the raid made excellent anti-German propaganda. In reality it was one of the very first effective strategic bomber raids and an example of what the RAF's own bomber chiefs had in mind for Germany, but had not the means to carry out. The Germans also coined a new word for a city so treated – 'Coventrated'.

In the London blitz many hundreds of East Enders had simply trekked out of the capital, heading east into Epping Forest and other inhospitable places. Similar exodus took place from some Midland cities and elsewhere. These raids as indicated were long before RAF's Bomber Command began its own real campaign of destruction across Germany, which until early 1942 was ineffective. Condemnation of British air raids on Hitler's Reich are really misplaced in the context of that war. The Luftwaffe's attacks caused most damage and casualties to non-military and non-economic targets, unless of course one includes the workers themselves, who the British Air Staff eventually came to regard as legitimate cogs in the Nazi war machine – without them it would cease to operate.

But to the German air crews the arguments and niceties and theories did not matter, as Juventus points out:

'On that night [the Coventry attack] we took off at about eight o'clock I believe, it's all a bit hazy really as with so many raids night after night it all became a jumble in my mind and I grew exhausted and we were not often relieved. The way across England was clear, with little in the way of defences to contend with. There was a little flak here and there which was pretty or even spectacular at times. We saw the "lights" of Coventry long before we arrived and when we went in to bomb the fires were already blazing with all kinds of colours so we guessed metals had ignited in our targets. It really began to look like hell down there and I felt for those poor people in the little houses that we could easily see by the light of the flares and fires.'

Karl Haulmeier recalls that the night flyers slept most of the mornings, rising for lunch and some exercise:

'I borrowed a bicycle and travelled about the beautiful French countryside, even stopping in villages when I found a small bistro. For the afternoons we relaxed before briefings. These tended to grow shorter, for the target was usually London and we grew to know all the target areas by heart. In my case I had memorised the dock plan, so when I viewed it from the nose of our bomber by the light of the fires it was rather like looking at a model of what I had seen on the maps etc. We would take off at sunset so that by the time we reached England it was dark. We used the Thames as a guideline, but some units flew across southern England on a simple compass bearing. Then we were directed further afield, though some bombers continued to attack London nightly until about Christmas 1940 I believe. We flew to Hull, Liverpool, Birmingham, Manchester, Bristol, Portsmouth and Merseyside, some units going as far as Clydeside and Glasgow.

'In all these attacks I saw not one plane go down, although soon after we began raiding London the flak was suddenly stepped up greatly. This barrage was spectacular and took us by surprise but did little or no damage as it appeared to be random firing.'

The night when the London barrage came alive was 11–12 September, for the chief of Anti-Aircraft Command, Lt-General Sir Frederick Pile, decreed in response to criticism that every available mobile flak gun should travel the London streets carrying as much ammunition as could be taken in their limbers. The mostly 3.7-inchers cruised the suburban streets, blazing away two or three rounds at a time, before passing on a mile or so to repeat the process. The sudden tremendous crack of these weapons among the roads of London gave the inhabitants a nasty shock but boosted morale. Some 28,000 shells hurtled up into the London sky but did not bring down a single raider.

But, as Haulmeier points out, it did force them to fly higher and meant the crews had to go on oxygen, which was wearing and not good for the lungs in the long term.

Peter Kroller is of the opinion that the Luftwaffe chiefs believed a cheaper job could be done by night, which bears no relation of course to their original objectives. Kroller says the 'English flak steadily increased but losses were minimal due to enemy action, it was the wear on our health and accidents which caused difficulties.'

During all the months of the night blitz up to the worst attack of 10 May on London, Kroller enjoyed only one home leave:

> 'When my parents saw me they thought how ill I looked. This was due to the unnatural life I was leading. Sleeping through a large part of the day and preparing before teatime for the night's work. On a number of occasions we flew twice in a night to bomb London, and though these trips were not long they were very wearing.'

Georg Kessler recalls that his own pilot was already worn out by his experiences in the summer's daylight operations over Britain, and of one pilot who fell asleep at the wheel, only swift action by the Captain-Observer saved the plane from disaster.

> 'There were fatalities, it was inevitable, We had leave twice and in one of these my father pronounced that it would be a long war and looked at me meaningfully.'

Meantime, the fighter pilot Peter Winker had been carrying out escort duties of a different nature, accompanying other Messerschmitts carrying a single bomb under their bellies. These forays took them to the Thames Estuary and over Kent and did little harm to the enemy on the ground for as soon as the RAF fighters arrived the bomb-carriers jettisoned their loads and gave combat. The raids did continue to harass the defenders however, even if losses were few:

> 'I saw quite a few combats, but nothing like the great battles of the summer. And as the weather grew worse into October our flying hours became more restricted and we knew we had not beaten the RAF, but neither did we feel as fighter boys that they had beaten us. Rather did we see it as a contest between two worthy opponents – in other words a draw.'

Winker's unit was withdrawn from the Channel Front for a rest in Belgium and then into Germany, and:

> 'When the winter came we began to hear the most fantastic rumours of a war coming in the East which at first we refused to believe. But then we heard from an artillery officer that some kind of operations

were planned and would be carried out in the spring. However, I and my comrades fully expected to return to France.'

Winker's expectations were not fulfilled, for when the time came he was sent to the new Eastern Front: 'where insofar as air combat is concerned we were far superior to that enemy'.

Early in November 1940 the condemned Stukas were hauled out from under their covers, manned by Rudel and other crewmen and despatched once again across the English Channel, their target British shipping. Two whole fighter Wings were used to protect just twenty-seven Stukas. Over three attacks the dive-bombers achieved some success but three days later lost a quarter of their number to Spitfires because their escort arrangements had miscarried. It marked the end of the Stuka story as far as Britain was concerned. Hans Rudel went back to Germany with his comrades, in June 1941 he would begin his extraordinary stint of action on the Russian Front. In the West the Luftwaffe's attack continued, but on a steadily reduced scale because of the weather.

The statistics tell the true story.

In August 1940 the Luftwaffe flew 4,779 sorties against Britain, dropping 4,636 tons of bombs. For September the figures rose to 7,260 flights and 6,616 tons of bombs, plus 669 mines laid in estuaries and harbours. In October, 9,911 sorties were flown and 8,790 tons of bombs dropped, with the laying of 610 mines. Thereafter the number of flights and bomb tonnages dropped owing to weather conditions. By February 1941 it would drop to a mere 1,401 sorties loosing 1,127 tons of bombs. By that time the great fire raid on the City of London had taken place, but it was over Bristol that Horst Juventus nearly came to grief:

> *'By then I had a new plane CO called Karl who told me that he thought the British would soon give in. That was before we were struck by flak over Bristol, he was a little more sober after that.*
>
> *'We had just dropped our bombs when a particularly loud burst of flak occurred near us and I felt the aircraft rock in the blast. One wing dropped but I retained control although I had to increase speed. Then I saw by my instruments that we were losing fuel from a wing tank so decided we must get back as soon as possible. I cut back the throttles and began a long glide down from our height of about 12,000 feet. We soon left the flak zone and reached the sea, we were by then stationed at Vannes so did not have too far to fly. But by the time we crossed the French coast we had lost a great deal of fuel and were forced to make an emergency landing at the Abbeville fighter base where the lads were very hospitable to us. Our Heinkel was repaired and we flew back to our own base soon after.'*

For the attack on the City on the night of 29–30 December, Karl Haulmeier recalls that the crews were briefed that the raid was justified on the grounds that much of economic importance to the British war effort went on there. In other words, there was no question of attacking military targets or factories, it was simply an administrative and financial centre, and arguably a legitimate target since essential to the enemy war effort. The aircrews may not have realised of course that the City of London also contained much else of interest that had no connection whatever with war-making, such as a myriad of little bookshops and other places fascinating to the browser and indeed the student of old London.

Not that this would have made the slightest difference, soldiers are trained to obey orders.

'I believe we hit our target and caused great damage, but as to its importance in the war effort, this was quite another matter. It did of course stir up a great deal of resentment on the part of the British and caused them to determine a great reprisal against our cities. When I saw the great fires springing up below us I thought of the people trying to save what they could, but wondered if in fact our commanders had been correct in telling us it was a commercial area.'

It was probably the biggest and best known 'commercial area' in the world, but Haulmeier's sympathy for any people was not displaced, this author's own cousin was bombed out in the area three times up to 1944. Being a Saturday night all the business and commercial premises were well secured and it became very hard in some cases for the firemen to gain access to fight the fires raging within. Added to which there was no effective fire-watching system in operation, but that did not stop Home Secretary Herbert Morrison from castigating bosses for their tardiness in making no provision for such an emergency, and very soon the national fire-watchers scheme was introduced which made it compulsory for every firm to organise nightly staff in such duties. The classic photographs taken of St Paul's cathedral surrounded by a sea of fire made excellent war propaganda for the British, yet there was no doubt that the Luftwaffe had struck the British capital a grievous blow.

After the bad weather in January–February the German air attacks were gradually stepped up, by March the Luftwaffe had learnt the better tactics of trying to concentrate their raids into a much shorter space of time, so that by the early hours both British citizens and their own aircrews could look forward to some sleep. The raids in March–April therefore became much livelier, sharper affairs, with low overcast after dark often enabling the bombers to fly lower, though by now the flak and night fighters were beginning to score some successes.

But by early May the transfer of Wehrmacht units to the prospective Eastern Front was well underway, yet before it became a reality Hitler decreed that an attempt must be made to deceive the British by applying even greater pressure with one last really devastating Luftwaffe attack. Every available bomber was scraped together and 'the beams laid on

London': the German radio-direction beams that would guide the pathfinders ahead of the main force. British attempts to 'bend' these beams had had some success, as had the laying of dummy fires, but it was impossible to divert the Luftwaffe from a target as large as London, and the pathfinders were hardly necessary.

Horst Juventus:

> 'By the Spring of 1941 I personally felt worn out through all the sorties I had flown over England. Then we were told that a heavy blow was to be struck against London, which we assumed had already suffered irreparable damage but was still to an extent functioning. Certainly our reconnaissance photos showed damage, but it seemed to me to be scattered and owing to the size of the city it obviously needed a far larger force of bombers than we possessed to deal it a real knock-out blow. All available bombers took part in the attack, I believe around 500 or so.'

The sirens sounded across London at 11 pm, their howling note initiated by 500 police stations, which had been alerted that a sizeable force of German bombers was heading for the capital in bright moonlight. Two minutes later the first of KG100 pathfinders dropped its load of incendiaries on long-suffering West Ham in East London. Unlike the very heavy attacks of March and April, this raid was spread all through the hours of darkness and in fact the last bomb did not fall until 5.37 am (on Scotland Yard). By then it was obvious to the authorities that it was by far the worst air raid the capital had suffered. The British estimated fairly accurately that around 500 German bombers had attacked the city, in fact official Luftwaffe returns show that of 541 sorties ordered 358 took place in the first wave and 147 in a second, making 505 bombing runs across London. These caused nearly 2,200 fires including nine conflagrations, twenty major fires rating up to thirty fire pumps, 210 medium fires, in all destroying 700 acres which was on a par with the Great Fire of 1666, though spread over a much wider area for bombs fell everywhere across London. Whatever the German aircrews were instructed or claimed then or later, damage was most among private housing and buildings not directly concerned with the war effort, plus the usual destruction to a host of public utilities, hospitals etc. Firemen were severely hampered in some areas, notably near the Thames by ruptured water mains, and attempts to draw water from the river itself proved difficult as the river was at low tide.

Casualties were heavy: 1,436 people were killed, 1,800 seriously injured, some of whom died later; 12,000 were made homeless, but this only included those requesting shelter from the authorities, others made their own arrangements, for 5,500 houses were totally destroyed with a further 5,000 damaged beyond repair. The cost was estimated at £20 million (1941 value).

It cannot be denied that in all that damage some injury was caused to firms engaged in some kind of war production, but for the Germans this was a bonus. What needs to be borne in mind here is that the attacks on British cities were in essence no different to those carried out on Germany by the RAF bombers later – whatever the original aim, they ended up as area attacks in which it was chiefly the civilian population that suffered the most. It has become fashionable in recent years to castigate or at least question RAF bombing policy, there are some in Germany and elsewhere who consider British bomber crews as 'terror flyers' who were really guilty of war crimes, with 'Bomber' Harris their chief as the most culpable. The Luftwaffe's campaign against Britain was carried out by an air force originally conceived and wholly trained and devoted to military operations in the field of battle that came to be used in fact as a 'terror weapon'; the attempt by the Germans to overcome the British people by air bombardment was feared by Churchill before the war came about. In short, the Germans initiated such warfare and as Harris stated publicly during the war, they did indeed reap the whirlwind.

Georg Kessler:

'We had flown over the London fires, the flak was especially intense and our pilot was taking evasive action. In my rather open position on top of the fuselage it was particularly frightening when the shells burst close to us and I kept my head down as the splinters splattered through our thin metal skin. Owing to the glare from a very large fire and the need to take evasive action, I believe our pilot failed to see another bomber dead ahead of us. Not until the very last moment did the captain shout a warning and then it was almost too late, for one of our propellers just caught the top of the other plane's tail fin and we shuddered and fell away at once, partly due to the pilot's reaction in turning the wheel hard to port. But the other plane was not seriously damaged I believe and flew off, perhaps unaware it had been struck, although their gunners should have reported it.

'When we reached our base we found our prop slightly damaged, otherwise we were OK.'

Horst Juventus comments that some crews had to fly more than one raid that night in order to make up the ordered number of attacks, and that it was a very wearing night that led to increased accidents. Tactics he says had changed so that crews flew much closer together and 'that was fine for us as we were often back in our beds well before dawn and were able to lead more normal lives'. Yet the German bombers streamed over England for many hours on the night of 10–11 May 1941, though Juventus comments:

'We were told that the defences would be swamped by our great force and would not be able to cope with the fires, and to some extent I believe this proved to be true. While we were always briefed to bomb certain targets such as docks and factories and railway stations it was not

always possible to restrict bombing to such points for various reasons. We had no really adequate equipment, the weather played a decisive part and other factors such as flak also interfered, though I never once saw a night fighter in this period. It has to be admitted that there were those crews who were less caring and dropped their bomb loads all over the city, which was unfortunate in more than one way. The civilians inevitably suffered, which bred hatred of the German airmen and also enabled the British to more easily mount similar and worse attacks on our own cities.

'In my case the raid of 10 May was a watershed. We took off normally into the darkening sky and flew over the Channel with others of our unit in sight until the blackness of the night swallowed them up. As we flew up the Thames the flak grew more fierce and we flew as a slightly rocking, zig-zag course but could not deviate much owing to the risk of collision and the need to enter the target zone from a prescribed direction. There were few searchlights but they caught one of our planes – a Dornier I believe – and we saw it trying to escape the glare, with shells bursting round it. It was not hit. Then we saw flares and incendiaries over the target and knew we had arrived. The scene was spectacular as the river Thames was lit up by the white light of the incendiaries and the first orange glow of fires and flashes of exploding bombs.

'We flew steadily on course and could hear the wump-wump of shells exploding near us. We were at about 8,000 feet and could see the houses of London and Big Ben lit up in the eerie glow of increasing fires and the flash of bombs and gunfire. We bombed the East End dock area and I carefully swung the Heinkel to port into a gentle dive, keeping a very careful watch for other planes. We now headed due south, straight for the coast, and at that moment, just as we were leaving the London area, a final burst of flak exploded just off our port wing which went up in flames. This was very alarming as we found we were lit up for the defenders to see on the ground and of course any patrolling night fighters.

'I was terrified in case the wing fuel tanks exploded, even though they were supposed to be self-sealing and made of composite rubber. I dived the machine but the fire grew worse and our captain ordered the gunners to prepare to bale out. We were down to about 4,000 feet and still descending and I felt I would have no chance to escape. The Heinkel was vibrating badly and I said a short prayer that we would be saved. I imagined the machine exploding into a thousand fragments and me with it.

'But a miracle happened – the fire went out and I pulled the bomber onto an even keel. As we crossed the coast a few more shells came up at us but we escaped back across the Channel and reached our base. On the ground again in great relief we examined the plane's wing and found that although some of the metal skin had burned away the fuel tanks remained intact.'

Wild claims were made next day as to the number of Germans destroyed, later re-guessed at eight; in fact the Luftwaffe lost fourteen bombers. Juventus recalls that the very next day many faces disappeared from his unit, despatched eastwards for the big build-up against the Soviets, most being killed later. Georg Kessler refers to these days as 'the great migration east', most never to be seen again:

'As for those left, life changed as we no longer had the strength to continue large scale raids on England. But we did our best, being directed to the usual targets including Bristol and Liverpool. In our off duty times we were occasionally able to borrow a car or truck and make little tours of the countryside and stop in a town for some refreshment. It was quite safe to do so at the time, though we were always alert for the first Resistance activity had begun, or so we heard, though it did not really affect us. But when I went home on leave I was dismayed to find my lady friend had gone off with a Captain of the army, so that was that. I did not find another girl friend, I was too upset. But back on the base we found we had frequent problems as the British began raiding our bases both by day and night. These attacks after dark were potentially very dangerous as in some cases our pilots were followed back to their bases and then attacked as they landed. All this added to our nervous fears and soon after that we crashed, though none of us was killed.'

How this came about will be explained shortly. When Karl Haulmeier went on leave his parents asked him about the attacks on England and what it was like:

'I told them it was almost a safe routine and that we were doing a lot of damage to the British war effort, but that London was a very big place. So my father asked me this: "Isn't it true that life has come to a standstill over there?"

'So I told him that if it had then there was no point in our continuing. He took my point and I further enlightened him that the invasion was "off". He realised that we had lost a lot of planes and men in the battle and seemed rather sobered by it all. He had not been in any fighting in the earlier war but had no illusions as to its reality. When I went out and met old friends they told me how proud they were of the Luftwaffe and wished me luck and told me that the British would surely soon give up. I said nothing to this but merely laughed.'

When Horst Juventus went home his parents amazed him by telling him of a big operation they had heard pending in the East:

'Of course by then the Balkans thing and Crete had come and gone, but they told me of local lads on leave from the army who spoke of something much bigger about to break. This is how the rumours began at home, though it's fair to say that few on the home front knew any

details. I already knew that something was in the wind, but told my parents it did not concern me. I knew they always worried about me, and then my younger brother was called up and he too went into the Luftwaffe but in a ground trade and did not become involved in any fighting.'

Georg Kessler crashed following a test flight:

'For some reason I flew, though it was not essential. I believe we had a new engine installed and as we were not on operations that night we all strolled out to the Heinkel and climbed aboard. It was mid-afternoon and all very routine. I think I just went along out of boredom and nothing special happened until our pilot had completed the flight and found everything satisfactory. But when we came in to land the new engine suddenly cut out completely and the loss of power caused us to lose height dramatically. I was in my gunner's position on top and suddenly aware of a lurch to one side and a descent that seemed far too rapid for safety. I looked round in alarm and at that instant we struck some bushes, we were that low. The undercarriage broke off completely and we flopped along the ground on our belly short of the airfield.

'We came to a bumpy halt and I leapt out over the fuselage and waited to see if my comrades were in need of help. There was no sign of fire, but it was safer to get out just in case. My three friends quickly ejected from the plane and we all slid off the wings onto the grass and ran clear. In a few moments the base firetruck and other vehicles and staff had reached us and we were safe. The Heinkel had to be dismantled to be taken away for repair and next night we flew a different machine which we christened Dora-May.'

Too many accidents claimed the lives of these young airmen. Karl Haulmeier describes some he witnessed:

'One of our Dorniers had just taken off and had barely cleared the field when it lost an engine and went straight into the ground, caught fire and blew up at once; there were no survivors. On another occasion a Heinkel from another unit tried to make an emergency landing on our field but overshot the runway and came down in a field. We ran towards the spot but it caught fire at once and we could hear the cries from inside the plane. The top gunner escaped, but the other three perished. That was horrible and reminded us of the dangers we ran. There were very many crashes all over the countryside, though some were minor and cost no lives. Then, as the Tommies became bolder and reached for our bases we saw some of them shot down and met some of the RAF aircrew who survived. I recall the crew of a Blenheim which came down not far from our base. We found them and brought them back to our field where we gave them some beer and coffee. They seemed quite cheerful and interested in all they saw. In fact, we let them climb

into one of our bombers and sit in the cockpit, which they found very interesting.

'On another occasion a Spitfire pilot was brought in after he crashed not too far off and we had him in our mess. He was a young Sergeant, from London I believe, happy to be alive and in good hands. When I asked him in poor English how he viewed the war situation he shrugged his shoulders and said, "You can't win, you know!" so we laughed and gave him some more tea.

'I believe two thirds of our bombers were sent East, and for many of the men it would be the end and we never saw them again. I remember an Observer who was an old friend from my training days who I knew very well indeed. After going to the new front in the East he wrote telling me of his experiences and how vastly different it all was and how he hated it and longed to be back in the West. His letters became less frequent and then stopped and I never heard from him again, but learned later that he had been killed after transferring to fighters. In our case we considered ourselves to be fortunate to be left behind in the West to carry on our little "private" war against England, even though our efforts were so much smaller and obviously no more than a nuisance to the British who grew bolder as the weeks went by in attacking our bases.

'On one occasion several of our bombers were returning in the early hours when we heard machine-gun fire and saw tracers light up the sky. Then a plane caught fire and crashed not far away and it proved to be one of our own. All the crew were killed.'

For the British the great raid on London in May 1941 was one more climacteric, another the same night being the arrival of Deputy Führer Rudolf Hess in Scotland where he had flown in a crazed attempt to persuade the British to make peace with Hitler before the attack on Russia. But on a very personal level one of these German witnesses experienced his own extraordinary affair. Horst Juventus:

'After I returned from leave to my unit at Vannes I found a local lady friend, a French woman who I had seen in the town. I often visited a nice little restaurant in the town with my friends where the patron was very civil to us. The food was sparse but delicately prepared and we enjoyed the breaks from service life. The patron's daughter was a little older than myself and always rather friendly to us and myself in particular. I must say the population behaved very reasonably in the circumstances. Of course, during 1941 the Resistance began to expand and make itself felt, but it did not affect us at that time, only later did we have to take more care.

'The girl's name was Marie and one evening I remained behind talking to her after my comrades had left to return to our base. She agreed to meet me so we could go for a walk and talk. I knew only a little French but somehow we managed to pass the time. Of course, I realised that to be seen together would perhaps place her in disfavour with her people,

although I knew her father did not object. In fact, I met her on the edge of town when very few people were about and we did enjoy a nice walk into the countryside. After a few more meetings we were in love and this was very agreeable to me, but she became increasingly apprehensive that there might be some repercussions among the townspeople. As for my own comrades, I had to undergo a certain amount of joking comment, but this did not bother me.

'I became much more careful in my flying duties, not that there was much I could do about the danger, but this is to indicate that being in love had made me much more aware of the frailty of my existence and the fact that I did not want to be cut off from Marie. She was dark and pretty and quite petite, gentle and loving and perhaps a little surprised to find herself consorting with an enemy airman. But when we came together we had no time for the war, only for ourselves. I had no idea that it would end tragically, but felt increasingly vulnerable and aware of the difficulties we faced. In fact, my CO warned me not to become too involved because of the normal security risk and the fact that she might suffer as a result. I tried to brush aside such fears, but the thought did nag at me increasingly.'

Juventus remarks that he continued to fly over England, taking part in raids that were small by comparison with those of 1940, though they cost his unit three or four aircraft.

'We raided Belfast one night and this was a very successful attack as our reconnaissance pictures proved. But the cunning British had learned how to bend our radio beams and lit dummy fires and these often led to crews going astray. Some regrettable incidents occurred when some crews bombed Eire and Dublin in particular, which was very embarrassing for our command. I believe great apologies and even some compensation was made.

'There were also attacks on other British cities and in some of these it was possible to see people fleeing from the flames for we often flew lower in these night attacks. This was quite distressing I must say as it brought home the reality of the air war in such localities once a large fire took hold. The fires were like magnets to aircrews carrying bombs and they tended to drop their loads on them rather than search for 'legitimate' targets, regardless of whether the fire raging below was a military objective or not. So civilians were certainly the main sufferers.

'I recall flying over Manchester one night, there were some quite spectacular fires burning and we could actually see the firemen doing their best to put out these conflagrations while the bombs continued to fall among them. We certainly admired their courage. I feel the German people need to be reminded of such things when they think and talk of the later Allied "terror" raids on their own cities. We of the Luftwaffe carried out raids on all the principal towns and cities of Great Britain

long before the Allies had the strength to do such things. It should be understood quite clearly that in that kind of war the raids tended to get out of control, and this happened as early as during take-off, by which I mean that although we would be notified as to this or that target, once the bombs started to fall and action was joined it soon got out of control. When you are under fire the nerves take over, from fear it is perfectly possible to adopt a very different attitude, one is driven by the instinct of self-preservation. Let's drop our eggs and escape! Anywhere as some aircrews did, this was inevitable, whatever they told their officers on return. And of course if their plane was damaged or under attack by flak or a night-fighter then jettisoning the bomb load came first. Many civilians suffered, it was inevitable. The Allies developed the bomber as a decisive weapon, but we did all the experimenting in 1940–41 when the RAF was doing little or nothing despite all its efforts and hopes. We had no strategic air force and no night bomber fleet in 1940 so had to do the best we could and to a degree achieved a lot in a short time considering our complete lack of training for night operations. I know we did a lot of damage to the British economy, but also to the civilian population who suffered greatly as a result of our attentions to their cities. So it is no use bleating about Allied terrorflieger, the air war on civilian centres was begun by the Luftwaffe, there is no doubt of that.'

It is unfortunate that such views have not been disseminated today, a rather one-side picture of the bombing war seems to have been promoted by the media, especially in Britain.

But for Horst Juventus his own personal experiences at the time were far more concerned with the immediate, and especially his lady love:

'After a few months, at the end of 1941 came the great blow which ruined the life I had led in France. Dangerous though it was at times, it was in some ways very comfortable, for in my off duty times I met Marie and we had some fine afternoons and evenings together. In fact, I had by then been able to stay the night with her above the restaurant, making sure that I arrived after dark and curfew time, leaving at a suitable hour next day. Her father was quite agreeable, and since he was a widower there was no woman to cause problems. I used to give him comforts of German beer and cigarettes and he seemed quite happy with the arrangement.

'Then one evening when I arrived I found him in some distress and he told me that Marie had vanished. I was thunderstruck and wondered what could have become of her. Then while I stood there speaking to him a note was pushed through the front door, it was from the Resistance and it said simply: "Death to traitors!"

'We were both very, very distressed by this which we could only interpret in one way. I had no idea what to do, but, after a few tears, was forced to return to base where some of my comrades noticed my

distress, and when I told them the CO sent for me and said, "I warned you, didn't I? Now perhaps you have learned your lesson!"

'*I was in no fit state to fly and was given a week off duty but told to remain on the base. I believe the French police became involved, but I don't believe any trace of Marie was ever found. This event had a terrible effect on me, and even though I was able to resume flying I became a changed man and for a year or so had little time for anything. In fact I did not even go home on leave and my parents became very worried about me, although I did write and explain that I could not get home to them. All in all it was a very difficult time for me and my CO was rather displeased to say the least, and at one time threatened to send me to the Eastern Front if I did not pull myself together. My comrades did their best to pick me up and involve me in their activities.*'

Hans Bender piloted a Heinkel to Bristol in the Spring of 1941:

'*We bombed the target and turned away south, intending to begin a long gliding descent back to our base in France. But at that moment a flak shell burst very close to us, rocking the plane and damaging our port engine badly so that I had to shut it down and feather the propeller. We were uninjured, but I had doubts as to getting back on one engine. We were already losing height and well below 15,000 feet, so after some discussion with my captain I changed course slightly to the south-west, intending to take the shortest route to north-west France where if we reached it we could, we hoped, make an emergency landing.*

'*The night was very dark and the flak and fires at Bristol were soon far behind us as we left the coast of England and flew over the western Channel. The plane was not too stable but still flying though we continued to lose height too rapidly and after a while I warned the captain that I did not feel we could reach France. The crew stared out into the blackness and then the radio operator sent out an emergency call, and we received a position report and course to fly for one of our bases in north-west France. So I adjusted our direction and we flew on into the darkness. But then the starboard engine began running roughly, and I warned the crew that we might have to ditch in the sea.*

'*Eventually, we were down to about 2,000 feet and still descending when our captain in the nose shouted that he could see the blacker mass of land ahead. But it was too late, for just as suddenly he saw how close we were to the sea and I shouted at them to take up crash positions, which they did – hurriedly. I braced myself and then we struck the sea with a great jarring crash. It all happened in a few seconds, the nose was smashed in and the water rushed at me as I tried to undo my straps. The men behind me were yelling as they attempted to scramble out of the top hatch, but with the sea water flooding around me I found it hard to move quickly enough. But I managed to reach the hatch where my captain helped me out. As I climbed onto the top fuselage the gunners were launching the dinghy off the wing and in a moment we were all in the water and struggling as the Heinkel began to sink. We had one paddle and moved away rapidly, soaked and cold and saw our plane vanish. We could see the darker landscape and hear the surf but did not realise how close inshore we were until we saw little lights and realised some rescuers were climbing down the cliffs.*

'In a few moments we had reached the beach where we found soldiers about to launch a small boat. We were soon in good hands and flown back to our own base next day. Soon after that we were sent to the East, I alone survived.'

Georg Kessler's unit of Heinkels was transferred to a base near Nantes in western France, the hope being that they could intercept British shipping in the way that the larger four-engined Focke-Wulfs had been doing for some time.

'But we achieved nothing so returned to our original base near Arras. By then we only seemed to be going through the motions of air war, the raids on Britain were mere pinpricks. But then in 1942 came the larger RAF raids on German cities including the great attack on Cologne which caused great consternation, not only across the country but in the Luftwaffe bases. We were very surprised that raids of such size could be mounted and wondered as to the truth of the British claims. But we soon heard stories as to the extent of the damage at Cologne, Lübeck and Rostock, so became very concerned.'

Indeed, no matter how much the Göbbels' propaganda machine attempted to deride the British claims, rumours based on hard facts passed across the Reich. Air Marshal Harris had taken over Bomber Command in February and at once begun a shake-up and campaign to show both Germany and his mentors at home that he meant business. With new aids and tactics plus sufficient new four-engined bombers he mounted successful attacks on Lübeck and Rostock, cities placed on the north-east German coast and easy to find. At the former town, apart from war industry the old town was burnt out, and at Rostock the Heinkel factory knocked about. Well over 900 bombers were scraped together from Bomber and Training Commands to visit Germany's second city and much of Cologne was razed. When Kessler mentions doubts he is of course echoing genuine disbelief in Germany that raids on such scale could be carried out; the problems of routeing one thousand planes (as the British claimed there were) would have seemed formidable. But the Germans should have known via their intelligence that their enemy had been designing, testing and then operating four-engined strategic bombers for some time, and by then they surely had no doubts as to the British determination to use every weapon at its disposal to smash Nazi Germany. All the Nazi leaders and their commanders could do was promise suitable reprisals, even though they knew their air force was now dispersed to several fronts.

Kessler:

'We were ordered to carry out reprisal raids on British cathedral cities, which seemed a very bad idea. We had a few ideas of our own as to better targets but were obliged to follow orders. So we flew to Exeter and Bristol and a few other places. Although we did some damage and fires were started they were not war targets and the raids did nothing to hamper the enemy war effort.'

As Juventus points out, by that time the British defences had greatly improved:

'We always had to be on top form when we entered enemy air space and a crew with a pilot pining for a lost love was no use at all. I began to see that I could prove a real danger to them and in due course requested to be taken off flying duties. My CO agreed to give me a rest and posted me off to a training school as an instructor. This was not too good as I was in no mood to instruct novices as to the realities of the bombing war, but I had to do my best. I travelled to a sub-unit outside Paris where there was a school for qualified pilots undergoing pre-operational training. There were a few bombers on the base and these were used as hacks for the pilots to learn the tricks of the trade which I tried to teach them along with the other instructors. It was there that I began to improve and I must say I had all but forgotten my old girl friend in Berlin. My parents knew her well and induced me to write to her, and so began a new episode of romance and when I finally went home at last on leave I met her and this helped a great deal. I could never forget Marie but seeing Helga was a healing balm. I could not tell her about my French lady friend but she assumed I had been scarred by some war experience and said nothing but tried to cheer me up. In this she succeeded and I did not feel so bad on returning to my unit. In fact, by mid-1942 I had returned to Vannes and resumed operational flying which I found quite refreshing.'

'I believe we lost about a dozen crews over a year or so through accidents, mostly on the base at night. There were of course accidents all the time and it was the same for the RAF and inevitable in wartime conditions. I remember one of our Heinkels that crashed on take-off in mid-June 1942, just as we were about to get away ourselves to England. It burnt out in a very short time. The crew as usual were killed so it was a very bad start to the night's work. Then one night after we had returned from a raid another base called up to warn us of a Dornier overdue which they said might attempt a landing at our field. In due course the plane came over very low so all the runway lights were switched on, just long enough we hoped to get the pilot safely down before the enemy arrived to try and interfere. The danger from British night-fighters was constant.

'We all stood outside in the darkness as the Dornier came in for its landing, but it seemed to be damaged as the engines were missing badly. We heard a thump and saw a bright flash as it hit the ground at the edge

of the field and as it struck the ground more fully it blew up. There was nothing we could do, it was a routine occurrence. We simply went off to bed. Next morning we viewed the bits and pieces scattered across the edge of our field.

'*In this period the British night-fighters proved a real and increasing danger, with Beaufighters and then Mosquitos intercepting us with radar. It was highly dangerous work flying over England and we did all we could to avoid detection, also attempting to attack known fighter bases, but it was a hopeless task as we had no idea which were in use by night fighters and they were blacked out anyway. Our losses began to rise and although the replacements came they were not as competent as before. So many crews had been sent to the Eastern front which was swallowing up our air force, then of course there was the Mediterranean and Balkans.*'

The Luftwaffe bomber crews had been saddled with obsolete equipment for too long in their estimation, not that the new types could make much difference, as Karl Haulmeier indicates:

'*At last we began to receive the Dornier 217 which was faster and had better equipment, but otherwise was not greatly different to the old model. Our attacks on Britain were now in the form of single sorties or in small groups and of little value.*'

The Führer Directive (14 April) following the successful heavy RAF raids mentioned had contained the phrase: 'preference is to be given to those (targets) where attacks are likely to have the greatest possible effect on civilian life.'

This led to the attacks on so-called 'cathedral cities' supposedly selected from the Baedeker tourist guide book. But the Luftwaffe had proved too weak and frustrated by British defences. For example, in the raid already mentioned on Exeter bombs fell over a wide area owing to overcast, only one bomber actually hitting the city. This was during the night of 23 April, though there were other attacks which caused cultural damage, Bath and Norwich being two notable examples of this raid series in which the planes involved were mostly Junkers 88s of the latest type and Dornier 217s which preferred to operate against undefended targets by moonlight, often carrying a new type of incendiary bomb canister containing 140 2.2 lb bombs, the casings operated by barometric fuse which allowed unprecendented concentrations of these fire bombs in small area. During an attack on York a new device was tried out by the British defenders, the so-called 'Turbinlight' Havoc night-fighter illuminator which was a failure. But by that time Britain's defences included 935 static and 465 mobile 3.7-inch AA guns. Of these 416 were of the 4.5-inch calibre plus 144 obsolete 3-inchers. Naturally, most of the heavy guns were located in places of vital importance to the war effort, such as Liverpool where one hundred weapons could put up a formidable barrage. Horst Juventus:

'*I remember one night when we attacked Liverpool, but it proved a fiasco as long before we arrived the British had lit their dummy fires (code name Starfish) and confused the pathfinders by interfering with the radio beams so that bombs were scattered over several different points, wherever the crews thought the target was because of the fires they saw on the ground. In fact that city was easy to find in strictly navigational terms because of its location on the north-western seaboard, but because of the enemy's countermeasures and the weather all kinds of difficulties arose. That raid was a failure.*'

There were other, like failures, such as when *Starfish* fires diverted the Luftwaffe from Plymouth, most of the bombs landing on Hayling Island.

'*On another occasion we had taken off to attack London when the weather grew much worse and we became lost over the sea. This seems absurd, but it is easy to get disorientated in wartime circumstances. We lacked good navigational aids and did a fair amount of guesswork, for compasses could prove unreliable at times and with interference on the radio wavelengths it could be very dangerous.*

'*I could see nothing at all out of the cabin windows but blackness and decided to go down to try and catch a glimpse of the sea. We were all very alert as the Heinkel dived down through the cloud, aware that the British were probably following our progress and trying to trick us into landing on one of their fields. This was the sort of thing that could and did happen. At last we thought we saw a light in the murk but were not sure if it was a town showing lights contrary to blackout regulations or ships at sea. I flew towards the spots of light but all of a sudden they seemed to be moving – and then it dawned on me that they were the exhaust flames of another aircraft! We had no idea if it was one of ours or theirs, but followed it for a short time until it vanished in the cloud. By now we were becoming seriously worried as although flying on the correct compass bearing we had no idea if we had reached England or indeed any land that we could recognise. Eventually our captain decided we must turn back, so I turned the plane and reversed course, hopefully back to France. But as we made progress on the new heading one of our gunners reported flashes behind us so we turned back and sure enough saw flak bursts, which by our course had to be over England. Hopefully, we thought, this could be the coastline.*

'*But in a few moments the flashes had stopped and all was blackness again. But we flew on, direction north-west, hoping for a glimpse of the coast – anything – even shellfire. But we saw nothing, not a glimpse of the Thames or the sea, and after a few minutes we were forced to give up and turn back. In due course we were given a homing signal by our beacon and when we reached our field it was briefly illuminated for us to touch down. I was completely exhausted and had wasted two hours of our energies and precious fuel to no purpose.*'

Even when the German bombers did penetrate British airspace they were often too hounded by the defences to make any worthwhile attacks. Karl Haulmeier mentions that one night he and his crew had reached the Midlands with the intention of attacking Birmingham, but one of the gunners spotted a night-fighter, and by the time they had completed evasive action their chance had gone. So on the way south again they bombed London.

'Since the British had radar night-fighters and we had no such equipment the enemy held a distinct advantage and we felt very vulnerable. In any case I felt I was about superfluous for it now became impossible for us to fly on bright moonlit nights for fear of night-fighters. This meant that we hugged the clouds and our attempts to find targets were so fleeting that it gave us no time to do our job properly. I had no desire to carry out indiscriminate attacks and always tried to find proper targets, but this was becoming increasingly difficult.

'When we raided Bristol great damage was done to the port which although not large I believe handled a significant amount of cargo. I have heard that some of our crews flew low enough to machine-gun the streets, which is reprehensible, but I must say that the heavy RAF attacks on our cities tended to make our feelings run high and of course as a war progresses so does it tend to become more savage. In most cases we held no animosity towards British civilians and the airmen we captured were always fairly treated throughout the war.'

With the exception, it has to be said, of those Allied airmen murdered by the Gestapo and in some cases civilians. But cases of ill treatment of Luftwaffe aircrew are known, though reports of two being killed after parachuting cannot be proven. But two German aircrewmen who parachuted into the Thames mud during the big raid of 10 May were beaten-up by Home Guards before being taken away.

CHAPTER TEN

'DROP THE BOMBS AND GET AWAY'

O ther German airmen were engaged in the battle in the same
hemisphere but on a different front. Robert Kanafuss went
into the Luftwaffe in 1940; in 1942 he joined a Ju 88 group
operating against British convoys en route to Russia:

'*My home was in Bremen where I lived after my parents died. I
was conscripted and had a great interest in aircraft and wanted to
fly a bomber. But, as it turned out, I had no aptitude as a pilot so
I was trained as a radio operator-gunner and sent to a Ju 88 unit in
the West.*

'*The war had entered its mid-phase before Germany's defeats began,
and at the time I was stationed at Bardufoss in northern Norway, which
was hardly what I had expected. The climate was quite harsh and one
had to adapt to it, especially when winter came and everything was
freezing, but when I arrived at the base in July 1942 it was not too bad,
in fact quite warm at times. The whole purpose of placing bomber units
there was to attack Allied convoys taking supplies to Russia, either to
Murmansk or Archangel. When I arrived I joined a new crew from a
training school and was introduced to them.*

'*My captain was called Karl and had a very commanding presence.
The pilot was very young, about nineteen or so and called Robert like
myself and we got along very well. The other gunner was Herbert and
from Hamburg and always grumbled about the cold. A Sergeant-Major
explained the uses of our unit which was equipped with torpedoes as well
as bombs. The former weapons were an experiment already used to good
effect by Heinkels from the same base. The NCO told us it was vital to
interrupt the flow of supplies to the Russian Front and that once we
had carried out a few local familiarisation flights to get our bearings he
himself would teach us convoy attack techniques using two old steamers
which had been brought up specially for training purposes.*

'*All this was contrary to what I had expected. I had heard about the
Junkers 88 "wonder bomber" long before the information services had
begun to make great play of the new weapon early in the war when
one of them had supposedly sunk the aircraft carrier Ark Royal. So
here we were, almost in the Arctic Circle, and contrary to my hopes of
dive-bombing attacks on the British Fleet in English harbours we were*

sitting about for hours waiting for news from our reconnaissance unit and the radio intercept service of Allied convoys. But we had our orders and the same day went off with the Sergeant-Major for some local trips which I must admit were very spectacular from the air, quite different to the ground life where we were apt to think of personal comfort most of the time.

'Within the week we were armed with dummy torpedoes and flying on the tail of the Sergeant-Major who showed us how to attack a ship. The problem was that our target was stationary, so this made it all much easier. My job of course had nothing to do with dropping weapons or piloting, I was only an Observer with a machine-gun and manning the radio at times in case of any special orders or directions which came to us.

'We flew at 150 feet at cruising speed and then slowed as we neared the large wreck and dropped the dummy torpedo, at which point the pilot was required to hit the deck so to speak in order to try and avoid enemy flak which was something the Sergeant-Major did not mention, though we soon discovered later how bad it would be. An alternative was to drop the weapon and do a smart turn about, but this entailed exposing the underside of the plane a little too much.

'We flew every day until our pilot and captain–Observer felt they had mastered the art of torpedo dropping as far as they could in practice. So all we needed was some action – but then we learned that the main ordeal was to be boredom; the Allied convoys were infrequent and there were no alternative targets, so we had to kick our heels waiting. We played cards, read books, attended a few compulsory lectures on various topics, not all concerned with flying but about the war in general including Germany's aims. We wrote letters to family if we had one, or to lady friends. In my case an old school friend had promised to write to me, a girl I respected rather than loved, and we had some interesting correspondence.

'It must have been two months before we received an alert and attended a briefing where our CO showed us a wall map and the present position of an eastbound convoy and its expected position a few hours later when it would be within range of our bombers. We had about twenty Junkers 88s and a similar number of Heinkels on the other side of our base; we had seen these other lads and expected to play football with them shortly.

'Our reconnaissance planes went off at dawn next morning and these included Dornier seaplanes which were moored off the coast but, although of the Luftwaffe, were controlled by the navy. A few hours later we were alerted and took off one by one in what for us was our first taste of action. It was about midday, the weather was gloomy but for a lemon-coloured horizon. The sea looked leaden and very uninviting and I thought of our chances of survival if we crashed into the sea.

'The Ju 88 was very cramped and my seat backed onto the pilot. I faced backwards against the radio sets with my machine-gun over the *top sticking through a hole in the rear cockpit roof, while my fellow gunner had his position below me and was even more cramped. I believe our pilot and the captain were the most comfortable.*

'*We flew a course in one large formation, the Heinkels had already gone off ahead of us and disappeared. The noise in the cabin was always very great, one long uninterrupted roar which wracked the senses. We carried a few sandwiches and some boiled sweets for the trip which would last some hours, as well as flasks of hot tea and coffee which we passed round. I believe the captain also carried a flask of schnapps for special occasions. We flew at about 8,000 feet, and although at that height we should have had good views in all directions as the clouds were above us the light was poor, a kind of twilight which needed adjusting to in those climes and was rather straining on the eyes. In those circumstances it was everyone's duty to keep a sharp watch for the convoy or anything else of interest, though needless to say we flew very many miles and saw nothing but grey sea. But the position of the convoy had been given and one of our large Focke-Wulfs was following it and sending position reports so our formation leader was able to stay on the right heading.*

'*Then at long last our leader waggled his wings which was the signal for us to break into more open attack formation and this we did. We were somewhere in the middle of the group and I watched the other planes spreading out into a long, broad column. Those pilots knew their job as all had seen similar action before so the drill was quite familiar to them.*

'*At first when I looked ahead I saw nothing, but as we flew lower I spotted a lot of ships silhouetted against the lighter skyline. The group now went into an even more open formation, there was no sign of the Heinkels, so we assumed they had already attacked. There was a certain amount of smoke on the horizon, but it was impossible to tell if it was from damaged ships or not.*

'*We drew nearer to the convoy, which appeared to consist of about sixty ships, and in a moment the first flak came up near us, the first I'd seen and it looked harmless enough – small puffs of black smoke. Then I saw flashes from some of the warships which were now quite visible and realised that the first Junkers were already on their way in. It was an extraordinary sight to see the myriad lines of tracer curving across the sea at our first attackers which I could no longer see as their shapes had merged with the grey sea. Our captain gave course corrections to the pilot and pointed out a likely target. We had no idea if there were any escorting fighters with the convoy, sometimes they had small aircraft carriers with them, so I kept a very careful eye open, especially to the rear.*

'*Then I heard the first distinct thump of exploding shells and we were skimming nearer the surface of the sea. I glanced over my shoulder past the pilot and was amazed to see all the flashing lights on the dark objects on the sea before us. All the ships were firing weapons of various kinds,* and then I saw a larger flash and a waterspout and smoke as one of the torpedoes from a leading plane struck home. Our captain was shouting at the pilot and our plane banked through a column of spray though whether this was from a flak near miss or our own torpedo dropping I had no idea. The coloured lines of fire seemed to shoot straight for us and then whip by and I tried not to look ahead as it seemed impossible for them to miss us.

'Then the plane climbed sharply and banked to the left and I knew our torpedo had gone. I heard the captain shouting and saw a great line of flashes from the flak and heard a rattling sound along the fuselage. Then we were racing away over the sea at low level. My heart was thumping and looking down I saw Herbert grinning and clapping his hands as if we had hit something. I had no idea, but I did know that in those moments I had been very frightened.

'Then the pilot shouted, and looking out of the cabin window to the right I saw one of our Junkers on fire, flames were streaming back from it and it went into a climb and two men jumped out – I knew this when their parachutes opened. Then I saw a puff of flame and smoke and bits of the plane were falling into the sea. I felt terrible as I thought of our comrades dying in that mess and wondered if the ships would pick up those who escaped – I doubted it. They were some way off. Then I remembered our seaplanes, but the ocean was so large and their chances of being rescued about zero. It was very sad to be so helpless and unable to help those survivors.

'We flew back in loose formation and when I counted then I realised we had lost two planes, I could only see eighteen so assumed a second had been shot down, though it was possible our comrades were somewhere behind us. I had no idea if we ourselves had hit anything; to lose two planes for one ship possibly sunk was not a very good result in my opinion.

'At last we arrived back at our base – by some miracle – I could never stop marvelling at this navigation business, but I knew some crews got lost and this was easy once darkness fell in that inhospitable area. After we had landed we went to a de-briefing session and I heard crews reporting hits on three ships, the CO remarked that U-boats would confirm this or otherwise as they were now taking over the attacking. Someone had seen the missing Junkers disappearing in a curtain of flak on the other side of the convoy and since they had not returned we had to assume them lost. Very few aircrew survived such events.

'I assumed we were then free of this for some time, but to my surprise the CO then told us to get cleaned up, have a meal and some rest as we were to fly off again within hours. I felt very disappointed. We ate quite well and then I went to my hut for some sleep but it seemed no time at all before we were being woken up and told to get ready. The planes had been rearmed and refuelled and take-off was in thirty minutes. I felt very sleepy and at that moment bitterly regretted the kind of life

I had let myself in for and thought of all the things I could be doing in a safe, comfortable job.

'*We took off again, this time flying a new course, for the convoy had moved on. It was quite dark and as we climbed to the same height, direction north-east, our calls were received by the shadowing Focke-Wulf Condor which relayed the convoy's latest position to our formation leader. I heard these exchanges over my radio and passed notes to my captain. The flight seemed interminable and when we finally arrived in the target area I was almost asleep and very cramped. But this time I knew what to expect and all at once the Jus had split up into the dawn light and we started to attack.*

'*Once more I marvelled at the great rash of tracer which seemed even more spectacular than before as the first Junkers went in. But almost at once as I glanced round to watch there was a brilliant flash which was one of our planes blowing up. We went on without a word being spoken and made our attack on a tanker. The worst sights were yet to come. As we banked away our captain shouted and looking round I saw a huge red and yellow flash from our target. I also saw a long trail of black smoke going down to the sea which was another of our planes going in. But our tanker blew up in a large gush of fiery smoke and flames. It was quite a fantastic sight and we all shouted in amazement and triumph as we climbed away and circled for a moment to watch. It was very spectacular but I thought of the poor devils on that blazing ship and trusted they would be rescued.*

'*Then we were climbing away, and this time we flew back widely dispersed and when we eventually reached our base the planes were all over the place and took some time to get down. At de-briefing we confirmed that two of our planes were missing, but three ships were claimed as hit including our tanker, this being confirmed later by our U-boats which finished it off.*

'*We had breakfast and went to our beds exhausted. Since the convoy had now passed out of our range we were free and would be bored again for weeks. At that time it was not considered policy to bother about the ships returning to Britain empty, so these were reported but not molested. Later on this changed as it was realised that shipping space was of vital importance to the Allies, so these westbound convoys were attacked and many ships sunk.*

'*Then we were granted leave, half the crews went home to Germany, travelling by truck and then train. I had no special plans but returned to my flat in Bremen where I was in time for an RAF raid which was not bad and nothing compared with those later. I met my lady correspondent a few times but nothing developed and in fact I ceased to keep in touch with her. However, as I was somewhat a free agent I decided to spend a day or two in Norway, so went back early via Copenhagen, which I found interesting, and then took a bus into Oslo which disappointed me. I spent a night in a Wehrmacht hostel before travelling back to my base, meeting two comrades on the way, so the long journey was enlivened by games of skat and tales of our respective leaves.*

'After our return we were assigned new duties, patrols were to be flown down the western coast of Norway to watch out for enemy attempts to land commandos or agents etc, so this helped to fill time, though despite the spectacular scenery this too became boring in time.

'Then another convoy was reported by our reconnaissance and intelligence, and within a few days we flew off to attack it. The intention was a co-ordinated attack by ourselves and U-boats so that the convoy would be thrown into confusion. But this was difficult to achieve as contact between us and the submarines was not close enough. However, the subs did make an attack just as we came on the scene and though it was a little disjointed we gained an advantage and many ships were sunk, some of them in spectacular fashion, blowing up and sending huge columns of smoke up into the clouds. I learned later that rescue ships accompanied these convoys, so hoped that some of the survivors were saved.

'When crews arrived on our base as replacements it was our job to show them the ropes, just as we had been shown, and this made a change. In my case I instructed the radio operators in the use of local frequencies and what to expect from occasional interference from "natural phenomena" in those latitudes. All this helped to save me from utter boredom.

'I had an aunt who was always very solicitous of my well-being and sent me woollen comforts she had knitted, one of these being a multi-coloured pullover which I took to wearing under my thick flying suit. Up there we were provided with fleece and fur-lined clothing, all leather covered which was fairly good, but in winter nothing could stop the cold seeping into the body.'

Robert Kanafuss took part in one more convoy attack in which the unit lost two more planes, the Heinkels four.

'At this point I requested a transfer and after some discussion with my CO this was granted, though he warned me that I could be sent back to them at any time as it was an unusual privilege. In fact, I had landed myself in a worse mess as I was sent to the Eastern Front, and that tale is outside this scope. Suffice to say that it was worse in many ways and I was lucky to survive.'

All the threat of defeat which had inexorably loomed towards Germany late in 1942 became a reality early in 1943 as the 6th Army under General Paulus was surrounded and destroyed at Stalingrad. Meantime, the Allies under General Eisenhower had landed an army in north-west Africa, this force would link up with the triumphant 8th Army under General Bernard Montgomery, which chased Rommel's desert remnants one thousand miles to beyond Tripoli. And in north-west Europe the Allies began their 'round-the-clock' bombing of the Reich.

Georg Kessler:

'The year 1943 was a traumatic one for us as one defeat came after another. And when the summer came my poor parents were killed in the Hamburg air raids. It was a while before I received this terrible news and I was sent home on leave. I could hardly believe the sights I saw, the heaps of ruins and the thousands of people outside the city who had either been evacuated or left in panic. My home was a heap of rubble and I trudged about in tears searching for some clue or relic, but found little. The firestorms had reduced everything and I was not able to see my parents' remains as the authorities told me they were not identifiable and my task was a hopeless one. From that moment on I went about like a robot, and at my base I was a fairly useless individual, and although I flew I don't believe I was of any use to my crew.

'Eventually my captain requested I be removed from operations and this happened. I was given a desk job dealing with records of ground maintenance and never flew again and was thankful for that.'

By then the old Heinkel 111 was obsolete, yet still flying. Horst Juventus:

'It had been good enough in 1939, but years had gone by with very little change, its bomb load was quite small and I wondered at the point of so much effort to deliver such a puny quantity of bombs on the enemy. It did not seem worth it. Other units had the superior Junkers 88, even the Dornier had been developed, though neither of these aircraft carried much of a bomb load. We seemed to be fighting a cinderella war to no good purpose, for the raids we made were tiny affairs, quite often single excursions by individual bombers roaming all over Britain, giving nuisance value but nothing else. This sort of thing through 1943 had a curious effect on our morale, for while we were thankful to be living a life of comparative luxury compared to the poor devils on the Eastern Front, we seemed to be doing no good in the air war.

'In 1942 the RAF under Air Marshal Harris had become strong enough to develop its own kind of raids over the Reich, which became very serious. The first thousand-bomber raid hit us like a bombshell; I heard the news with my comrades and found it very hard to believe. Our listening service we knew could tune in to the enemy crews taking off etc, but it was unable to determine just how many planes were involved, though obviously at the receiving end a fair assessment could be made. The tales concerning the damage at Cologne were very bad, and we compared our own miniscule effort to that of the RAF. After all, despite all Göbbels' propaganda, even if only half of the claimed one thousand planes took part in that raid it was still a very great effort and of course the RAF bombers carried a heavier load than we did, especially the four-engined types. So we became very apprehensive for our homes and families, though I did not see great danger to Berlin at that time in 1942, but as to the future – who could tell?

ombing east London, with West Ham dium in view.

Dorniers over Gravesend, Kent, 7 September 1940.

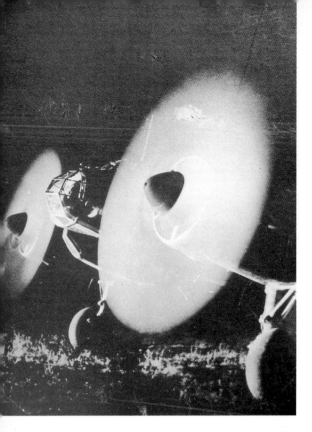

Night start for a Junkers 88.

A German artist's view of heroic *Luftwaffe* aircrew battling through searchlights, flak and night-fighters to bomb Britain.

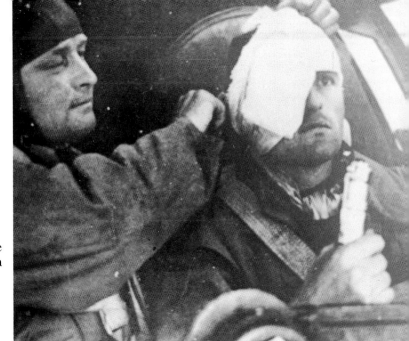

crewman tends the
ounded pilot of a
einkel.

urvivors paddling to an English shore.

ircrew prisoners at a London station
rminus.

German high explosive bombs of 50, 250 and 1000kg. These carried a greater weight of explosive than early British bombs, though a proportion failed to explode.

Incendiary bombs burning in a British street.

The Heinkel 111H series were adapted for experiments with balloon-cutting equipment; this cumbersome example was shot down in 1941.

The burnt-out remains of a Junkers 88.

New blood for the *Luftwaffe*.
TOP LEFT: The Focke-Wulf 190
ABOVE, a Junkers 188.
LEFT, a Dornier 217K2.
BELOW, a Messerschmitt 410.

The troublesome Heinkel 177 with its four coupled engines.

A He177 crew prepare for take-off.

Young aircrew at a briefing during the 'Baby Blitz' of early 1944.

Already becoming obsolete by 1941, the Heinkel 111 soldiered on, being adapted to carry the VI 'doodlebug' flying bomb later in the war.

The German lead in jet warplane development is well illustrated by the Arado 234 reconnaissance bomber which overflew Britain in the final months of the war.

'It soon became obvious that the war was lost – Africa, Stalingrad, then the increasing Allied incursions by air. I remember standing on our base as the first American bomber formations came over. We were very impressed, and wondered how they would fare in such daylight attacks, judging by our own experience, not very well. Our own defences had been steadily improved with an ever-increasing number of fighters stationed in the West, and soon we saw the first American bombers being brought down. This was later in 1942 after they had begun to extend the range of their excursions.

'I remember watching a B-17 Fortress as it struggled to maintain height and get back over the Channel, but it could not make it and came down some miles away. I believe the crew survived. After that we saw many more as our fighter comrades got the measure of the Yankees, who I must say were very brave to even attempt such attacks by day in those large aircraft. The cost to them became enormous both in terms of machines and men lost.'

Juventus had taken part in the raids on the British 'cathedral cities', admitting that he and his comrades knew perfectly well that they were not war targets:

'If the Nazi government hoped to deter the British from further raids on Germany then they were much mistaken; the attacks grew worse and soon all our towns were devastated and very many thousands killed. It was a terrible reckoning for Germany and in a sense worse for us as we felt so helpless and unable to assist. We knew there were increasing recriminations against the Luftwaffe, but there was nothing we could do.'

Karl Haulmeier records the depression felt when in 1943 it became obvious that the war was lost. Yet in the occupied territories on the West life went on as before, except that the German personnel were no longer able to go about alone outside their bases and all contact with locals was forbidden. Then there was the fear of actual attack by the Resistance, British commandos and agent activity. But the units kept flying over England, but as losses grew so they were weakened.

The new ideas adopted by the Germans as a response to ever-increasing Allied air raids but especially the RAF bombers' assaults were puny but in some cases deadly. In 1940 the Luftwaffe had used so-called 'oil bombs', apart from the regular high explosive, incendiary and air-dropped mines. By 1943 it had added to its weapons inventory the small anti-personnel bomb – a sinister item nicknamed the 'butterfly' bomb by the British since it contained small metal 'wings' which opened after release by canister, this enabling the bomb to flutter to earth rather like a winged seed pod. It was a cylinder measuring only 3 × 3.5 inches and weighing 4.4 lb, and, typically, one canister could hold 108 of these bombs, which were deposited on civilian targets as a terror weapon. Some of the bombs were set to explode thirty minutes after impact, or when touched. As a result, when such bombs fell on Grimsby they caused 163 casualties and many thousands of man-hours were spent searching for them.

Like the RAF, the Luftwaffe also used 'Window', calling it '*Düppel*', that is, metal foil strips used to confuse the enemy's radar system. Interestingly enough, the Germans name for this item in the air war was derived from a little town in Denmark where examples of the RAF version were first discovered. But the Luftwaffe's technical innovations were as nothing compared to those coming into use by the RAF, as shown by some of the 'larger' scale attacks made on Britain in this period. When thirty bombers tried to raid Norwich they were so shaken by gunfire that all their loads fell outside the city. And when a mere twenty bombers raided London four were destroyed and little damage done.

However, advanced ideas were progressing in Germany, and the first radio-controlled bombs were used by the Luftwaffe in the Mediterranean against the defecting Italian Fleet, the battleship *Roma* being struck and sunk while en route to Malta. But later, when the Luftwaffe tried to attack British warships, such as the battleship *King George V* moored in Plymouth harbour, they were foiled by weather and smokescreens.

But, if a few German bombers were risked to roam over Britain by night, by day the Luftwaffe posed a further small but in some ways more serious problem. Again, purely as reprisal and on a very small-scale, fighter-bomber units were organised near the continental coast to make what became known through the British media as 'tip-and-run' raids (the Americans dubbed them 'hit-and-run'). The main weapon in these pinpricks was the formidable Focke-Wulf 190 fighter, first encountered by RAF Fighter Command over the Channel and France in mid-1941. The type at once outclassed the current Spitfire, the Mk V, and it took some while for Vickers Supermarine to bring out the Mk 9 Spitfire which could match the deadly new Focke-Wulf on equal terms. Even so, the new German fighter was a menace, as exampled by the great air battle which took place over the Channel during the Dieppe raid (16 August 1942) when over 90 RAF planes were lost.

As will be seen, the problem with catching the FW190 as a fighter-bomber was not easily solved.

Herman Kanzler was one of these pilots in 1943, having been called up the year before and after the usual recruit training achieving his wish, he was assessed as suitable for training as a fighter pilot. Following his initial flying training and qualification as a pilot he was sent straight to another school to learn the ropes on a Focke-Wulf 190 where the ground and air training was thorough:

'*By that time the Luftwaffe was building up its fighter force as defence against Allied air attacks, in the West and of course in Germany itself. But when I joined a unit in France as a novice early in 1943 I was assigned at once to a fighter-bomber squadron and told to prepare myself for raids on England. I had received no training at all in that kind of thing, only as a pilot for air combat, so I was surprised and very disappointed. But the other pilots told me that there could be opportunities to fight though our task was to avoid interception by the Tommies or Yankees.*

'*So after a few initiation flights using dummy bombs over a range I was ordered to undertake my first mission in a FW fighter-bomber, which was very fast and once free of its bomb load well able to take care of itself in a dogfight. At the briefing we were shown a map of south-east England and told that because of the Allied and especially RAF attacks on civilians in Germany we had to retaliate, which was why it was our duty to hit the British as best we could in short, sharp raids that would cause them great nuisance. In view of the fact that the assigned targets were coastal towns with no mention of military targets it was obvious to me at once that this was a purely revenge attack.*

'*The CO pointed out the various towns dotted along the English coastline – Dover, Folkestone, Hastings, Eastbourne etc, and remarked that there were few heavy flak guns but a number of 40mm cannons which might cause problems. Because of our speed we would be over the target for seconds only and then make a low level, weaving escape. I realised that all this was very routine to the old hands of the unit. One of them, a Sergeant, told me to stick close to him and to watch out for RAF fighters which were quick off the mark, but we should be able to get away before they could catch us. It all sounded very unsatisfactory to me and obviously the whole intention was to drop my single bomb on some houses or whatever and flee without offering combat at all.*

'*I did a little calculating of my own and reckoned that we would have fuel in plenty to do a little mixing with the RAF, if they appeared. But my new mentor the Sergeant seemed to guess what was in my mind and warned me that I must follow orders as the CO was very strict on that point.*

'*Our base was just outside Abbeville and we took off one morning just after ten o'clock, twelve strong, and set off at once across the Channel at about 100 feet in order to try and avoid radar and arrive undetected off the English coast. It was spring, but the weather was not too good, quite chilly outside though I was already sweating in my cockpit, partly from nerves but also from the heat of the great BMW engine in front of me, which although powerful was very noisy. We flew at about 370 mph, close to our limit, and knew that we would arrive in a very few minutes, our intention to arrive off the English coast and allow conditions to dictate targets. If we saw any ships in a harbour all to the good, our formation leader would waggle his wings and make his intentions clear. Above all we had to maintain radio silence as we knew the enemy listened in constantly.*

'*It seemed no time at all until I saw our leader waggling his wings, the first signal to change formation so we moved into pairs. Then I saw a grey line in the mist which soon changed into white cliffs and my heart thumped with excitement and apprehension. I felt sure the British must have spotted us, and sure enough a line of fiery red balls came zooming out over the sea, just as our leader waggled his wings again and we dropped into line abreast formation. I was so busy concentrating on my flying that I had no time to watch this new phenomena of light flak, coloured lines that streamed after us, and then puffs of smoke near us. Then we were turning at great speed alongside the cliffs themselves and ahead of us I saw buildings in a kind of blur and made ready to drop my bomb. I had been warned that very quick reactions were necessary and that I must watch my leader and of course the altimeter – it was easy to misjudge and crash into the sea at low level.*

'In a few more seconds the planes ahead of me were jinking madly, some of them zooming up and down as a whole screen of coloured lines whipped up and then among us. I saw a mad whirl of buildings on a seafront and then my leader was turning away. There was a bright flash to the right as a bomb exploded, and then I had let go my own load and kicked the rudder pedals to skid the plane to the left, close behind my Sergeant friend.

'I then heard loud thumps and bangs and we were shooting over the sea at an even lower level and I saw a trail of smoke issuing from one of the Focke-Wulfs ahead. Behind me were two more of my new comrades and one of them flew up beside me and pointed to the rear of my plane. I did not know what he meant and tried to look round, but at that low altitude it was too dangerous to take my eyes away from my course. One slip and it would all be over. We flew back with no more trouble and landed, and then I discovered a large hole in my tail fin, which, however, did not extend into my rudder so the plane's flying had not been affected.

'That trip was the first of many I did with that unit, every one highly dangerous, especially one I recall.

'The first target I learned had been Folkestone, the next was Brighton and this took a little longer to reach. We were probably expected because we arrived off the coast further to the east and followed the cliffs to our target. The flak was intense and I tried to sink into my seat as we swept on towards the town. And as we dropped our bombs on seafront houses I caught a glimpse of several dark shapes racing over the town and at once one of my comrades shouted "Fighters!"

'They were Typhoons and as we turned away over the sea at very low level I sensed that these very fast machines were on our tails. We split up all over the sky to try and make it harder for the Tommies. Then I heard the sharp rattle and bang of cannon fire behind us and then a terrible sight took my breath away as a Focke-Wulf behind came hurtling past at an even greater speed and enveloped in flames. I could see the pilot struggling to get out but in

a second his plane had crashed into the sea in a great cloud of spray and smoke.

'On that day we regained our base with only the one loss, but soon afterwards one of my comrades, who I had come to know quite well, was shot down by flak.

'We had bombed Eastbourne, which looked a very nice town from the glimpse I had of it, and as we turned away I saw the usual flak bursts and lines of tracer following us, and then one of our planes pulled up in a steep climb with smoke billowing from its engine. It had almost disappeared into the low clouds when the hood fell away and the pilot fell out. But he must have been wounded, or else struck the tailplane as no parachute opened. Both he and the plane fell into the sea.

'After some months of these futile attacks I requested a transfer to a combat unit, and this was granted.'

To try and counter these low flyers who brought only casualties to civilians, sometimes machine-gunning promenades, the RAF put Typhoon and a special new Spitfire squadron on permanent standby, with pilots at readiness in their cockpits throughout the hours of daylight on a shift rota. As soon as word of incoming raiders came the fighters were scrambled and roared off at low level and maximum boost to give chase or hopefully intercept the Germans. The Typhoon was able to overtake the Focke-Wulf by its superior speed and one good burst from its four 20mm cannon was usually enough to destroy a raider. The other fighter used and introduced specially to combat the FWs was the Griffon-powered Spitfire Mk 12, which likewise had the speed to catch the raiders if scrambled in time.

Rudolf Sendtler was another FW190 pilot in this period who made similar raids on England's south coast as well as on London:

'These attacks were purely of a nuisance and reprisal value and of no military significance at all. Our orders were simple – to go in fast, drop the bombs and get away before the Tommies could catch us.

'On one occasion we swept along the south-east coast until we reached Eastbourne and then saw some Spitfires which were on to us before we could drop our bombs. This was a very dangerous situation for us so we jettisoned our bombs into the sea and were forced to fight as we tried to escape over the Channel. The atmosphere was misty and the coastline vanished as soon as combat was joined at quite a low level.

'I had never been in such an action before and although I had trained as a fighter pilot my only experience had been in a fighter-bomber unit. In fact, until that day I had never seen an enemy fighter, except those that flew over our base or were shot down nearby. So I was in considerable excitement and terror as we weaved this way and that. The Spits were very fast and manoeuvrable and had clipped wings. One of these fastened on my tail and though I tried to escape I failed. He fired his guns every so often and at such moments I thought it was

the end, but the smokey streams of tracers missed and I thought my best chance of escape lay in zooming to almost sea level. Some of our machines had been shot down or damaged and I saw one Spit go into the sea.

'But my pursuer would not give up and all at once I felt a horrible bang on my rear fuselage and a sudden loss of control, but when I glanced round the Spit had banked away. I knew I had been damaged and seriously as the plane was vibrating badly and would not climb. I was only a few metres above the grey waves and became very alarmed, but I felt if only the plane would stay in the air a few more minutes I would be over friendly territory and could put down anywhere.

'However, the FW seemed reluctant to climb even a few feet so I had visions of my striking the French cliffs. I saw the coast before me and hoped I would not be fired on by our own flak. There was no sign of my comrades.

'I saw the French coast loom up before me and managed to sideslip as the plane was too low to get over them, and I saw only one chance, which was to land on the beach. Otherwise I could try to fly alongside the cliffs until I reached some point where I could cut inland and put down in a suitable field. But all such ideas were dispelled as the FW began to shudder and fell even lower, so I tightened my straps, said a prayer, and braced myself to hit the beach above the obstacles that the army had constructed to deter Allied landings. I lowered my flaps to the full, shut off the engine and hoped for the best.

'I was unable to check my speed sufficiently before the plane's belly struck the beach, the machine bounced along, scraping the sand and stones with a terrible noise and I saw my right wing fly off as it hit a bump. Then I had crunched to a halt. I threw off my straps, jettisoned the canopy and leapt out. The plane was smoking and then my legs buckled under me, so I rolled over the sand and struggled clear, and saw that the plane's tail had been shot away.

'In a few minutes some soldiers came running along the beach and helped me up. The FW did not catch fire but was a wreck. I had somehow sprained my ankle getting out of the plane and as a result was off flying for two weeks.'

It is not inappropriate to remind ourselves at this point that the once most powerful air force in the world, which had been conceived and developed solely as part of a blitz battlefield juggernaut, had, in the West at least by the mid-war years, been reduced to making tiny sneak attacks on genteel English spa towns (even Cheltenham), and to knocking down a few seaside dwellings – such as at Hastings, with some fighter-bomber pilots using cannon and machine-guns to spray the promenades. The Luftwaffe seemed incapable of dealing any kind of effective riposte to the ever-increasing Allied air attacks, and the only really new equipment it received in the Western air

war in this period was the Messerschmitt 210 and its derivative
the 410.

Peter Mahlen piloted one of these machines to England after serving
as a night fighter pilot:

'Several Me 210s were sent to us for evaluation: they were quite
good, certainly faster than the 110 which I had flown, but not without
faults. I never flew one of these early models, though I examined them
and sat in the cockpit. I continued to fly the Me 110 and scored two
victories – a Wellington and a Lancaster. I was then invited to join one
of the new schnellkampf, fast fighter-bomber units equipped with the
improved Me 410, though it was of limited use and was never produced
in large quantities. The new unit was put together specifically for raids
on England, and I agreed to this change for various reasons. First, it
would give me a chance to fly by day, and secondly I did, I'm afraid,
have reason to seek revenge on the British as my lady friend had been
killed in an air raid.

'So about a dozen planes were assembled in this new SKB squadron
with a few in reserve and we made a few low level practice flights from
our base in Belgium, carrying bombs and attacking small targets on
the sea, but to little purpose as the type of raid planned was intended
to knock down buildings. It was October 1943 when we were briefed
for our first attack which would be on Dover, and if we saw any ships
we would bomb them, we were given latitude in these raids.

'We took off in loose formation, headed directly north at very low
level, then turned west towards Dover. I carried an Observer behind me
in the cabin whose job it was to report on any RAF fighters, bomb bursts
and anything else of interest. When we were a mile off the English coast
we went into line ahead formation and I made ready. I was excited and
felt I would hit the enemy in some way and do something worthwhile to
avenge the death of my lady friend. It was a naïve and simple thought,
but I was a rather uncomplicated type of young man.

'We raced straight at Dover harbour and at once saw the coloured
balls of light flak, which were at first behind us and then ahead, and
by then we were running in at great speed over the harbour and I had a
brief glimpse of a few small boats and a steamer, people running along
a wall and flashes from flak guns. Then there were multiple explosions
as our bombs went down, some among the boats, others on the harbour
wall and buildings nearby. I had to make a violent swing to avoid one
of my comrades as he changed course and then we were over the sea
again and my observer Franz reported bomb bursts all over the place.

'In a moment the flak had lessened and we were racing back to
base in a sweat and relief. It had been but a few seconds of high
tension and excitement and I felt we had done our job. A little later
we made a number of night attacks and in these we flew individually
or in pairs though we did become separated over the sea. I tried to

attack the airfield at Hawkinge one night but the landscape was totally blacked out and I could see nothing. The flak came up so we returned to the coast and bombed an unidentified town. These raids were very haphazard, achieved nothing and cost us some aircraft.'

Relics of these tip-and-run raids remained in England, a piece of one Focke-Wulf which went into the sea off Eastbourne now resides in the town's war museum.

There were still a few veterans among the Luftwaffe's airmen on the Channel Front, but even these succumbed to the hugely, near impregnable British defences in the second half of the war.

Richard Pahl made his first solo flight in 1940 and by the time Operation *Barbarossa* began he had been promoted to Lieutenant and flew a Junkers 88 in Russia where he received many decorations including the German Cross and a special prize from the *Reichsmarschall*. Pahl was wounded three times, shot through the lungs and barely survived. After months in hospital he returned to active service, this time with the Ju 88 *Edelweiss* unit in France, but transferred to the Me 410 SKB squadron. On 16 April 1944 he wrote a farewell letter to his family, having a presentiment of his imminent death, and during the night of 18–19th was shot down and killed by a Mosquito night-fighter, his plane crashing on Brighton cemetery. This was during the last gasp of the Luftwaffe's 'Baby Blitz' of 1944, more on this will be covered shortly.

During 1943–44 the Luftwaffe copied the RAF tactic of trying to intercept enemy bombers over their own bases, a ploy which held great promise and if carried out on a greater scale might have brought very considerable difficulties to Bomber Command. Among the aircraft types used by the Germans was the night-fighter derivative of the Dornier 17 bomber – the Do 17N night-fighter. Rudolf Zimmerman piloted one of these machines during night intruder sorties:

'This Dornier was just coming into service in the summer of 1943 to help combat the great and growing British night bomber attacks. I had been in an Me 110 night-fighter unit and after a spell of success I was invited to transfer to this new Dornier squadron and I accepted. I left behind my old comrade and gunner in the Me but found two more friends to fly with me in the Dornier, one of whom would reload the nose cannon. The plane was an adaption of the old bomber with cannon and machine-guns concentrated in "solid" nose.

'I did a simple conversion course. The great advantage of this new plane was its radar, which although primitive by later standards was of considerable use when it worked properly in night interception. However, my CO told me that he planned to use the type not only over the Reich but also over England too. He pointed out that the RAF bombers were extremely vulnerable over their own bases both on take-off and when returning from raids. The best plan was to get among the bombers as

they flew back over the North Sea and follow them back to their bases. We had the fuel to do this and remain over the enemy bases for a while. I was perfectly willing to do this experiment, even though I had never flown a larger plane to England or in fact the Me 110, though I had trained as an escort fighter before switching to the night-fighter role when my few successes were achieved over Holland.

'Soon one evening we were standing in the ready room listening to the running commentary on an RAF raid on the Ruhr. We were stationed at Gilze-Rijn, which also housed Me 110s and a few Ju 88s, all night-fighters. Then my CO came in and told me to take my crew to the plane for take-off as the enemy bombers were now heading back across the North Sea. So we climbed into the Dornier and in a few minutes had taken off, reached the sea and begun to search for the enemy. Then we saw the exhaust glows of many aircraft scattered above us, so we continued climbing into their course, which was north-west at first and then west. After a while we were at the same height as the Tommies, which now showed as pinpricks of red light (from their engine exhausts) as they began descending into what they assumed to be friendly sky.

'Although we knew we might encounter enemy night-fighters we felt safe in the bomber stream, though of course they had come from a number of different bases so were now tending to spread out as they made for them. So I decided to select one bomber and follow it and see what happened. Fortunately, the sky was free of cloud but quite dark.

'Within half an hour we had reached the English coast and dropped to a much lower altitude as we followed the four-engined type which was not yet identifiable as it made for its base. My crew pointed out several other bombers at various distances, these also just visible by their engine glow. Now I concentrated my sight on the bomber ahead as it began a wide turn over a beacon which was flashing a letter below us. The enemy crew suspected nothing and continued their almost gliding descent towards their base. Then our radio operator told me he had managed to tune in to the enemy wavelengths, the ether was full of messages as the bomber crews requested permission to land.

'I told my crew to stand by as we closed in on the still unidentified plane ahead, concentrating on the four pairs of lights from its exhausts. Then I could just make out the great shape of the monster and at once set my sights and made to fire. In a second or two the cannon and machine-guns roared and a tremendous light filled the air before us. The tracers lit up a Lancaster which took the full force of my fire in its tail. There was a great glowing cloud of smoke and sparks and the entire tail assembly of the Lanc fell off. The plane bucked over sideways and went straight down, flames shooting from its engines. I banked away, climbing, and thought the plane would somehow recover, bit it didn't and went straight into the ground, causing a tremendous flash below us. Obviously, the people on the ground and other crews

for miles around must have been alerted. We had scored a victory and felt elated, though sorry for the airmen shot down who must have been tired after their long flight. But we had to steel ourselves, this was war and these same boys had killed too many civilians in our country.

'So I banked the plane around the sky, looking for fresh targets, and soon saw another set of exhausts pulling away from me to the north. Our fuel state was still satisfactory so I gave chase at top speed. I had no idea if the Tommies had seen us but I dropped down to come up below them. The enemy was flying straight and level and as I neared them I hauled up the nose of our Dornier and opened fire. The blaze of light and tracers lit up a Halifax which blew up at once in a tremendous cloud of flame as its fuel tanks were hit. I pulled away violently, but even so bits of flaming debris fell all round us and I thought we must be damaged. Some of the pieces were very large and fluttering earthwards as I dived to the east. We reached the sea again and reached our base without incident.'

The Germans' attempts to belatedly develop a four-engined heavy bomber is a story in itself. The Focke-Wulf Condor was an adaption from a pre-war civil type, and used on a small scale to prey on Atlantic shipping, it was never intended to be a strategic bomber for use over Britain. So by painful experimentation the Luftwaffe used the Heinkel 177. It would be difficult to find any warplane of the period which suffered more development problems and which proved less popular with aircrews.

General Wever was something of a lone voice in the mid-1930s when the Luftwaffe was still in its own formative stage; he insisted that the air force needed a strategic bomber, and since his opinions carried some weight a specification was issued by the Reich Air Ministry calling for such a plane. From this came the Dornier 19, the Junkers 89 and the Heinkel 177. The first two types proved unsatisfactory, and following the death of General Wever in an air crash his fellow planners scratched the Heinkel, preferring to concentrate on medium-range aircraft to support the army which as explained was within the doctrines already laid down.

The harsh lessons learned in the Battle of Britain when the bomber types produced found themselves at the mercy of RAF fighters led in part to the resurrection of the Heinkel 177 concept, and the real problems began. A number of errors, partly resulting from a change in the RLM specification brought about by techical difficulties. The Luftwaffe was obsessed with the dive-bombing mode of operation, so even this large bomber was deemed to need a dive capability of sixty degrees. This led to a conventional aircraft but with four engines coupled in pairs, and this arrangement led to the worst problems encountered with the type, not the least being the lives and machines lost and of course the cost. Propeller shaft vibration and fires were common, the latter usually caused by the lack of firewalls fitted behind the engines so that a fire could spread unhindered to the wing spar and fuel lines.

The V1 prototype crashed and was destroyed by fire in April 1940. The V2 disintegrated during diving tests in June, while the V3, which was being tested for Lufthansa, also crashed in April. The V4 fell into the Baltic following a propeller gear failure. The V7 reached an operational unit for testing but proved a failure also, and in May 1942 the V8 suffered a disastrous fire in both engines which cost the crew their lives.

Despite all this, a series of pre-production aircraft were produced, but no less than seven of these machines crashed through various causes, with the death of seventeen test crewmen. From the many flight tests, 170 major and 1,395 minor modifications were made on the plane, and a few better characteristics led to the bomber finally being put into production. Yet problems continued, and this situation led General Udet to call a halt to further production until the bugs were ironed out. But as soon as Udet committed suicide production resumed, several different versions were planned, and other firms were co-opted to help in producing the machine, with Arado turning out 130 of the A1 version. But the crashes continued, with nineteen of the Arado-built Heinkels being lost, most due to power plant seizures due to poor lubrication. The Rechlin test centre discovered fifty-six causes for engine fires. Yet, amazingly, the few reports received from Luftwaffe crews who managed to operate the plane were quite favourable.

This was the sorry tale of bad design and inadvisable persistence with this aircraft before Karl Richter took to the air in one and engaged in one of the very first operations over England.

'It was still very much in the experimental stage and was first used for high level reconnaissance and then small raids over England. In the summer of 1943 I made a reconnaissance sortie with a full crew over England. We did not want the type to fall into British hands, which seemed a possibility owing to its manifold faults. The Command felt that a malfunction of the troublesome engines could entail a forced landing in enemy territory, which would not be advisable for the crew but in the eyes of the higher-ups would be disastrous as the plane was still secret.

'We took off from Amsterdam airfield and climbed in wide spirals overland until we had reached about 18,000 ft and still climbing as we set course over the sea, our target was the Midlands arms factories. We had three high-resolution cameras fitted and one of my crew had a cine camera which was his prized personal possession. What he hoped to film I didn't know as there would not be much to see – unless we encountered enemy planes, and then we would be much too busy as in trouble with no time for film-making.

'I believe we crossed the English coast at almost 30,000 ft, heading

*inland and fully aware that the enemy were watching our progress. The
Heinkel refused to climb any higher, this was not good as I felt there
would be some kind of fighter which could reach us. The weather was fine
with only a little scattered cloud and ideal for our purpose. My captain
and navigator plotted our course for Rugby, which we would photograph
before passing on to Birmingham and then perhaps Manchester, or if we
saw any Allied air bases we would photograph them also, though these
were not of prime interest to us.*

*'In about thirty minutes we changed course and began our first run-up
over the photo target. So far we had seen no sign of enemy reaction, but
then as we passed high over Derby the first white puffs of flak appeared
well below us. This surprised me as they were so inaccurate, but then
more bursts appeared behind us and I felt they would soon have the
range. The bursts would also act as a guide to any enemy fighters.
And then as we made for Birmingham one of our gunners reported the
start of a contrail a little below us at about five miles range. This was
not good and I tried to coax the Heinkel to climb higher, but it refused
so I gritted my teeth and hoped for the best.*

*'In a few minutes we were about to make our run over Birmingham,
with the enemy plane still below us but gaining. He may have been
trying to catch us by surprise from below. Well, we made our photo
run and as the Heinkel had good speed I turned away and put on full
boost, racing for the sea again at at least 350 mph.*

*'At this point the other plane's contrail seemed to vanish, as if it had
perhaps given up and dived away. Nevertheless, we stayed very alert all
the way to the coast, but apart from a few flak bursts as we crossed out
at some 20,000 ft we saw no more sign of that enemy plane.'*

A few days later the same crew again visited Birmingham – but this
time carrying two 2,200lb bombs: 'They made impressive explosions.'
Pilot Richter took his Heinkel home via the south coast of England,
just in case the RAF were waiting for them to the east, and saw no
interceptors at all.

The venerable Me 109 was not entirely eclipsed by the FW 190 in the
Channel battle, even joining in the tip-and-run raids, as Rolf Neumann
relates:

*'I flew a 109G which for a short time I used as a fighter-bomber, the
intention on the raid I will describe was to try and catch enemy planes
on the ground in south-east England, but it did not work out at all.*

*'In our first briefing the CO pointed out the various RAF airfields
and told us that a surprise raid should prove profitable. We had our
doubts but climbed into our planes which carried a single 500 lb
fragmentation bomb under their bellies which would prove useful
against parked aircraft. We took off from Calais-Marck and flew
over the Channel, direction north-east, intending to sweep west over
southern England and bomb the first airfield we saw. We had no need*

of maps as our leader was very experienced and had often flown over the area.

'No sooner had we turned left and raced over the English coastline than someone shouted "Fighters!" and we began looking this way and that, wondering where they were and if we should jettison our bombs. Then our leader waggled his wings so we guessed he had seen a target ahead; in fact it proved to be Manston.

'Then the flak tracer came up at us from all directions and I saw one of our planes turn away and suddenly vanish in a cloud of smoke. Then I saw a runway right in front of me and we were racing over an RAF field in open formation, firing our guns and dropping the bombs. I saw a hangar already going up in smoke so pulled up a little and released my bomb, at the same time pressing the firing button and sending a stream of lead into the hangar roof. I had not seen a single plane on the ground, but was so busy flying the plane I did not have time to look around the field.

'Then we were speeding south again, and at last the reported RAF fighters appeared from our rear quarter and we at once opened our throttles to full boost. But the Spits caught us up as we changed course and one more of our Mes was hit and went straight into the sea. I was in great fright as I tried to get down even lower and yet jink the plane, and then a great gout of splashes went up over the sea in front of me as one of the Spits fastened on my tail. I felt sure I would fly straight into this line of fire – but it didn't happen. The Spits gave up and we reached our base without further loss.'

This attack was an exception in the general rule of Luftwaffe tip-and-run raids, being partly successful, though Manston had on occasion taken greater damage. The base, being situated on the north-east tip of Kent, was used as an emergency landing field by all types of aircraft including four-engined bombers and on occasional mornings could be seen crowded with planes scattered into every corner.

Only rarely did the Focke-Wulfs penetrate further inland, such as on the late afternoon of 31 October 1942 when thirty Focke-Wulf fighter-bombers delivered a low level attack on Canterbury, these were escorted by a similar number of fighters in close escort and with more behind. The German planes took only three minutes to reach their target city from the coast, and twenty-eight bombs landed in and around the town, killing thirty people and injuring forty-eight. Despite the great speed of these events RAF fighters and the flak defences were able to bring down three of the attackers, while at Canterbury itself 'Z' or rocket batteries had been in action, the smoke trails left by the missiles making a criss-cross mesh in the sky which appeared to one German pilot as wire fencing.

It may seem strange that the Luftwaffe would commit such a comparatively large force of planes to hit a cathedral city and for such paltry results, but that was the state of play when the fighter-bomber units in the West were ordered to carry out reprisal attacks. As for the heavier bomber squadrons, their night efforts were usually even less effective, especially now that the British had begun operating radar-controlled guns and searchlights. On the same night as the raid mentioned, twin-engined German bombers tried a follow-up attack on the same target, causing little damage and only nine casualties. As an aside, and this was unique, Germans stationed on the clifftop at Cap Gris Nez took infra-red photographs of the daylight raid on Canterbury, using a telescopic lens. One picture shows smoke rising from the city, barrage balloons and radar towers on the white cliffs of Dover.

The total casualties caused by German air raids in 1942 were 2,326 killed and 4,148 injured, a figure only one-fifth of the previous year. But tragedies there were, small incidents which bred hatred for the enemy, such as a more daring raid by twenty-eight Focke-Wulfs on 20 January 1943 aimed at London.

This was the first attempt at the capital by a sizeable force since 1940, and by a series of mischances the true nature of the attack was not realised by the defenders, especially as some of the raiders split off and headed for Maidstone in Kent. The rest raced on to London at low level, to find the balloon barrage on the ground: eight bombs fell on Lewisham, two on Poplar and twelve on Deptford, Bermondsey and Greenwich. At Lewisham a school was struck, and since the defences had been caught napping the children had not had time to reach shelter. Thirty-nine children and five teachers were killed, sixty were seriously injured. According to one British periodical published soon afterwards, one of the Luftwaffe airmen, a Captain Stuhmann, had broadcast his version of the raid over Berlin radio, stating: 'We dropped our bombs where they were to be dropped.'

CHAPTER ELEVEN

THE 'BABY BLITZ'

B y January 1943 the Luftwaffe's heavy bomber force in the West comprised only some sixty of the latest Dorniers (217K and M versions), plus a similar number of Junkers 88s, these were usually the A14 type, soon to be superseded by the 188 and later 288 with streamlined nose like the Dornier. These planes comprised KG2 and KG6, and it was these groups which, on 17 January, had carried out the heaviest attack on London, since the great raid of 10 May 1941.

But by the end of 1943 Göring's own stock had fallen dramatically, both as 'economic Führer' of the Third Reich and leader of the once all-powerful Luftwaffe. As a driving force and organiser of German war industry he had proved a failure, and his boasts of the early war period resulted in him becoming a joke. A measure of the Luftwaffe chief's failure in the West can be seen in some figures produced by Winston Churchill's scientific adviser Lord Cherwell in this period concerning German air attacks on Britain:

- On average the Luftwaffe had sent its bombers to raid Britain only once in eighteen days.
- Only four-fifths of those enemy planes crossing the British coast actually bombed.
- One bomber in eleven was destroyed.
- Therefore: the Luftwaffe was using one bomber and four aircrew to drop one ton of bombs in order to kill one Britisher, while every five persons killed on the ground cost the Germans two airmen.
- Finally: for every fire raised by the German bombers some thirty resulted through routine human causes.

But by December 1943 Göbbels was able to record in his diary that his rival Göring had been routed out of his luxury home at Karinhall and despatched by the Führer to the West to organise a large-scale reprisal attack on Britain. In fact, Göring summoned his bomber chiefs to a conference in Berlin to appraise them of Operation *Steinbock* (Ibex).

Göring told his audience that he had promised Hitler that the first attack wave of bombers would begin operations in two weeks. Yet, as a measure of the Luftwaffe's weakness, once more the aircrews would be called upon to fly double night missions in order to make up the prescribed weight of attack. This was a daunting prospect for the young airmen in face of the hugely improved enemy defences; the 'milk run' days of 1940 had long gone. What remained of the German bomber force in the West was about to be sacrificed in a futile gesture.

Yet the Nazi leaders had great hopes of *Steinbock*, especially as the Luftwaffe now fielded an increasing number of the new Heinkel 177s, its predecessor the ageing He 111 being all but demoted to second-line duties, though it would enjoy a small new lease of life carrying V1 robot bombs to England. The two groups of He 177s could use two 5,500 lb bombs per plane, these missiles containing the special new 'England mix', a more powerful explosive comprising Trialen and Hexagon. The Germans had also developed a new radio guidance system called Egon, similar to the British Oboe, employing two transmitter stations which required the bomber to fly a semi-circular course. The German system was supposed to guarantee an accuracy of three degrees at a range of 170 miles. In addition, extra guidance was supposed to be gained by tuning in to the British Gee radar sets carried in bombers. The war of technology was continuous, the Germans having suffered a serious setback when one of their Junkers 88 night-fighters equipped with the latest radar landed by error at RAF Woodbridge in Suffolk, the crew allegedly believing it to be the base at Venlo in Holland. This event would be surpassed much later by the disclosure of another Junkers 88 whose crew defected with their radar-fighter from Denmark at the supposed instigation of the British Secret Service, the plane being met and escorted to an RAF base in Scotland by Spitfires and subsequently seen at various public displays in post-war years.

The new wave of raids on London and a few other localities would be under the command of Colonel Peltz, now called *Angriffsführer England*, his task being to co-ordinate the raids but with little in hand to carry them out. His first move was to organise a new pathfinder group, KG66, but his own plan to bomb selected military targets was frustrated by the Führer Order which stipulated reprisal raids on British cities.

The two veterans Karl Haulmeier and Horst Juventus were both involved in the so-called 'Baby Blitz' of early 1944. The former recalls that:

'We received reinforcements for this heavier assault which did not go well for us owing to the heavy defences over Britain.'

Juventus also provides comments on the events:

'We were told that a reprisal bomber offensive was to be launched against Britain, principally against London. A few more crews arrived with planes from the training schools, and we were told by Peltz to do our utmost whatever the difficulties, for the honour of the Luftwaffe was at stake. It seemed a very dubious proposition, but I believe we were as prone as anyone in our desire to hit back at the British for their terrible raids on our cities which were doing a very great deal of damage to the war economy, apart from the civilian population.

'When we flew the first attacks early in 1944 we soon learned what we were up against, for by then the British had perfected their defences with many radar-assisted night-fighters and ample flak batteries including rockets. We crossed over the Thames in a great barrage which forced us higher and into taking evasive action, it was by far the worst flak we had ever seen and gave us great problems until we were over the city itself and able to identify the dock area where we were told there would be supplies massed for the projected invasion. I must say that by that time many German airmen had but one thought which was to drop their bombs anywhere on English cities, and in some small way pay back the enemy for his attacks on Germany. So, inevitably the bombs went down all over the place, but partly as a result of the enemy flak. And as soon as we were clear of the target area we saw several combats, with bright bursts of tracer followed by a plane going down in flames to crash on the ground below. Then we ourselves were followed by a night fighter, which one of our gunners saw silhouetted against the glare of searchlights for a moment. I dived the plane and opened the throttles as we made for the coast at full speed.'

Juventus was one of the few still flying Heinkels it seems:

'But the fighter was faster and soon closing within firing range. Some instinct made me swerve the Heinkel to the left just as a great burst of tracer fire swept past us. I dived the plane steeply, hoping the enemy fighter would lose us, but of course they had the cursed eyes of radar and our gunners saw the fighter's exhausts following us.

'But then we were saved by a miracle, though not one that was good for another German crew. The fighter was diverted from us as the crew saw another of our bombers trying to reach the coast and opened fire on it. There was a large whoosh of bright flame and then debris falling to earth. This saved us and we flew back over the Channel in peace.'

A German bomber struck by the fire from the four 20mm cannon and four machine-guns of a Mosquito stood no chance.

Juventus states that the raids continued over the following weeks of 1944.

'But our losses grew so that the bomber force was whittled away and without any real gain. We saw two more of our planes go down in that time, one of them over London itself, the other over the Channel. By then I had reached the rank of Captain and received the Iron Cross, which was almost a routine formality for long service. I had been flying for years and felt worn out, and when I went home on leave to devastated Berlin my poor parents looked on me with anxiety. Yet they had suffered most, whole areas of their district had vanished and their apartment block was almost isolated. My morale suffered accordingly and I longed for the war to end.'

The former Luftwaffe Commander West, Hugo Sperrle, had been relieved and gone into retirement, his successor, newly promoted General Peltz, had been pessimistic from the start of his tenure, and soon found this attitude justified. His grand assault was first postponed from December 1943 and began on the evening of 21 January 1944 when 227 bombers set out across the Channel dispensing Düppel as they went. The bomber stream crossed the coast between Hastings and Folkestone, being harassed by the defences all the way; of 245 'incidents' reported on the ground, no less than 201 occurred outside the London area – in Kent, Sussex and Essex. Little or no results were obtained in the intended target area, twenty-five bombers were shot down and a further eighteen lost in accidents.

Apart from attempting to raid London, the Luftwaffe force tried to bomb the 'invasion ports' – Torquay, Weymouth and Falmouth included. And when ninety-one bombers raided Bristol in May, of the 83 tons of bombs dropped only a mere 3 tons actually fell on the port. Bristol had, however, suffered greatly over the years, on some occasions the Luftwaffe crews had been bold enough to fly at very low level so that witnesses later reported seeing the crews in their cabins by the light of fires on the ground.

But despite the inauspicious start on 21 January there was no question of giving up the attack on London, though bad weather frustrated the bombers until the 29th when 285 bombers achieved more success, with 345 fires being started in the capital. Yet, in these two raids only one hundred people had been killed; regrettable though it was, that was the best way of determining the enemy's success, damage to the war economy was slight. In the second raid fourteen more bombers were shot down or written off and Hitler, exasperated and sarcastic, referred to the Heinkel 177 as 'a load of rubbish'. These were the last weeks of the Luftwaffe's bomber force in the West, its demise hastened by the removal of its fighter-bomber groups to the Mediterranean theatre. But these planes were used in a new angle dreamt up by Peltz before they left for sunnier climes.

Focke-Wulfs were sent to infiltrate RAF bomber streams returning from Germany – and a fiasco resulted: four of the FWs landed on or near RAF fields in error, a fourth crashed near another base, and two more vanished. All this was due to the German pilots' inexperience in flying night missions and their inability to make proper use of signals from the ground stations in France. The continued use of these small night interlopers was discouraged by RAF night-fighters and the sterling work of No. 80 Wing who jammed every known Luftwaffe frequency. Even a resumption by the Germans of the old *Knickebein* (crooked leg) system using thirty-four channels was foiled.

Yet the Luftwaffe persisted: ten more raids were flown in February with mixed success, that of 18–19th being the worst from the British view when 200 sorties were flown against London which received 140 tons of bombs. The authorities noticed the larger calibre of bombs arriving and the greater areas of blast damage. In these raids the bombers were routed to High Wycombe in Buckinghamshire, making a sharp turn south-east to pass across London, bombing from up to 29,000 ft before entering a shallow dive to escape. In February 961 people were killed and 1,712 injured, the Germans paying for this by the loss of 72 bombers – an absurd proportion. Four more raids were made on London in March before the targets became Hull and Bristol, these two raids were unsuccessful. After a lull the Luftwaffe returned to London on 18 April which proved to be the final manned bomber attack of the war.

By May the Luftwaffe had lost 300 bombers and 1,200 aircrew in Operation *Steinbock*, or 60 per cent of their strength at the start. The aircraft were replaceable, but not the airmen due to the run-down of the bomber crew training programme. When the bomber veteran Hajo Herrmann referred in his memoirs to '20,000 pilots under training' he was certainly not alluding to bomber pilots.

Incredibly, for every five British civilians killed in Operation *Steinbock*, the Luftwaffe lost one bomber and four aircrew, an unsustainable equation. In his original orders, Göring had stipulated that although the operation was 'to avenge the enemy's terror raids', apart from cities, targets could include industrial areas and ports, leaving his staffs to work out details, so in the case of London the dock area around Millwall (code-name *Hamburg*) became the prime target, though in the event and for various reasons bombs were scattered far and wide. However, although the actual results were poor and not really the 'heavy shock' predicted by Göbbels, there is no doubt that the lack of Luftwaffe activity had produced a sense of false security in the British civilian population, so that real shock and even some panic did ensue when the raids began anew in greater strength early in the year.

How then had the troublesome Heinkel 177 fared in this last attack on Britain? Karl-Ludwig Ernst was a pilot in one of the two units involved. Ernst had been conscripted into the Luftwaffe in 1942 following the usual Hitler Youth and Labour Corps training, and soon made known his interest in planes ('the bigger the better') to those above him. Having been assessed he went into pilot training and passed out in due course as capable of handling larger machines. By 1943 he had also learned to pilot old Heinkel 111s, and of course realised how badly the war was going for his country. Fully qualified and proud of his flying certificate and pilot's badge, which were handed out on a big parade, he went home on leave to his shattered city of Hamburg:

'We could not really see the purpose of the air raids on our city even though we knew there were factories there which had been destroyed. My family were fortunate in owning a little bungalow outside the city, but sad to say my girl friend was killed in the huge raids. This was a very bad loss for me and naturally enough I and many of my comrades felt that the British should pay for the destruction of our cities. Despite the razing of Warsaw and Rotterdam it was not our way of doing things, though I must admit we were rather naïve and did not realise that a lot of indiscriminate bombing had been carried out by our Luftwaffe.

'When I returned to my unit near Mannheim we were assembled and told to prepare for a new task. We received travel orders the same day and went off to a specially prepared base fifty miles away where on arrival we learned there were to be two new units equipped with the strange mottled and black camouflaged bombers we saw on the field; these we learned were the new Heinkel 177s we had heard about, the tales we had picked up about them were not too good. After our reception and meal we were shown to new hut barracks and a senior NCO told us to report to an instruction hangar next morning.

'Next day we found a stripped down Heinkel 177 in the hangar and were shown over it. The plane had a very curious engine arrangement consisting of four motors to drive two huge, four-bladed propellers. We thought this very unusual and soon learnt that the scheme had given a lot of trouble, it was far too complicated, but the bombers were in production and there seemed no turning back. So we began ground instruction followed by some taxying trials around the airfield. The engines were very noisy and needed very careful handling. I was very apprehensive of the plane and although I had an instructor at my side I thought if anything should go wrong we would be in serious trouble. After a few days I sat in the cockpit of one of these monsters ready for take-off with the same instructor next to me and a full crew. We carried no bomb load, first I had to learn how to fly the thing.

'I opened up the throttles, released the brakes and away we rolled until we had gained at least 90 mph and began lifting off the runway; I was surprised that the monster took off so easily. Once the great double undercarriage was raised I began making a gentle turn over the field, with the instructor making helpful comments in my ear. After a few moments he told me to try a landing, so this I did, coming in at the minimum recommended speed and touching down quite gently. I was very relieved, the Heinkel seemed quite easy to fly – providing the engines behaved.

'From then on we flew most days, sometimes without a crew who went off for ground instruction; I made long distance flights across Germany, direction south and low to avoid Allied fighters. Then came the first night take-offs. I was very nervous indeed, but the instructor flew with me for the first two or three flights, after which I was on my own. All went fairly smoothly except on one trip when we suffered *a drop in engine power before take-off, so after a delay we changed planes and went off in another Heinkel. We then flew as a squadron but obviously could not operate like that by night, so our training after dark continued. We made dummy sorties on various places in Germany and the occupied territories, occasionally being interrupted in our flight schedule by enemy air raids. But by the end of 1943 we were declared operational and transferred to a base outside Brussels where we learned we would take part in probing flights over England. These would be by individual aircraft and I would be one of the first to go.*

'By then we knew the British defences had greatly improved so we were rather apprehensive. But our flight would be up the East Coast and then inland at about 25,000 ft, flying towards the Midlands and avoiding the London defence zone.

'On that winter evening we wore as much clothing as possible and took off after sunset to be over Britain in the early evening. I set course and we settled down for the long flight. We carried a tail gunner but because of the very cramped position there he only moved into it when we reached the coast of England.

'We flew up over the North Sea until we reckoned by our radio beam signal that we were in position to turn westwards. It was pitch black outside and all we could see was a faint glow from our engine exhausts. Actually, as we reached the enemy coast we did see one or two pinpoints of light, but not a shot was fired at us, so we thought this could mean the British could be directing their fighters on to us. We had a warning device fitted in the plane but were not too sure of its effectiveness.

'After an hour or so we reckoned we had reached our turning point over the Midlands, and so far had seen no sign of any defences, which seemed a little odd. We warned the tail gunner to be especially vigilant as we turned south-east. When we passed the estimated position of London some searchlights sprang to life but some way from us and we decided they were looking for another plane. So we flew on with no problems at all until we reached the sea and picked up our beam signal once more and were able to navigate home again. I landed the plane without difficulty by the light of the briefly illuminated flare path, and before long we were taking hot coffee and rolls.

'Two more crews landed and reported peaceful trips, so we guessed the enemy were not bothering to intercept single raiders, though we knew they had the means to do so. For us it had been a mere training exercise, we had only carried practice bombs to test the plane under operating conditions, and now we wondered what our COs had in store for us.'

Ernst soon found out. Bad weather interrupted flying for a while, but then he flew another sortie over England before learning of Operation *Steinbock*:

'. . . which would soon commence with a greatly reinforced Luftwaffe bomber fleet in the West. We would fly at great height in attacks

co-ordinated with other units including a few old Heinkels but also newer Dorniers and Junkers. On our first raid we carried a heavy load of bombs including one 2,000 lb high explosive plus incendiaries. With this and a full fuel load I felt we were almost overweight, but we managed to get into the air and then kept careful watch for other planes as the fear of collision was always there. We had already seen one disastrous ground accident in which a whole crew was killed. There were many planes in the air that night over a small area so much care was needed. Some had switched on their navigation lights, but I felt this was too risky because of the risk of British intruders.

'We climbed away into the night sky and had reached 25,000 ft over the North Sea, heading for the Thames. Before we reached it we began to see searchlights and flak bursts and then markers released by our own pathfinders marking route beacons in two or three places. We flew over the Thames, intending to come in over London from the north – and this we did.

'But before we turned back towards the centre of the city and the dock area a great storm of flak erupted. We were completely new to it of course and were very frightened and impressed as the streams of fire seemed to be shooting in all directions with many explosions directly over the city. Then we saw the first explosions and fires starting below and were soon ourselves in position to bomb. The flak was very fierce but seemed to be bursting below us so we grew less nervous. I warned the tail and other gunners to be alert for night-fighters and had hardly spoken when I saw a long streak of flame going down to our left as one of our bombers was hit and hurtled earthwards. It was a very sickening sight and shook all of us.

'Our plane leapt upwards as we released our bomb load and our Captain and Observer Heinz told me to get away as fast as possible. So I pushed the stick forward a little and increased speed to the south-east part of the city below and at once we seemed to be surrounded by flak bursts, which was very frightening, and we could hear some of the closer explosions above the noise of our engines. But we soon left this denser zone of fire and sped for the coast in great relief, even though more flak came which seemed to be following us as we sped lower at about 300 mph. Then I saw a faint glimmer of the sea, the last flak burst behind us and we were over the Channel and adjusting our course accordingly. I felt relieved but as we neared the French coast some of our own defences opened fire on us. But we followed the coast until reaching Belgium where we soon found our base and landed unharmed.

'We judged that attack to have been a success, but then had to repeat the process over succeeding nights and found it every bit as wearing and frightening, especially as the flak seemed to get worse and we saw several air combats with night-fighters in action. When we were re-routed and came out north of the Thames it was hair-raising as the flak followed us all the way into the Estuary where a barrage met us head-on and I

*was forced to take swift evasive action. We had several planes put out
of action through splinter damage and engine problems, and heard that
a lot of the smaller types of bomber were being lost in the raids which
decreased in scale over the weeks. But we flew on, though not always
in the same plane for our own machine developed various problems.*

*'Then came the night when two of our machines went missing and I
believe crashed into the sea as their crews were never heard of again. And
on one night we saw a Mosquito chasing another bomber and shooting it
down in a spectacular explosion like thousands of fireworks going off
at the same time. It was not good for our morale.*

*'In these months I had but one leave which did not go too well because
of our low morale and we knew the Allied invasion was near. There was
talk of our bombing the invasion fleet and I believe some units did make
the attempt to bomb Portsmouth and other places of embarkation, but to
no effect. Then the invasion came at last and we heard terrible rumours
of bomber crews being transferred to the infantry, which was frightening.
This did not happen I'm glad to say, and we carried on making individual
raids over England but with ever increasing danger from flak and night
fighters. After one such raid from which we returned safely one of our
bombers crashed on the edge of the field, it burned and all were killed.
Fortunately we had gone to de-briefing and refreshments and did not
witness this event.'*

But a number of Luftwaffe men as well as naval personnel were being
drafted to make new infantry battalions; though the biggest transfers of
men would not take place until later in 1944 when German territory
became threatened with invasion. The very idea of being sent off to
fight as infantry was, of course, worse than anathema to the airmen.
Karl Haulmeier:

*'It seemed madness to us, with the enemy's air effort getting ever
stronger our bomber fleet was being run down to nothing. Of course,
all our production was being concentrated on fighters for defence, and
we could not hit back with those. The promised "revenge" weapons
were, they told us, of great power and would inflict terrible defeats on
the enemy. Of course, this never happened.*

*'When the invasion finally came we made a few sorties over the
beach-head, but the flak was so terrible we stood no chance and lost
some planes. It was really the end of us, yet we were not disbanded and
continued to raid by night.'*

The raids spoken of were not on Britain but the Allied supply centres
etc on the continent. By then the V1 campaign against Britain had begun.
Horst Juventus:

*'We assumed it meant the end of the Luftwaffe's bomber force, and
we were not far wrong. But after a while we were shown how the new
flying bombs could be launched from our bombers and a few crews*

including our own were moved to another base in Holland where we were instructed how to fly a set course over the sea in order to launch the V1 which was attached to the underside of a Heinkel [111]. It was obviously a very indiscriminate weapon and to no good purpose. But we had our orders.

'With the V1 attached the Heinkel's performance was of course weakened. We flew off from Gilze Rijn over the North Sea for some distance before igniting the V1's motor and releasing it. The things could be a positive menace as they did not always fly true, and we felt in great danger with the contraption beneath us. I was sure some crews released them as soon as they were out of sight of land in order to be free of them.'

Karl-Ludwig Ernst heard that his unit might have to re-train to carry the flying bomb, but this never happened:

'There were too many surplus bomber crews anyway. But a new problem came as we ran short of fuel, which meant that our raids became fewer and fewer, and as the Allies advanced we were forced to evacuate our base back into Germany, in fact to a field near Wilhelmshaven from where fresh attacks carrying larger bombs were planned. There was a great deal of indecision, with operations scheduled but cancelled at the last moment, until eventually we could see no point in them at all. Very few crews made any more raids on Britain. I recall my own last flight when we flew across the North Sea, heading for the port of Hull which we bombed from nearly 30,000 ft with a great deal of flak bursting below us. This was in March 1945 and a completely futile gesture. We dived away and beat a hasty retreat before the night-fighters found us.'

It was Ernst's last operation against Britain, his unit transferred East.

Belatedly, German aircraft firms produced a range of four-motor heavy bomber designs, but two factors served to inhibit such developments – the advent of 'wonder weapons' such as missiles, and the jet plane. Apart from the well-known Messerschmitt 262, the world's first and most successful jet fighter of the war (others being the Gloster Meteor and Heinkel 162 *Volksjaeger*), the Luftwaffe operated the first jet bomber – the Arado 234.

Richard Endlass had trained as a bomber pilot and flew operationally in later versions of the Dornier 217. Later in 1944 he was transferred to the Rechlin test centre with three other pilots and shown over some jet aircraft projects:

'By then the Me 262 was operational and enjoying some success, but facing difficulties in other ways owing to Allied bombing and shortage of fuel and trained pilots.

'One of the new machines we saw was the Arado. Of course, jet propulsion was all very new to us so we attended a short course of

instruction on its principles and saw a number of engines in action, some in the planes themselves. We were tremendously impressed and told that Germany was well ahead of the Allies in this respect. Then we learned that a new unit of Arados was being formed on an experimental basis and we were free to join it if we wished. I had a great interest in flying and the technical side so I volunteered at once. Although my experiences over England had been far from enjoyable I was far from being worn out and felt that flying a jet plane would be an amazing new experience. Two of my companions also agreed to join the new unit, but the other declined and so returned to his old base at once.

'We three volunteers were then sent to Warnemunde where we found the new unit had six of the Arado machines which were being evaluated and we were introduced to the manufacturer's representative and two test pilots. The CO told us that various ideas as to make use of the new jet had been put forward: one of them in the reconnaissance role over Britain, another was as a fast, low-level bomber. Well, the first idea appealed to me so I was placed in that category and told that an Observer would be assigned as second crewman.

'But first I had to learn to fly a jet, so we began our ground instruction which lasted about a week and included taxying an Arado round the airfield and learning the various controls. One of the test pilots showed us how to start up the engines, which were very noisy. Soon we entered our flight experience with the test pilot at the controls and this was very exhilarating. The take-off and climbing speed were outstanding, and I thoroughly enjoyed every moment of it. The all-round view from the cockpit was excellent and I felt I would have no problems, and after some practice at handling the controls and engines I was ready to take-off with the test pilot beside me.

'I opened the throttles, adjusted the fuel mixture, released the brakes and the jet began to roll along the runway and was soon thrusting forward at a tremendous speed and take-off came in no time at all. I hauled up the undercarriage and climbed away with no problems and in a very short time had reached 10,000 ft. The instructor then suggested I try a dive down to the sea which was near us and fly for some distance before turning back. The plane responded well and we were soon hurtling over the waves at about 100 ft, the machine was so fast I became nervous in case we went too far from our base, and the instructor told me to do a gentle climbing turn before flying back. This I did and found the controls excellent. There was always the danger of an engine failure – a "flame-out" as they call it in jets – and I wondered how we would cope in such a situation as the Arado had a comparatively small wing area and I felt it would not stay up long with insufficient power. But we reached the field and I managed a touch-down without trouble.

'Our flying training went on for a few days but was then marred by a crash when one of my fellow pupils suffered an engine cut-out in his plane and was killed with the same test pilot who had flown with me.

But this was war and we were used to crashes. I completed my course of instruction with another test pilot, who was a grand fellow and a much decorated bomber pilot.

'Then the CO called us together. By then another volunteer had joined us as a replacement who made excellent progress in his tuition. We learned that an Erprobungsstaffel (experimental squadron) would be sent to Holland, to a base in the north-east not yet menaced by the Allied advance. From there some operational flights would be attempted with the new jet, including, it was hoped, some sorties over England, which interested me. Some of my comrades would attempt the low-level bomber role. So I studied maps of England with my CO and it was decided I would fly a high-level reconnaissance sortie to England, crossing the coast at the Wash and heading for the Midlands. We felt confident that the British defences would not catch us. I was then introduced to my Observer who had never flown in a jet before, so we made a few local flights to let him get the feel of it. And then came the day of our first sortie. I believe this may have been the first by a jet bomber, apart from those with the Me 262 which was then being experimented with in that role.

'It was mid-morning when we took off and climbed away in a north-easterly direction up to 25,000 ft and by then we were leaving a contrail, but we were too fast for any Allied fighter to catch us. I then turned westwards, still climbing, and soon we were above 30,000 ft and doing about 450 mph which was far from our limit (max speed Arado 234 B,460 mph (26,000 ft) and max speed Arado 234 C (4 motors) 542 mph (19,000 ft)). We carried two cameras on board and these were the responsibility of the Observer who had already undertaken such flights over England in piston-engined planes.

'In a very short time we had crossed the North Sea and reached the English coast exactly on track and saw the Wash pass beneath us and I set course for the Midlands. The sky was blue with variable scattered cloud below us. We flew at such a great pace that we almost overshot our target area. Of course, the real object of the flight was not to take pictures but to test the plane's performance. But since we were over the English Midlands with the right equipment we made two photo runs, one from east to west, the second in reverse. We then set course back to the sea. At no time did we see any flak or fighters, so re-crossed the sea to Holland where we landed back at our base where the camera film cassettes were removed for development.

'I was well pleased with the Arado's performance, which was excellent in every respect, and I felt the plane had great potential. I made one more flight soon afterwards, this time to Scapa Flow, flying up the North Sea from Holland before turning west towards Scapa. Then came a lull in operations while various proposals were examined and in this delay, which was long, very little flying was carried out, which disappointed me. The ground war hotted up, two pilots were lost in accidents and we

were forced to withdraw back to Germany where no more flying was done at all.

'A great new weapon was wasted through indecision.'

The historic first flight had taken place in October 1944, and, as Richard Endlass states, the great lead the Luftwaffe had in jet aircraft was thrown away. The fact that the enemy possessed such an advanced plane was never publicised in Britain, only in 1945 were the prizes of war in the shape of some of these German jets brought back and put on display. But in terms of secrets the following is probably one never before disclosed.

Already well-known among aerophiles is the fact of the Luftwaffe's special squadron of captured Allied planes, the RAF had their equivalent and both air forces used these enemy machines in demonstration flights to combat units around the country. Peter Grabener flew several Allied planes during the war:

'A Spitfire 2, Spitfire 5, a recon Spit, several Hurricanes, a Blenheim, Wellington, Typhoon and a Tempest, as well as several American types including the Thunderbolt, Mustang and B-17 Fortress. These models had fallen into our hands almost intact or comparatively undamaged and were used for demonstration purposes and evaluation as to counter-tactics etc. But there was also a plan to fly one or more of these types over England including some wild schemes which never reached fruition. The first was to actually land agents, another was for reconnaissance purposes, a third to follow and report on enemy formations by day. This last did happen, using an American B-17 which was successful to a degree until the Americans got wise to it.'

Such incidents of 'mystery Fortresses' which appeared over the North Sea near American formations en route to Germany have been described in various histories. Eventually, the Americans fired on them if they were in range.

'Then, on one occasion the captured Wimpey (Wellington) was used for a quite exhaustive flight across Britain, and this was rather dangerous as all air movements were watched and we wondered if the British would tumble us. I was the pilot and I took off with a full crew: An Observer who acted as captain, a rear gunner and a radio operator-gunner. We made our landfall in the early hours over England, just as it was beginning to get light and in the middle of a British bomber stream returning from Germany. We flew across East Anglia, noting any airfields we saw, turned north over Lincolnshire and to Yorkshire. We then turned out to sea on a roundabout course to be met by an escort of Messerschmitts to make sure we passed over our own defences unmolested.

'During a further flight I used a Boston in daylight which was even more dangerous, the intention was to photograph Allied bases at will. This we did but really unhindered by fear of discovery. Our flight was

timed to coincide with the return of American formations over the sea and we flew at lower level. There was a lot of Allied air activity that day and we felt one more plane returning at a low altitude would not excite comment. We photographed Hawkinge and several more airfields from about 3,000 ft and flew up to Essex where we repeated the exercise before flying out to sea.

'The mission was a complete success.'

CHAPTER TWELVE

HITLER'S LUFTWAFFE FAILED

I n the summer of 1940 Göring's boast that his Luftwaffe could subjugate Britain may have seemed like music to the ears of his Führer who, as is known, had no enthusiasm for an invasion of Britain. But Hitler was in some ways a pragmatist and for all his praise of the German Air Force which had performed so well in its previous campaigns he may have had doubts.

By all that is militarily sensible, the Wehrmacht should have conquered Britain. But so amazed and dazzled was its leaders by the headlong rush to the Channel and Atlantic coast it was in no state to continue its march across the sea into Britain. In any case, it had never seriously laid plans for such an undertaking, even though ideas and 'feasibility' studies had been carried out earlier. In the field the Germans proved masters of the lightning decision, its forces were highly mobile and trained for blitz war, yet the collapse of France rendered it suddenly incapable of further action. This was largely a mental attitude, and, it has to be said, a desire of the military themselves that peace should break out. Having re-geared itself and breaking free of its inertia following the British refusal to parley and receipt of Hitler's orders, it set the wheels in motion to break England or at least render it incapable of further offensive action.

The facts of what followed are well-known, but what really happened?

Propaganda at the time and ever since, including the testimony of countless historians, has set down the simple fact of a German defeat in the Battle of Britain, the Luftwaffe failed to gain the air supremacy necessary for an invasion, so that was that. Let us look further at this before assessing its performance and the effects as a whole.

By and large the Luftwaffe gained *sufficient* mastery over the Channel itself to permit the despatch of ground forces. The Royal Navy was denied use of the narrow strip of sea well before September 1940, and there is no doubt that the Germans succeeded in their first objective. The British destroyers were removed from their usual patrol areas to safer havens, just as the Luftwaffe and U-boat threat had forced the Admiralty to evacuate the Home Fleet from Scapa months earlier: the battleships, cruisers and destroyers that would be sorely needed to repel an invasion fleet, which would certainly have included German heavy units, were hundreds of miles away in the Clyde. This force would have needed many hours sailing time (even after preparation) to reach the Channel in order to intervene.

Also, most of the big air battles in that summer took place over the British mainland, not over the sea; the Luftwaffe's momentum, it can be said, carried it over the enemy frontier where battle was joined. Note that RAF Fighter Command became fully stretched as the struggle intensified, so much so that when crunch point came Dowding had to confess to the Prime Minister that no reserves were available. By then the British fighters were having a hard time simply trying to prevent the destruction of their own airfields and many young pilots were being thrown into the battle to be lost through very inadequate training and of course inexperience. It was at this point that an invasion launched across the Channel must have stood a very good chance of success, for Royal Navy intervention must surely have been thwarted by Stuka attack, as the dive-bomber was the deadliest weapon in the Luftwaffe armoury when properly used. It would have been a tremendous race but with the Luftwaffe throwing everything into the struggle success would have been probable. It has been recorded that with practically no artillery left after the disaster in France and only one infantry division intact (the Canadians) there was little to repulse a German landing in force. The forces landed along England's south coast would have thrust on to link up with the Luftwaffe airborne divisions dropped south of London. The new Local Defence Volunteers or Home Guard would have proved less than nuisance value.

The contention is that the Luftwaffe failed to win a victory in the Battle of Britain, its supreme test, and that it failed to win air supremacy – so the invasion was called off by Hitler. This cannot be the truth, for the heart of the matter lay in Hitler's will, a force in itself with great power. Invading Britain was never one of the Führer's 'irrevocable' decisions; half-hearted about it from the start, whatever his pronouncements, he needed little excuse to call it off for his mind was and always had been on the East, this is well-known via his assertions in *Mein Kampf* that Germany's destiny – its need for 'living space' – must be fulfilled in that direction.

To most German veterans of the period the *Kanalkampf* ended in a tie, a stand-off; from belief their opponents were almost beaten came the unpleasant news that this was far from the case, yet they never knew how close they had come to success. But this kind of thinking ignores the fact that *total* air supremacy was not needed in order to ensure more or less safe passage of sufficient forces across the Channel, only enough to keep the enemy air force at bay. And in 1940 the RAF simply did not have the kind of aircraft capable of annihilating shipping at sea. A reasonable degree of control of Channel air space should have ensured success for the Germans, and this certainly was achieved by the Luftwaffe. It was not the fault of the German airmen that Hitler in effect declared their sacrifices to be in vain, it was the dictator's lack of determination which rendered their struggle a waste in respect of the invasion. As to assertions that the Luftwaffe was bled white and never recovered from its losses, this is hardly borne out by its highly effective campaigns that followed when yet again it did everything expected of it until the ever-increasing tide of sheer weight of men and material sent against it in the East and West wore it down.

In the air war against Britain the Luftwaffe did a reasonable job in a situation for which it was not really fitted. Designed as a tactical force its role became more and more compromised as it was called upon to soften up an enemy protected by a formidable water barrier. Just as it had success within its grasp it was switched to a very different kind of war through the vacillations of its masters – a strategic war and worse – by night. In view of its almost total lack of training it performed very well, if one can speak of such an effort involving death and destruction in those terms. In this new kind of assault the Luftwaffe was greatly aided by the research carried out in navigation by radio beam; the *Knickebein* (Crooked Leg) system placed it far ahead of RAF Bomber Command and there lies a paradox. For it was the British not the Germans who laid great faith in a strategic air war and planned for it before war came. The Bomber Barons embraced the theory of winning a war by eradicating the enemy's war potential by aerial bombing, and soon discovered in practice that such a war could only be carried out in darkness. But, unlike their enemy, the RAF navigators were forced to rely on 'dead reckoning' or at best primitive aids which more often than not meant they missed their targets by miles. The German countryside received far more bombs than did that of Britain.

The Luftwaffe proved in its night blitz of 1940–41 that it could mark and bomb any target in Britain, and despite certain British successes in 'bending' the *Knickebein* beams and the use of decoy fires in the 'Starfish' system, every major city in Britain suffered damage, in many cases severe. It would be another two years at least before the RAF received radar aids that enabled it to achieve some greater measure of accuracy in its attacks on Germany, raids which met with the whole-hearted approval of the great majority of the British people led by Winston Churchill and his War Cabinet.

Once committed to the experiment, for it was the first sustained aerial bombardment of civilian centres in history, the Luftwaffe pulverised British towns and cities in area attacks; it was indeed the Germans who inaugurated this form of warfare. By then no invasion was contemplated: Hitler's attention was riveted eastwards and the gigantic operations contemplated, which from mid-May 1941 necessitated the switching of most of the German squadrons from the West Front. Any notion that the Luftwaffe was to any extent weakened by its exertions in the summer of the previous year had been expelled by its constant attacks by night through the autumn and winter, attacks interrupted only by bad weather early in 1941. Of course, these assaults were hazardous for the German aircrew only in the main through accidents on their own bases, not by the attentions of the British defences which were ineffective. And as a grand gesture designed to deceive the enemy rather than as some parting shot, the Luftwaffe was ordered to mount a far more devastating raid on 10 May 1941, more damaging by far to London that is; in terms of proportionate effect those on some other British cities were more effective by virtue of their smaller size which meant greater concentration – that on Coventry for example in November 1940. In view of the continued debate and criticism concerning Allied bombing of Germany in World War II no excuse is needed to point out the results of just one Luftwaffe attack, the one cited of May 1941, the swan-song of the enemy's air force in the West, though the battered British people were not to know this then.

Unlike recent raids, this terrible assault extended over some twelve hours, during which time 2,200 fires were started, 1,436 people killed and 1,800 injured. The number of German bombers taking part has been quoted as 500, this of 2,300 bombers of all types available for operations, a number exceeding RAF bomber strength by a wide margin, and confirming yet again that the Luftwaffe had far from used up its strength in the Battle of Britain. Hitler had apparently ordered the attack quite suddenly, his excuse that of yet another pinprick RAF raid on Berlin. The Führer was therefore sticking to his promise to eradicate British cities if the RAF continued to raid German towns. Otherwise, it is said that Hitler's real wish was to mount a last great spoiling attack by air on Britain before opening his campaign in the East; the decision does seem to have been primarily one of deception.

Whatever comments have been quoted by the responsible Luftwaffe commander Hugo Sperrle, a 'monocled giant of a man' as one writer has called him, the Field Marshal is said to have believed in his motto 'Is there a foe that bombing cannot break?' (much like Air Marshal Arthur Harris). It was Sperrle who had firmly believed in the sustained assault to knock out the RAF's fighter fields, only to see his tactics ruined by his master's interference just as success was within his grasp. The German commander believed in deluging targets with a mix of high explosive and incendiary bombs, and there can be no doubt that from the professional point of view the RAF bomber chiefs must have been envious of their enemy's success, for whatever delusions they were under concerning their own achievements against Germany, they were perfectly well aware that the scale and concentration of the Luftwaffe effort far exceeded their own. By the Luftwaffe's standards in the kind of war then current Bomber Command was akin to an amateur gentlemens' club, with the class-ridden aspect still well to the fore.

It must be obvious that if the Germans had maintained a similar scale of aerial assault on Britain throughout the war instead of switching most of their effort to the East then the civilian casualties would have been as great or greater than those suffered by the Germans at the hands of the RAF which have been such a topic ever since, for to many Germans the RAF bomber crews were indeed *terrorflieger* and therefore war criminals, waging war on civilians – to their distress and bafflement. The 60,000 Britishers killed by German air raids must be seen in the context of what was largely the Blitz period of 1940–41.

Obviously, it is wrong to try and assess the Luftwaffe's attack on Britain in terms of an air-to-air battle, with tables of plane and aircrew losses, which is why the other part of the equation has been brought in here. To ignore the *effects* of the assault is like omitting part of the whole story, it leaves an unbalanced picture. The ex-Luftwaffe aircrew witnesses quoted have given honest accounts of their own experiences, but too often the effects of their actions have inevitably been ignored. They flew to England for one purpose, encountering defenders on the way, the objects of their endeavours lay below them, and whatever their intentions, hopes and belief later, the plain fact is that most German bombs fell on civilian areas. Indeed, in all too many cases the attacks resulted in no encounter between Luftwaffe and RAF but became Germans versus civilians.

It was pointed out and stressed many times since that in World War II the civilian population of Britain entered the 'front line' for the first time; this is true, the official publication detailing Luftwaffe attacks was aptly titled *Front Line* (HMSO 1943). It had indeed become a civilians' war, the Home Front was in the firing line, the population under fire by day and night, as Winston Churchill had foreseen could be the case, though not on the scale of 'frightfulness' envisaged in the 1930s.

The Blitz did not of course commence with the big raid on London on 7 September 1940, other areas of Britain had long suffered sporadic and quite terrifying Luftwaffe attentions. But as soon as France fell and many fresh bases became available the enemy air force stepped up its scale and range of attacks so that before long the south-east coast of England became the focus for the most intense raiding activity to date and was never surpassed in that respect. It is therefore to the county of Kent that one must look, for example, as to what the effects the Luftwaffe's activities really meant; Kent became a 'front-line county' and from its annals come a few examples of the reality of events in those amazing days when the nation's fate seemed to hinge on the heroic defence put up by a few squadrons of young fighter pilots. It is not the intention here to present a catalogue of 'bomb stories', but the other side of the picture presented earlier.

Lenham is little more than a large village of just over 2,000 souls some three miles east of Maidstone, the county town. At 4.30 in the afternoon of 1 June 1940 a high explosive bomb fell on the Congregational Chapel, thirty minutes after a host of schoolchildren had left it. Considerable damage was done but no casualties resulted. Lenham is about three miles from what was the then RAF airfield at Detling, and much farther still from another base at West Malling, so no excuse of a 'near miss' existed.

Although the main Luftwaffe assault was not scheduled to start until Eagle Day on 12 August (actually misfiring owing to bad weather until the next day), bombs fell on many localities well before as indicated. On 17 July a German bomber dropped its load on Ashford New Town, possibly aiming for the railway workshops (closed only recently). A baby boy and a lad were killed.

The Luftwaffe staff chose targets from its military geographia books, issuing suitably amended British Ordnance Survey maps to aircrews to find the objectives chosen. The first listed every city and town in Britain, together with its military and economic facilities such as gas, electric and water works, and though special large target maps were prepared for important objectives such as ports etc, finding or choosing particular buildings etc from the air, especially if under threat from the defences, could be difficult. These questions arise despite the alleged Luftwaffe object to knock out RAF airfields, and such are the ways of historians that the reality of what went on in this battle is often sidetracked. Whatever damage was achieved at RAF bases, that incurred in towns, villages and even on remote farms was more extensive by far. No matter how many formations made for the RAF airfields, there were always other, lone raiders overflying other areas.

When these solo operators attempted to bomb what they believed to be factories, railway workshops, barracks etc, they were all too often striking at no such targets – or usually missing them altogether. Then, as happened often enough, once combat was joined in the sky the German bomber formations became broken up, some turning back, some damaged, the crews anxious to escape, especially with wounded aboard. Bomb loads were hurriedly jettisoned, often with fatal results to civilians below. Otherwise, if for reasons of weather or RAF interception alternative 'targets of opportunity' were chosen, the results were usually the same, with the greater percentage of bombs landing in residential areas, this was inevitable. It was not then the enemy's intention to bomb civilians, but that was the result.

Not all the German bomber groups made for RAF airfields, far from it, the attack widened and the Luftwaffe flew round the tip of the Kent coast and many bombs were released on the towns of Whitstable, Margate, Ramsgate, Deal and Dover of course where shipping was a legitimate target. At Northfleet six generations of one family were wiped out by a bomb; bombs are not choosey and a school was struck in the same town.

'Either purposely or accidentally, much damage was done to residential districts in Kent,' a wartime account told, with many photographs to back up the claim. To stand in the street or garden watching events in the sky was to ask for trouble: one man watching a raid through binoculars had a splinter enter his jacket sleeve, others were struck and injured. An

AA shell landed to explode beside an air raid wardens' post in a cricket ground at Gravesend. Neither was Sunday sacrosanct: a congregation in the same area found a stained glass window of the church blown in on them by a near miss. Then too, some German airmen saw fit to make low-flying sorties, machine-gunning people on the ground. Farm workers watched a lone German plane one afternoon which swooped low over East Kent as they were gathering crops: 'A moment later the pilot machine-gunned people in the next farm,' quoted an eye witness, adding that a local AA gun caught the enemy machine which came down at Godmersham Park, three miles south-west of Canterbury.

One German aircrew survivor happened to be recovering in a West Kent hospital when windows were blasted in from a near bomb hit. The story goes that when asked his reaction he put both thumbs up in approval. Others were less fortunate, many crashing with their planes, the machines sometimes smashing into townships, such as one which struck Hardy Street in Maidstone on 5 September. One German parachuting to what he hoped was safety struck a rooftop in the same town and broke both legs. Yet another German aircrewman who escaped from his aircraft after a raid is quoted as saying: 'I thought I was bombing a barracks!', a type of target frequently claimed as hit in Nazi communiques. In this case the bombs had demolished several terrace houses in a village remote from obvious targets, though it is possible that a military camp lay nearby. But aircrews roaming in the hope of finding suitable freelance targets could mistake the roofs of a village hall, a covered market or a bus station for military accommodation.

On the other hand train crews could expect to find themselves in the thick of it – and often did. One loco crew from Dover were detailed to take a train from Ramsgate to Charing Cross in London, they were bombed from behind, from the front and either side, and at one point an oil bomb landed on the tender; they put this out with their hose. They arrived at their destination with blackened faces. An RAF officer delayed at Charing Cross by disruption to timetables remarked that such train crews had 'more guts than I have'.

Hundreds of bomb incidents looked on by many citizens as wanton enemy action brought tragedies as possessions and lives were lost. When one Victorian terrace house was totally demolished all that remained was a clutch of dresses clinging to the remains of a wardrobe on an upstairs party wall. As any rail traveller could see then as now, the greater part of the landscape is free of buildings, yet time and again Luftwaffe bombs seemed to hit country dwellings. One of these was reduced to a heap of rubble and sticks, just a couple of chairs and a sofa remaining.

Captain Bligh of *Bounty* fame once lived in a manor house at Farningham, some fifteen miles west of Rochester where the British branch of Short Brothers built Sunderland flying boats for Coastal Command just north of the Kentish Downs – the area was not known for military targets. Yet according to one account three Dorniers engaged in dive-bombing in the area were shot down by a 22-year-old British flak gunner. The wreckage of the bombers, including their bomb loads, was said to have fallen from the sky 'like hail'. Houses and a school were damaged and a wool shop wrecked, while sixty bombs fell in one field alone, certainly small calibre or incendiaries, some dud or time deviced, which caused traffic diversion on a main road nearby.

Then, after an incendiary bomb fell close to a church the congregation filed out, only to be machined-gunned as they left. So stated the wartime report, which it must be said is of a kind not necessarily factual, for when action is in progress overhead and machine-guns can be heard it is all too easy to imagine the worst, a fact this author knows from experience. Then, of course millions of spent bullets fell to earth in this period; it could have been one fired from an RAF or German plane diving in combat which struck Miss Nellie Coulston in her car. A school teacher, she was on her way to play the organ in the church mentioned; she died later in hospital.

On 12 September a German bomber flew over Tunbridge Wells, unloaded its missiles, the target if any unknown. Hits were scored on the Kent and Sussex Hospital (also struck by fire bombs later), the garage of the volunteer American Ambulance Corps, the Roman Catholic Presbytery, and the Salvation Army Citadel. As to economic objectives which might have brought inconvenience to the Royal town, the Deputy Borough Engineer's house and garage were hit, as well as a wholesale grocers. Twelve people were killed and sixteen injured, one of the fatalities being an eleven-year-old choirboy engaged in a newspaper round. Curious blast effects occurred, and women shoppers found their baskets torn away so they were left only holding the handles.

A Messerschmitt 109 fighter executed crazy manoeuvres on its own account after the pilot baled out, flying a loop and swerving violently before diving straight for a group of farm workers who scattered in all directions. One of these people happened to be the farm owner, proprietor and owner of the *Kent Messenger* newspaper, a man who spent much time 'in the field' in this period and experienced much of the action at first hand. The Messerschmitt missed the workers, burying itself deep in the earth and exploding into fire. Nevertheless, the Kentmen ran forward despite the flames to ascertain no other Germans were trapped in the wreckage, not being too conversant with Luftwaffe aircraft types and how many crew they carried.

It was the same newspaper editor who was able to claim story and pictures, since very familiar to many, of 'the one that got away' – Franz von Werra, whose fighter came down in the heart of the Kent orchard and hop country at Curtisden Green, south of Maidstone. Despite their ordeal, it was hard to find Britishers imbued with hatred for the enemy when face to face with them, though this could flare up if suffering became bad enough. One man who did express more extreme feelings was the Yardmaster at Herne Hill just over the border in the greater London area. The Southern Railway trains passed through his busy junction from Kent and he had seen plenty: 'I hate them, I hate every one. They've tried hard to kill me and my family, and many's the time I've wished I had something to hit back with.'

This worker, a Mr Doorne, claimed he had heard a thousand bombs fall, not counting incendiaries, the nearby rail tracks at times lit up as if someone were striking matches on them. At the start of the war he had wondered how he would stand up to bombing and was scared stiff when the sirens sounded what proved to be a false alarm on 3 September 1939; thereafter he found he was too busy to worry.

The old city of Canterbury with its famous cathedral did not have to wait until 1942 and German 'Baedeker' reprisal raids for its baptism of fire, one more tale of a 'Nazi pilot' raking streets with machine-gun fire made the news early in September. It may seem strange that some lone German raiders were able to roam around over localities for up to half an hour, this was possible when great Luftwaffe activity was in hand, as it proved impossible to catch every single interloper. Such an event occurred in mid-September when a raider, probably making use of early autumn cloud cover, trailed its coat low enough across Ashford for the townspeople to make out its insignia. Finally, after thirty minutes it made one more pass, the Observer perhaps trying to positively identify the railway workshops which must have been plain to see against the many tracks beside the station. Then several rifle shots rang out as local Home Guards let fly a pointless fusillade; the bombs came down, to hit the New Town area, causing devastation and casualties.

As indicated, those Britons who had suffered most were more inclined to take a less charitable attitude to German aircrew on the ground. The story of one unfortunate German killed by a mob in London's dockland area is not confirmable. But another German who parachuted down into a Kentish hopfield at Selling is reported to have been welcomed by a very angry crowd of female hop pickers taking their annual working vacation from the East End. The enemy airman was rescued by police and troops. Similar episodes occurred later in the war with RAF aircrew in Germany.

When the night blitz began in September hundreds, then thousands of citizens of south-east London and nearby areas in Kent began sheltering in Chislehurst caves. It was the same at Northfleet where extensive chalk tunnels provided security and some crude comforts when fittings were later installed.

Trains and buses were machine-gunned, and as the Battle of Britain drew to a close in October the Luftwaffe began using Messerschmitt 109s as fighter-bombers. The aircraft carried a single 500 lb bomb slung beneath the fuselage, and the attacks were often indiscriminate for the German pilots objected to such encumbrances which slowed them up and were only too happy to be rid of the bombs as quickly as possible over England. When attacked by RAF fighters the Germans dumped their load and attempted to defend themselves in straight combat. Actual targets were not always RAF fields: death and injury resulted when Mes attacked Canterbury, and fifteen bombs fell, killing nurses from the Kent and Canterbury Hospital.

By the end of October, the casualties in Kent – Britain's 'Hellfire Corner' – ran into four figures, while in Britain as a whole 14,281 people were dead as a result of Luftwaffe action, with over 20,000 seriously wounded. Many more were to die or be maimed before the final 'Raiders Passed' sirens sounded in 1945, by which time the South had suffered many casualties from Hitler's V1 and V2 weapons. Göring's boasts had proved hollow, and there is no doubt that frustration drove the Germans in later 1940 to use the Luftwaffe as a terror weapon in the hope it would wear down the British population. Why else would German bombers attack Cornish fishing villages? From the beginning the inevitable errors in aerial bombing were compounded by recklessness which resulted in bombs being scattered all over Britain. In the towns and cities it was found that not only could the population 'take it' (given adequate support from the authorities), but that energetic measures could and did effect speedy repairs that enabled war production and general life to continue. The annihilating ruination of Coventry in November 1940 is a good example: with public utilities cut off and many war factories damaged, the government and local authorities did all that was necessary to enable life to resume. Industrial production in the twenty to thirty firms in some way incapacitated re-started in two or three weeks, for it was found that while roofs and other parts of factory buildings could be razed, so long as the essential machine tools remained work could continue.

The Luftwaffe's assault on Britain was historic in the sense that it marked the first sustained campaign of destruction from the air against a civil population, for this is what the German blitz amounted to not only from 7 September 1940 but also to a considerable extent before. Despite grievous damage and heavy casualties the people survived, as many an impromptu slogan at the time showed. Contrary to the enemy's propaganda claims, Britain's cities were not eradicated and neither did life cease to exist. Hitler's Luftwaffe failed in the strategy assigned it in error, it had not the equipment to do otherwise and the Führer's Eastern obsession made certain it never would have. From 1941 onwards Hitler allowed priority for the U-boat war as long demanded by Admiral Dönitz, this the one card in the enemy's armoury Winston Churchill knew could bring defeat to Britain.

In terms of equipment the bombers which had served the Luftwaffe so well in its previous campaigns proved inadequate when battle was joined in earnest against the British. The Heinkels, Dorniers and Junkers carried comparatively small bomb loads and were poorly armed for defence; by 1941 the first two types were already obsolete and incapable of real development. Only the radio beam system of navigation enabled the Luftwaffe to inflict as much harm as it did.

As for the airmen themselves, in 1940 the German aircrew were the best trained in the world for the jobs intended, well motivated and of high morale which did not collapse in the harsh reality of the battle across the Channel. It would be pointless to brand those young men as 'Nazi' simply because they had enlisted in a service new by comparison to its fellows. Neither would it profit to consider a good proportion of them as Nazi because they had transferred from the National Socialist Air Corps before the Luftwaffe's official birth in 1935, and in all probability the number going straight from the Party hierarchy into the air force was small. Political motivation can in any case here be coupled with national self-belief, though because of very different circumstances it was often expressed on a national scale far more stridently than that, shall we say, of Britain's belief and faith in the Empire. This belief in Germany's cause, whether from the national socialist point of view or simply through patriotism, was rarely expressed on capture in Britain. Aircrew who landed after combat were thankful to find themselves in one piece and certainly perhaps surprised by British 'correctness', politeness and solicitude for someone in bad luck, especially if wounded. For once in Britain the enemy became the underdog and was treated with that curiously English trait of fairness in all things, a kind word and a cup of tea must have bemused many Germans and especially those who were indeed fervent in their belief of Hitler the saviour. Even so, the type of arrogant Nazi so beloved of British propaganda who clicked his heels and snapped up the *deutsche gruss* or 'Hitler salute' would have aroused amusement and perhaps a kick up the back side, for pompousness and the bullying type in uniform cut much less ice in Britain where the armed forces were far less elevated as a national institution. Again, it must be recorded that some RAF types also received considerable kindness when forced down among enemy civilians, especially of the well-bred classes.

Although it has often been written that the Luftwaffe never really recovered from its blood-letting over Britain in 1940, it still remained a powerful force well able to carry out the tasks allotted it in the Mediterranean, Balkans and on the Russian Front where it became frittered away in endless operations. In the renewed 'Baby Blitz' over Britain in 1944 it suffered severely, for it had neither the strength, equipment or sufficient highly trained crews and its morale did plunge irretrievably. For the once proud and powerful bomber force the final curtain came when it was superseded by V weapons, with air and ground crews remustered into the infantry.

An interesting aspect rarely touched upon is the number of operations completed by Luftwaffe crews. In the Allied air forces 'tours' were limited to 25 or 30 operations, in the German air force most flew on and on until killed or incapacitated. In this way the survivors amassed hundreds of sorties in their log books. This does provoke further comparison in considering the much greater scale of the Allied operations over Germany and the resulting battles and the much increased strain on crews.

Memoirs by German ex-aircrew members are few, those published appeared more often in the 1950s, those by Major Hajo Herrmann (Airlife 1991) are fairly recent. This officer can be compared to the 'gung-ho', 'press-on' types of the RAF, the kind of men who most often came up for decoration, men like Guy Gibson and Leonard Cheshire who were both admired and often looked on askance by other airmen for their determination and coolness. Herrmann certainly believed whole-heartedly in flying to the limit for Germany, amassing a great number of operational hours and achieving considerable success as a Junkers 88 bomber pilot before taking a crack at night-fighter combat later in the war. His long tale of bomber operations against Britain includes one night episode when, after flying fruitlessly the length of eastern England trying to find a suitable target, he dropped his bombs at random from sheer frustration. There was no question of returning home with his load, and his 'target' remained unknown. It would be naïve to imagine this never occurred to RAF crews over Germany.

Rightly, it has been the activities of the Luftwaffe bomber crews which have taken up most space here, though their fighter comrades were far from mere onlookers they had in general no contact with the enemy on the ground. As to their conduct in the air, most behaved as honourably as the life and death struggle allowed, though it seems impossible to be aquainted with a wide knowledge of these events without coming across mention of German fighter pilots machine-gunning opponents who had taken to their parachutes during the Battle of Britain. Likewise, one reads of Allied pilots committing similar acts, though specifically able to quote of only one, a Polish airman who admitted that when occasion presented and no witnesses were around he tried to make sure the enemy in his parachute reached the ground dead. The Poles had far greater reason to hate the Germans.

Finally, what of those Luftwaffe airmen who reached British airspace only to find themselves shot down and taken prisoner?

CHAPTER THIRTEEN

ESCAPEES WERE SOON ROUNDED UP

T housands of Luftwaffe PoWs were transported to Canada, many going on to the USA where they enjoyed the fruits of American 'high living', lavish by European standards, even in wartime. Many would elect to stay on after the war ended. The reasons for sending these Germans out of Britain were on the one hand economic, on the other to prevent the build-up of a 'Trojan horse' situation, with too many disciplined, healthy military prisoners within the country in a certain situation they could prove a danger. This had certainly not been overlooked by the German command, which was why a scheme was hatched to have the entire German PoW population break out of their camps in December 1944, this operation to coincide with the Ardennes offensive. It was a wild scheme which could only be depended upon for even slight success by the iron determination of thoroughly Nazi prisoners at senior NCO and officer level in England. At its core lay a notion to seize British arms stores, bases, airfields – and even march on London. The Germans hoped that with the Allies so heavily committed in manpower on the Western Front that insufficient strength would remain in England to deal with such an uprising.

In the event the operation failed; the British became aware of something in the wind, though were unable to prevent it occurring. A certain number of Germans escaped, coercion and murder took place in some camps when Nazi PoWs suspected they had been betrayed by those in their midst not interested in the scheme, and in due course a small number of those guilty were tried and executed by the British. Of this period Otto Jufen recalls:

'*An officer briefed us secretly that there would be a great uprising in all of the PoW camps in Britain, and if we succeeded in escaping then a plan existed to march on London or some such nonsense. There were some really hard Nazis in the camp including Luftwaffe aircrew who really believed that we could achieve something. I was quite happy as an officer to do what I could, though I thought the whole scheme impossible.*

'*In the event we found ourselves confined to quarters, the guards were*

*doubled and machine-guns set up the day before the attempt, but I know
that escapes did take place on a considerable scale elsewhere and this
caused a certain amount of bother to the Allies, though nothing really
was achieved.'*

Indeed, all the escapees were soon rounded up by police and troops
including American units, and in a TV documentary on the affair in
later years some Germans who had taken part in the affair in Wales
described how their British guards, irritated at having their weekend
leave disrupted, made certain that those PoWs recaptured were made
to run the gauntlet through a double line of soldiers who administered
them a beating. But most Germans who escaped or were captured were
given fair or even extremely hospitable treatment by their hosts and
captors, as indeed it must be said of Britons in similar circumstances
in Germany. Used as we are to the multitude of escape tales from the
Allied side, it is refreshing to see the other side of the coin as it were,
concerning some of those Luftwaffe aircrew who came to Britain in the
latter part of the war.

Peter Neumann admits to having been 'something of a Nazi' insofar
as he believed in Germany's rights and aspirations though not learning
of Nazi crimes such as the existence of extermination camps until later
in England where the evidence shown them seemed too awful to be
believed.

Neumann had been captain and Observer in a Dornier 217K on one
of the London raids during the 'Baby Blitz' of 1944, and during one of
these in March had just escaped the worst flak zone when struck by
fire from a night-fighter which took the crew completely by surprise:

*'The plane burned at once and there was a scramble to escape. I fell
through the hatch and was hit by the cold night air and had not fallen
far when the burning bomber blew up with a roar with my friend the
pilot still aboard. I pulled the cord and my parachute opened perfectly.
I was in a state of shock, it had all happened so quickly. One moment
I had been lying in the nose of the plane congratulating ourselves on
escaping the London flak – then I was trying to escape from a burning
bomber.*

*'But the cold air pulled me to my senses and looking round I saw fires
in the distance which I assumed to be London, but below me it was total
blackness. We had been instructed to dive away after bombing and had
in fact descended to about 12,000 ft. I wondered as I fell in the night
air what had happened to my other friends, I could see no sign of them.
I also lamented the death of my pilot, and thought of his poor parents
in Berlin.*

*'Then I tried to make out the ground below and thought I could see
vague shapes and possibly a little road. Then trees came up at me very
fast and my feet struck some branches and I went hurtling through them
to hit the ground below. I lay there for a moment in some shock but*

seemed to be in one piece, so I stood up and looked around, removed my harness and tried to walk a few paces, but my legs felt weak and I put this down to fear. I had just missed falling into a small wood, I was in a field and could see hedgerows but little else. Then I remembered the road and wondered if I should try to find it. I knew the nature of the English landscape and knew I would find a road whichever direction I walked in. However, I felt undecided. There was no sign of the British police or troops searching for me. Then I saw a glow some way off and decided it must be the remains of our plane.

'*So I began walking along the edge of the wood, and when this ended I saw a high hedge I could not see through, so I continued walking until I reached a wooden gate, beyond that was a sloping field and I thought I could make out some houses. It was so dark it was hard to see much properly, I thought it might be a farm where I could perhaps hide for a while and even steal some food. So I climbed over the gate but then remembered my parachute which I had forgotten to hide. So I managed to find my way back to it, gathered it up and threw it into the trees. Then I walked back to the gate and had soon reached the bottom of the sloping field and the first houses, which I thought could be the edge of a village as I saw a lane and farther away a church steeple. I was thirsty and would need food and wondered if I could find my surviving comrades.*

'*But then I heard a vehicle, so I lay down in the grass not far from the white walls of a house near the lane. Then the vehicle came slowly into view, it was a truck and I thought it must contain soldiers or police looking for me or my comrades. The truck stopped for a moment and I heard voices, then it moved off again, moving slowly. So I moved off, climbing a fence and hoping to find out where I was. But I saw no signs or names on the houses as I moved along the road. Then I rounded a bend in the lane and saw the main village, so boldly went on until I came to what appeared to be a little shop not far from the church, and I thought I would try to steal something to eat and drink, perhaps some chocolate and beer or lemonade. But although I could see a name over the shop and felt it sold supplies the windows were covered and it was too dark to see anything much. So I crouched there in dead silence, unable to decide my next move. If I tried to break into the shop the noise would waken the owner, on the other hand I had to do something. There seemed no point in walking on out of the village. Also, even if I reached the sea I could think of no way I could get back across the Channel.*

'*Then I realised I still had my pistol so wondered if I could use it to break the glass of the shop door and get inside without making too much noise. I decided to risk it, so took the pistol from its holster, placed it against the glass and gave it a big thump with my fist. But nothing happened. So I tried again, harder, and this time it make a fearful crash as the glass broke easily. I then tried to remove the jagged pieces to get my hand inside and unlock the door, but although I found the handle I could not locate any lock. So in desperation I tried to remove larger pieces of glass but this was too dangerous so I gave up. And then I heard noises in the building so turned away and ran along the street as fast as I could until I reached the church where I passed through a gate and hid behind a gravestone.*

'When I looked back up the street I could see a light moving about in the shop I had tried to burgle. Then I heard the sound of the vehicle again and saw what appeared to be the same truck entering the village. I watched carefully and saw a figure come out of the shop waving a torch and stop the truck. Some men got out and I realised they were soldiers carrying rifles. There was an excited conversation and then some shouts and all of the soldiers got out of the truck and began moving along the street, some one way, the rest the other. My heart was thumping as I knew they were looking for me. I decided it was useless and to give myself up.

'I moved out of the churchyard with my hands up and walked slowly along the road until I was seen by the soldiers who came nearer until one of them shone a torch on me and shouted, "'Ere 'e is Bill, I've got 'im!" A whistle blew and they all came running.

'I was searched and my pistol given to a young officer, my flying helmet taken away and then I was marched back to the vehicle and bundled into the back. I learned later that the men were Home Guards, I had noticed that they were older men. After some conversation with the shop owner we drove off for a mile or so until reaching a policemen's house where the wife gave me a cup of tea. They seemed very kind and I felt sick after my experience and was glad of the hospitality. An hour later some younger soldiers took me away by truck to a camp where I was put in a cell and slept on a cot until morning. Then I was woken up by a guard, handed a plate of beans, bacon, tea with bread and butter and later taken to the latrine where I used the toilet under guard, had a wash and was taken before an officer who asked me a few useless questions in English before an RAF escort and MPs took me to London.

'I took part in the "great escape" in December, but did not get further than the nearest village in the north of England.'

Ulrich Schneider also took part in the 'Baby Blitz' of 1944 as the pilot of a Junkers 88 A14. It was one night in February and the crew had just bombed the dock area of London and were passing over the Thames in a shallow dive when they were struck by flak and both engines set on fire:

'As the pilot I could see we had no chance so called on my comrades to get out fast. This they succeeded in doing and the plane remained on an even keel, so I began trying to escape myself. I thought the burning bomber was about to fall away out of control if it did not blow to bits first.

'The plane gave a lurch as I fell out of the hatch and fell clear, tumbling over and over, seeing the fires and river below and praying that I would not drown. The flak was very noisy and I thought I might be blown up in one of the explosions. We had been at about 15,000 ft when hit and I had now fallen some way – the Junkers had disappeared. Then I pulled the cord and was soon floating down in comparative calm. There was a breeze blowing and I could still hear the hum of planes above me with the flak bursting not only over London but in all directions, which was frightening. The Thames was lit up by the fires and flashes of flak guns and bursting bombs. It was a spectacular sight, but now I grew nervous as I seemed to be falling straight into the river. I tried to control the 'chute but had no idea how effective my attempts were as the water was still below me.

'Then I realised that I might be lucky and just miss the river and land on the bank where I could see buildings. Then I saw roads and on one of these was a moving vehicle. But my immediate concern was my landing, as although I seemed to be about to miss the water itself the tide was low and I was heading for mud which looked black and quite menacing, and before I knew it my feet had hit this surface with a great "splat" noise and I fell over with my 'chute on top of me. I was winded and lay still as I realised the water was some yards away and there was no danger of drowning.

'Then, as I sat up to get out of my harness I heard shouts and saw men looking over a wall – and they saw me as my parachute was easy to see. The mud I had landed in was like glue and smelly and as I struggled to get out of it I nearly lost my flying boots in the muck. I half fell over as I heard the men stumbling down to get to me. Some of them were cursing: "Come on Fritz, you bastard, out of it!" "Get 'im Len!" called another.

'I was hauled up the slippery slope with the soldiers cursing as they slithered about until at last we were out of the stinking mess and on firmer ground beside the wall. There was a truck on the road and as soon we reached this the men started hitting me, calling me names and other curses I will not repeat. They used their boots to kick me in the shins and on my rear, and two or three used their rifle butts to hit me in the back and across the shoulders. One of them was a Sergeant, and at last he said, "All right lads, let's get the fucker in the truck."

'"Come on, Fritz," they said, and helped me into the vehicle with more curses and we drove off. We soon reached a large hall of some kind and I saw that the men were Home Guards and they sat me down while one telephoned the police I believe. There was a long wait and I felt hurt and quite faint and one of the men gave me a cup of tea and a cigarette. I did not really blame them for beating me.'

It is known that fighter pilots taken prisoner fared worse in confinement because of their temperament, and consequently were more prone to attempt escape. Such was the lot of Hans Martin, shot down in his Focke-Wulf 190 late in 1943 and sent to a Midlands PoW camp where he recalls he was fairly treated, but:

'I hated confinement and tried to get into one of the outside work parties but there was no vacancy at the time. If I had been patient there would have been no problem. As it was I could not stand to be cooped up and resolved to escape; I had no hope of reaching the continent, I just longed to be free – even to tour England! I was naïve and young and believed in myself and spoke to my senior officer about my idea, he said it was foolhardy, but I could try: "You lead a reasonable life here, why not sit the war out in comfort and safety?"

'I could see his point, but I felt the war might go on for years. So I told him I would try to escape and remain free for as long as possible. It would do me good, even if I was caught – I would have done my best. I saved some rations, including some chocolate, cigarettes, cakes and bread. I had a reasonable knowledge of English and knew there were many foreigners in the country. I also received some clothes given me by our Escape Club who liked to monitor all such attempts.

'It was mid-February 1944 and the weather was ideal for me, overcast and dark in the evenings which was the time I planned my escape as I thought the middle of the night was no time to be wandering about. I also thought that there would be plenty of people about that I could mingle with in the evening. Our camp was just outside Derby and I had a map of the area, plus a larger one showing the whole of England that one of our men had managed to steal when on an outside work party.

'So, with the good wishes of my comrades ringing in my ears one dark evening about eight o'clock I slipped out of the billet, made my way to the hedge and in no time had slipped through it without problems. The British were quite lax in some respects, perhaps they felt that with the war coming to an end and the invasion due the prisoners had nowhere to escape to.

'I knew where to head for through the directions given me by my comrades. There was a lane by the camp leading to a highway where I could catch a bus into Derby. I had about £2 in English coinage and the fare I understood to be two pence. I moved up the lane, past some houses, seeing no one, and reached the main road where I saw vehicles. It was dark and the traffic used masked headlamps. I walked a few yards and found the bus stop, there was a woman waiting, she carried a bag and had a little boy with her. I paced up and down as it was cold and there was no shelter. Then at last the bus arrived and I helped the little boy on, his mother following. It was a single deck bus and rather full but I *found a seat next to an older man reading a newspaper. The conductor came and I asked for Derby and gave him six pence and as expected he gave me four pence change. Nobody took any notice of me, the bus was not well lit and had blackout blinds over the windows. This meant that I could not see where we were, but I decided to sit tight and wait to see what happened, and in any case I didn't think the bus was going further than Derby.*

'After about ten minutes and several stops I realised we were in the town and most of the people got off, so I said to the man next to me, "Is this Derby?" and he said yes, it was, so I too alighted and found myself in or near the town centre. I had no plan other than to remain free as long as possible, so I decided to find a cinema; I had enough money and it would mean shelter for the evening. I would then have to find somewhere to spend the night as sleep was essential. I had no wish to roam the countryside, roughing it. If necessary I would steal to remain in condition, but that would come later. I had food for a couple of days in the little parcel under my arm.

'So I walked along the street some way, watching the people go by and looking in the shop windows, which was very interesting. And then I saw a cinema – two in fact – but I passed the first after examining the programme and prices, after which I strolled on to the other one to do the same. Then I returned to the first cinema and asked the pretty girl in the ticket booth for a one-and-ninepenny seat and went inside where a little man in uniform tore my ticket in half and left me to find a seat in the dark. This I eventually did. It was a comedy film, and though I could not follow all the dialogue I felt very happy to be in that place and free! I looked around at the people enjoying the film and wondered what they would think if they knew that one of those horrid Nazis was sitting among them!

'Then came the newsreel with war reports, which was most interesting, followed by an interval when the lights went on and I felt very vulnerable. But no one took any notice of me and when I saw there were better seats elsewhere I moved and became bold, opened my parcel and when the lights went out again I munched some biscuits. Then came a war film which was not good, but I was happy to relax and ignore the silly propaganda on the screen. Then it dawned on me that I was alone in enemy country with nowhere to go for the night. How were my comrades faring, and how long it would be before I was found missing.

'The programme ended and I found it was ten o'clock, and the comedy film was about to be repeated, so I was undecided what to do. I had a wild idea that I might speak to someone, make friends and that they would offer me a bed for the night. But then they would want to know who I was and become suspicious at once. I had no papers whatever, my escape had been such a simple one. Then I wondered if I could find a small guest house, but this too seemed too risky. I tried to think up a cover plan and recalled the famous escape of von Werra and all his

boldness. But I had no identification so it all seemed futile. I did think of pretending to be a merchant seaman whose ship had been torpedoed so that I had lost everything. But then, what was I doing in the middle of England?

'*So I almost gave up. But I knew the English valued their privacy so wondered again if I dared speak to someone and tell them some plausible tale? Suppose I had been visiting my sick mother – say, in Rugby? Or even Nottingham, and had missed the last train home to where? They would not likely know the train times. I could say I had little money and needed somewhere to sleep for the night and wanted to catch the first train next morning. But then, they would probably tell me to go to the station, or even the police! The idea of befriending someone, even a woman, persisted, someone who would be sympathetic. The idea of going home with an Englishwoman excited me, but I contained myself against optimism. People did not always speak to strangers, but I began to look around me to see if there were any likely prospects – a woman alone with an empty seat next to her. But I saw none, all the women seemed to be in company, so that idea was dropped.*

'*When I left the cinema I was still undecided. I had enough English to ask directions to a guest house, the alternative was to find a park, but it was really too cold to sleep out. Then I saw a little cafe and on impulse went inside. There were only two or three people in there, so I boldly went to the counter and asked the woman for a cup of coffee please, and when she served me I noticed some cakes which looked nice, so after checking my money I bought one and took my modest repast to a table and sat down. I felt warm comfortable, and almost at leisure.*

'*I spent half an hour in the cafe until I was the only customer and realised the women was about to close up for the night. So I decided to ask her the way to a boarding house, as the English called them. I went to the counter, carrying my cup and plate: "Excuse me please, can you show me a guest house, or somewhere I can find a bed for the night?" I asked her.*

'*"Just a minute," she said, looking very surprised, and going off out of sight. I heard her speaking to a man who then appeared with her, saying:*

'*"I don't know one round here. Not easy to find anywhere."*

'*They stood staring at me and were obviously of no help, and as I began to get nervous I thanked them and left at once. Outside it was cold and dark and I cursed myself for not having brought an overcoat. I did not know what to do and for the first time wished I was back in my warm cot in the PoW camp. In fact, I began to feel I had been a fool for leaving, or at least for not making a better plan. I walked the streets, looking in a few shops, but with the blackout it was not too good. Then I saw a policeman, and on a very foolish impulse decided I had nothing to lose by asking him the way to a guest house, or even the station where there would be a waiting room.*

'*He was a big man and I felt looked down on me very suspiciously as I asked him the way to a guest house or anywhere I could find a bed for the night. He stared at me for a moment, so I said hurriedly: "Or the way to the station?"*

'*This I believe set him thinking and made him even more suspicious and he asked me where I was going to, so I said London at once. He looked me over and I believe decided at once that I was an escaped German PoW. He looked very stern and said. "Can I see your identity card, please sir?"*

'*I knew at once that the game was up. I had nothing to show him at all, but told him I had been in a cafe nearby and must have left my wallet there. I felt in my pockets and told him I must have left it there. Could he help me please?*

'*Well, we returned to that cafe as they were closing up and the policeman made them open the door and they looked at me in surprise. The policeman took me inside and told them I had lost my wallet, and the woman said: "It's the first I've heard of it, it's not here, I've just cleaned up."*

'*The policeman looked at me as I tried to look innocent, saying: "I'd like you to come with me to the station sir to establish your identity."*

'*So at that point I gave up. I told them who I was and at once the pair in the cafe said: "We knew it! He looked a rum 'un, 'e did!"*'

David Sussman's parents had a trace of Jewish blood, but not quite enough to prevent him serving as an air gunner in the Luftwaffe. Late in 1944 he and his crew flew on a raid to Britain in a Junkers 88 and were attacked by a Mosquito night fighter. The bomber burned and Sussman was the first and last to escape by parachute; his comrades were killed when the bomber blew up right afterwards.

'*My 'chute opened and I came down in countryside near I believe Dorking in Surrey. I was in good condition and decided to try and stay free for as long as possible. This led to an unusual adventure.*

'*The night was clear, but with no moon, so after hiding my parachute I started walking along a road in what I believed was a northerly direction. I had a vague idea that if only I could discard my flying suit and get hold of an overcoat I might pass as a civilian and reach London where I would be swallowed up in the millions of people. But I was not to get anywhere near the British capital.*

'*Soon after I started tramping along the little lane a vehicle came along behind me and stopped. I had by then gone into a state of delayed shock and felt grieved over the loss of my friends. The car that stopped was a small one and the driver looked out at me in amazement. He was an older man and said, "Are you a German?"*

So I admitted I was. I had learned some English and French at school.

'"So," he said, "you'd better get in then."

'So I climbed into the car beside him, forgetting I had my pistol on my belt and he may not even have noticed it in the darkness. He said nothing at first, and I thought what an odd situation it was. But then he said:

'"I suppose you've been shot down then?"

'I said yes, it was a bad experience and my comrades were dead.

'"I'm sorry to hear that," he replied, "are you injured?"

'I said no, not as far as I knew. He then told me he was a doctor and had just visited a patient. We reached his home in a few minutes to find his wife waiting for him. She was astonished to see his passenger and I handed her my pistol. All she could say was, "My God Henry, what shall we do?"

'"You put the kettle on and make some tea," he told her, "I'll 'phone the police."

'So I sat down and waited in their very comfortable home, and took my boots off which had begun to hurt my feet, put my flying helmet on the table while I tried to take in this extraordinary and very friendly situation. It was not in the least what I had expected or planned. In a few moments the woman brought in a tray with three cups of tea and a few biscuits; there was some sugar, but not much, she apologised for this – it was the rationing. I was quite overwhelmed by all this and hardly knew what to say.

'Meantime, the doctor had telephoned the police and said they would soon arrive. He asked me how I felt and would I care to visit the bathroom? He helped me out of my overalls and left me to have a wash and brush up. Then I went downstairs again to drink my tea and eat biscuits while we conversed in general terms about the war, but this was difficult so they asked me about my home and family so I told them and showed them some photographs.

'And then I cried and they became very solicitous. I was suddenly overwhelmed by my experience, the loss of my friends, killed in that bomber and thoughts of my family. They did their best to comfort me until the police arrived, two plain clothes men and two uniformed constables. The policemen were very patient and seemed unarmed. They took me out to their black car and we went to a police station where I was allowed to wait in an office until two RAF officers arrived to take me away for interrogation. Then I went to a PoW camp where I met some old comrades and waited for the war to end.'

The Luftwaffe ranged far and wide in the new form of warfare and did great damage it must be said to not only war plants but also to many non-military targets and caused the loss of thousands of civilian lives which hardened the hearts of the enemy to what was to come when it was Germany's turn.

'. . . *the whole thing became a routine with little or no central direction, the bombers were simply unloading bombs all over England and Scotland, too often indiscriminately, the effect on their enemy was minimal. It achieved nothing in the long term, in fact the German air offensive was a failure from the military standpoint, though of course it had its effect on morale, but we saw that even this was to rebound on us, for to "take it" became a watchword in Britain and later in our own country. It is my belief that that kind of warfare is both wasteful and inhuman.'*

Johannes Fink

'The strategic air war against Britain could never have succeeded with the weapons we had, and at no time was a weapon capable of dealing a knockout blow developed – not even the V weapons.'

Hans-Jurgen Stumpff

APPENDIX ONE

LUFTWAFFE RANKS AND UNIFORM MARKINGS

LUFTWAFFE	RAF (NEAREST EQUIVALENT)
Flieger	Aircraftman 2nd Class
Gefreiter	Aircraftman 1st Class
Obergefreiter	Leading Aircraftman
Fahnenjunker-Gefreiter	Flight Cadet Lance-Corporal
Hauptgefreiter	Corporal
Unteroffizier	Sergeant (Junior Sergeant)
Fahnrich	Flight Ensign
Unterfeldwebel	Sergeant
Feldwebel	Flight Sergeant
Oberfeldwebel/Stabsfeldwebel	Warrant Officers
Oberfahnrich	Flight Ensign
Leutnant	Pilot Officer
Oberleutnant	Flying Officer
Hauptmann	Flight Lieutenant
Major	Squadron Leader
Oberstleutnant	Wing Commander
Oberst	Group Captain
Generalmajor	Air Vice-Marshal
Generalleutnant	Air Marshal
General der Flieger (Flak etc)	–
Generaloberst	Air Chief Marshal
Generalfeldmarschall	Marshal of the Air Force

Colours

Waffenfarben or colours of the arms denoted different branches of the service and were shown in two ways: as underlay on collar patches and officers shoulder straps, and as piping on NCO and ORs straps and peaked dress caps.

White   Air Marshals and General Göring Regiment
             (which also used red piping)
Deep Yellow Flying Branch

Bright Red	Flak Artillery
Carmine Red	General Staff
Rose	Engineer Corps
Brown	Signals
Dark blue	Medical Branch
Light Green	Aircraft Flying Control
Dark Green	Administration
Black	Air Ministry

Functional Insignia

A range of machine-woven trade badges in pale blue were worn by NCOs and men on the lower left sleeve of uniforms.

Qualified aircrew were awarded large metal pin badges to be worn on the lower left top uniform pocket (Pilot, Observer, Air Gunner, Radio Operator-Gunner), decorations in the form of pin medals (Iron Cross 1st Class, Wound Badges) to be worn above these.

During the war a range of 'War Flight Bars' were awarded in the various categories – Fighter, Bomber, Reconnaissance, Transport aircraft, in bronze, silver and gold denoting number of flights achieved, these pin badges to be worn above the left tunic pocket.

Commemorative sleeve ribbons were worn by some squadrons etc, the names machine embroidered in aluminium gothic script on dark blue, for fighter and bomber units – *Jagdgeschwader Richthofen, Boelcke, Immelmann, Hindenburg, Horst Wessel and General Wever*. The Luftwaffe also awarded its own version of the *AFRIKA* sleeve ribbon in the same colours, all these were worn on the lower right sleeve.

LUFTWAFFE AIRCRAFT

Brief descriptions of aircraft used by contributors in the text

TYPE	FUNCTION	MAX SPEED (mph)	BOMB LOAD (lb)
Heinkel 111P	Bomber	247	4,410
Dornier 17Z	Bomber	265	2,200
Dornier 217 series	Bomber	273	8,818
Junkers 88A series	Bomber	286	3,968
Junkers 188E series	Bomber	310	6,614
Junkers 87B	Dive-Bomber	232	1,540
Messerschmitt 109E	Fighter	355	–
Messerschmitt 109G2	Fighter	398 (at 20,000 ft)	–
Messerschmitt 110	Fighter	349	–
Messerschmitt 262	Jet Fighter	540	–
Messerschmitt 410A	Fighter-Bomber	388 (22,000 ft)	–
Focke-Wulf 190A3	Fighter	382	–
Heinkel 177A	Bomber	273	8,000 (approx)
Dornier 217N	Night-Fighter	320 (19,000 ft)	–
Arado 234B	Rec-Bomber	460 (20,000 ft)	–

GERMAN AIRCRAFT PRODUCTION AND LOSSES

German Aircraft Production 1939–45 (main types)

Dornier 17	506
Dornier 217	101
Heinkel 111	5,656
Heinkel 177	1,446
Junkers 52	2,804
Junkers 87	4,881
Junkers 88	15,000
Junkers 188	1,036
Me 109	30,480
Me 110	5,762
Me 262	1,294
Me 410	1,013

Total Production by Year all types

1939	1940	1941	1942	1943	1944	1945
2,518	10,247	12,401	15,409	24,807	40,593	7,539

Total German Aircraft Losses 1 Sept 1939–Dec 1944

Fighters	52,042
Bombers	19,923
Grand Total	71,965

Luftwaffe Aircrew Losses 1939–45

Killed and Missing	69,623
Wounded & Injured*	27,294
Total	96,917

* the figures include casualties in training

BATTLE OF BRITAIN

Luftwaffe Aircraft Strength 10 May 1940

1,120	Bombers
324	Dive-Bombers
42	Battle Planes (Ground Support Henschel 123)
1,016	Short-range Fighters (Me 109)
248	Long-range Fighters (Me 110)

Luftwaffe Losses in the Battle of Britain
10 July–31 October 1940

RAF Claimed Destroyed	2,692
Actually Destroyed	1,733
Actually Damaged	643
In this period the Germans admitted the loss of only	896

Extracts from Operational Orders issued by GOC 1st Luftwaffe Air Corps 6 September 1940 for attack on London:

'In the evening of 7.9 Luftflotte 2 will conduct major strike against target Loge (London) . . . Purpose of initial attack is to force English fighters into the air so they will have reached end of endurance at time of Main Attack. . . . In view of the fact that the [German] fighters will be operating at limit of their endurance, it is essential that direct courses be flown and the attack completed in minimum time. . . . The intention is to complete the operation in a single attack. In the event of units failing to arrive directly over target, other suitable objectives in Loge may be bombed from altitude of approach. . . . To achieve the necessary maximum effort it is essential that units fly as a highly concentrated force – during approach, attack and especially on return. The main objective of the operation is to prove that the Luftwaffe can achieve this.'

APPENDIX FIVE

LUFTWAFFE SLANG TERMS

EMIL-Messerschmitt 109E fighter, but some versions referred to as a FLYING BRICK. Others used were: CANOE, BOX, BATH TUB, and MOLLE, this last a large size glass in a Berlin restaurant. An all-metal aircraft was a BRASS DONKEY, a heavy bomber a PANTECHNICON (removals van). PUPPCHEN referred to various small aircraft as well as females of endearment, while a worn or clapped-out plane was called JUNK. FETCH and CARRY was a term used to denote the Ju 52 and other transport planes.

Pilots in general were sometimes referred to as EMIL, Observers FRANZ or even STAFF GOGGLES, while a young airman was a HARE. An ace pilot was a CANNON, a crew a FLYING FAMILY. Bombs were EGGS or CIGARS; to open fire with a machine-gun was to BLEAT, a flight over enemy lines a FRONTBRUMMEL – a 'spree' or 'joyride'. Searchlights were GLOW WORMS, AA fire FLAK or MEASLES; to be shot down in flames to DISMOUNT HOT. The Reich weather forecasters were called FALSE PROPHETS.

A TITBIT was a girl, a BLITZMAEDCHEN a Luftwaffe female auxiliary. A RABBIT was a fool of an officer, a DOG a workhorse NCO. A CREAMER was a lucky man or pilot, one LOKO had gone over the top or lost his nerve. As with the Allies the OLD MAN was the CO, a RIDER a woman who would, a BLONDE ARSE a homosexual. A low level flyer was a CLOUD BUMPER or EARTH MOVER, a LORELEI a dream of a plane. The Heinkel 111 came to be known as a COW, the Lancaster bomber FAT ARSE, the Focke-Wulf 190 BUTCHER BIRD.

Finally, head of the Luftwaffe, *Reichsmarschall* Hermann Göring was called ROUGE and FEATHERS.

LUFTWAFFE BADGES

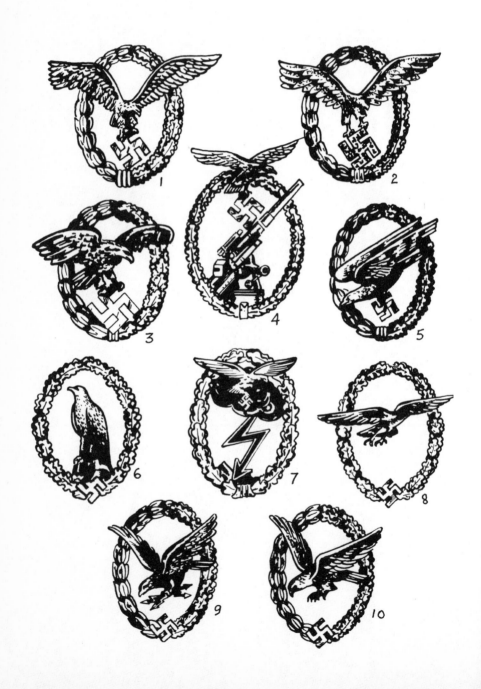

Left: 1 – Pilot 2 – award with diamonds 3 – Observer 4 – Flak crew
5 – Paratrooper 6 – Retired aircrew 7 – Ground combat 8 – Glider pilot
9 – Radio operator-gunner 10 – Air gunner
Above: WAR FLIGHT BARS (examples)
1 – Bomber 2 – Ground attack 3 – Transport/gliders
4 – Reconnaissance/Air-sea-rescure/Met squadrons
5 – Long-range fighters 6 – Fighters

INDEX

Advanced Air Striking Force 69
Air Force Association 56
Anti-Aircraft Command 54
anti-aircraft guns (available
  pre-war) 54–55
Ark Royal 60
ATS 55

'Baby Blitz' 168, 175, 176 etc
  202, 204
Baedeker guide book and raids
  151 etc
Baldwin, Stanley 46
Balloon Command 56
Baumbach, Werner 34
Boelcke, Oswald 18
British Expeditionary Force 69, 85
'Butterfly' bombs 162

casualties in air raids 193 (to Oct
  1940) 198
Chamberlain, Neville 38, 42
Cherwell, Lord 175
Christiansen, Friedrich 12
Churchill, Winston 41, 46, 60, 80,
  88, 141, 175, 193
Condor Legion 9
Coventry 135

Deutschen Luftsport Verbanden 10
Douhet, General 87
Dowding, Air Marshal 190
Dunkirk, 77, 78

Eagle Day 79, 81
Egon guidance system 176
Eisenhower, General 160

Fighter Command 54

Fink, Colonel Johannes 24, 53, 75,
  83, 84, 90, 112, 127, 211
Francke, Corporal 60
Fuller, General 87

Galland, Adolf 53, 113
Göbbels, Joseph 60, 80, 118,
  149, 175
Graf Spee 60, 84
Guderian, General Heinz 75
Guernica 41

Halifax, Lord 80
Harris, Air Marshal 192
Hart, Liddell 87
Heinkel 177 (development) 171
Herrmann, Hajo 200
Hess, Rudolf 145
Home Fleet 57, 61

Immelmann 18
Iron Duke (battleship) 65

Kesselring, General Albert 89
King George V (battleship) 162
KG3 Bomber Wing 77
KG26 Bomber Wing 31, 32, 54, 604
KG30 Bomber Wing 34, 61, 76, 104
KG66 Bomber Wing 176
KG100 Bomber Wing 127, 140
Knickebein beam system 178, 191

Legion Condor 41
Loerzer, Bruno 10
London (worst raid on), casualties
  192
Luftwaffe: strength in the East and
  organisation 1939 44
  strength in 1938–39 38

losses in Poland 53
strength in West 1940 89
losses in West 1940 89
number of sorties in Blitz 138

Maginot Line 73
Milch, Erhard 40, 86
Mölders, Werner 53
Montgomery, General 160
Morrison, Herbert 139
Munich Crisis 42

NSFK Nazi Air Corps 10, 11,
    12, 13, 20

Observer Corps 54
Operation *Barbarossa* 168
    Sealion 135
    Steinbock 175, 176
Orkney Islands 63, 65, 67

Paulus, General 160
Peltz, Colonel 176, 178
phoney war 54
Pile, General Sir Frederick 54, 136
Prien, Gunther 60

Rechlin test centre 171, 184
Richthofen Baron 18
Richthofen General Freiherr
    Wolfram 53, 73, 89

Roma (Italian battleship) 162
Rudel, Hans Ulrich 24, 35, 36, 72,
    85, 100, 101, 138

SA brownshirts 10, 13
Scapa Flow 57, 58, 60, 61, 63
Secret Service (British) 176
Seeckt, General Hans von 9, 10,
    40, 41, 86
Shetland Islands 61, 65
Spanish Civil War 41, 53
Speer, Albert 43
Sperrle, General Hugo 9, 89,
    178, 192
Stumpff, General Hans-Jurgen 69,
    86, 87, 88, 89, 104, 111, 211
Sylt (island of) 67

Territorial Army 54, 56
'tip-and-run' raids 163–9, 172–4
'Turbinlite' 151

Udet, Ernst 86

Versailles, Treaty of 9, 13

Werra, Franz von 118
Wever, General 43, 87, 170
Weygand, General Paul 80
'Window' (*Düppel*) 162